T0215291

This book is a welcome and important intervention into debates about digital culture and critical understandings of affect. It makes a persuasive case for the importance of psychoanalytic thinking in contemporary media studies, revealing through close analysis the sometimes messy underside of mediated pleasures. Jacob Johanssen charts a sensitive and astute route through theory in an excursion across mediated experiences of algorithms, reality television, social media, and data society, all the while bringing to life vivid images of emotional encounters and affective labour. He offers a creative and compelling account of the perverse enactments at work in digital culture, revealing that audiences invest in their mediated lives at both embodied and psychological levels. This book will be a truly absorbing read for anyone interested in human communication and its iterations in the digital era.

—*Caroline Bainbridge, Professor of Culture and Psychoanalysis, University of Roehampton*

Psychoanalysis and Digital Culture convincingly demonstrates the strength of psychoanalytical theory for the study of media and communication, without taking anything at face value. Grounded in an impressive mastery of the literature, the book moves beyond the rational by carving out its own route, making clear and well-informed theoretical choices, that open up ample opportunities for a better understanding of human communication. Its insightful engagement with affect, embodiment, inhibition and perversion, and with audiences and algorithms, make it a fascinating read.

—*Nico Carpentier, Professor in Media and Communication Studies, Uppsala University*

Johanssen's book is timely and a welcome addition to the growing interdisciplinary studies on new media. He deftly draws on psychoanalytic ideas and his own research in this area to help us to see ourselves more clearly as we engage with digital media. Its scholarly, yet accessible, style makes it an invaluable and rewarding read.

—*Alessandra Lemma, Professor, Psychoanalysis Unit, University College London, Author of The Digital Age on the Couch*

Turning a sharply nuanced understanding of psychoanalytic approaches toward digital culture, Jacob Johanssen carefully feels out the contours of an affective-skin-envelope that always stretches and folds the social and relational into particular bodies, situated contexts, mediating experiences, and more. Whether taking on big picture issues such as 'affective labor' and data mining & algorithms or zooming in more closely to 'embarrassing bodies,' Johanssen gathers up an impressive array of theoretical resources and parses their combined insights with clarity and creativity. This book offers us a truly refreshing model for the affect study of our contemporary moment.

—*Gregory J. Seigworth, Professor of Communication Studies, Millersville University, co-editor of Capacious: Journal for Emerging Affect Inquiry*

Psychoanalysis and Digital Culture

Psychoanalysis and Digital Culture offers a comprehensive account of our contemporary media environment – digital culture and audiences in particular – by drawing on psychoanalysis and media studies frameworks. It provides an introduction to the psychoanalytic affect theories of Sigmund Freud and Didier Anzieu, and applies them theoretically and methodologically in a number of case studies. Johanssen argues that digital media fundamentally shape our subjectivities on affective and unconscious levels, and he critically analyses phenomena such as television viewing, Twitter use, affective labour on social media, and data mining.

Jacob Johanssen is Senior Lecturer in the Communication and Media Research Institute (CAMRI), University of Westminster (United Kingdom). His research interests include psychoanalysis and digital media, audience research, affect theories, digital labour, reality television, psychosocial studies, and critical theory.

Routledge Studies in New Media and Cyberculture

For more information about this series, please visit: https://www.routledge.com

Psychoanalysis and Digital Culture
Audiences, Social Media, and Big Data

Jacob Johanssen

Routledge
Taylor & Francis Group

NEW YORK AND LONDON

First published 2019
by Routledge
52 Vanderbilt Avenue, New York, NY 10017

and by Routledge
2 Park Square, Milton Park, Abingdon, Oxon OX14 4RN

First issued in paperback 2020

Routledge is an imprint of the Taylor & Francis Group, an informa business

Library of Congress Cataloging-in-Publication Data
Names: Johanssen, Jacob, author.
Title: Psychoanalysis and digital culture : audiences, social media, and big data / Jacob Johanssen.
Description: New York : Routledge, 2018. I Series: Routledge studies in new media and cyberculture I Includes bibliographical references and index.
Identifiers: LCCN 2018033794 (print) I LCCN 2018035100 (ebook) I ISBN 9781351052061 (ebook) I ISBN 9781138484443 (hardback : alk. paper) I ISBN 9781351052061 (ebk)
Subjects: LCSH: Psychoanalysis. I Digital media—Social aspects.
Classification: LCC RC509.7 (ebook) I LCC RC509.7 .J64 2018 (print) I DDC 616.89/17—dc23
LC record available at https://lccn.loc.gov/2018033794

ISBN 13: 978-0-367-58418-4 (pbk)
ISBN 13: 978-1-138-48444-3 (hbk)

Typeset in Sabon
by codeMantra

Contents

Acknowledgements

This book could not have been completed without discussions with many people over the past years. Some rudimentary thoughts that would ultimately lead to this project began to emerge during my undergraduate degree, and I am very grateful to Lissi Klaus, Manfred Gabriel, and Thomas Carl Schirren for their inspirational teaching.

My thanks go to those who critically commented on my ideas at various stages of the book and the different research projects that form its basis, and offered valuable feedback. In particular Sara Ahmed, Lisa Blackman, Nick Couldry, Friedrich Krotz, and Matt Hills. Caroline Bainbridge, Siobhan Lennon-Patience, Yu-Kei Tse, Greg Seigworth, Diana Garrisi, Bonni Rambatan, Monika Metykova, Nele Heise, Cigdem Esin, Corinne Squire, and Heather Price have asked important questions and given advice at different times.

I am indebted to my friend and colleague Steffen Krüger, who provided extensive feedback on some of the book's chapters. Sharing similar passions when it comes to psychoanalytic media research and working on a number of projects together with Steffen has been very inspiring.

I am also incredibly thankful to Kylie Jarrett, who provided important feedback on Chapters 4 and 5. Chapter 5 is also based on some data from a research project carried out together with Diana Garrisi.

My PhD supervisors, Candida Yates, Darren Ellis, and Nicola Diamond, were a wonderful team. Their areas of expertise, motivation, and encouragement have helped shape parts of this book. I am happy to be part of the Psychosocial Studies community in the United Kingdom, and my thanks go to Wendy Hollway for telling me more about it over a conference breakfast one morning in 2011.

I am very grateful to all my CAMRI colleagues at the University of Westminster for their collegial support and that I am part of such a stimulating research environment. Particular thanks go to Christian Fuchs for his advice and support as well as to Anastasia Kavada, Daya Thussu, Tarik Sabry, Graham Meikle, Heidi Herzogenrath-Amelung, Mercedes Bunz, Winston Mano, Doug Specht, Maria Michalis, Alessandro D'Arma, Michaela O'Brien, Pieter Verdegem, Roza Tsagarousianou, Anthony McNicholas, and Xin Xin.

I am thankful for the members of the Psychoanalysis at Westminster reading group and that we have created a space of intellectual calmness amongst the accelerated academy: Dawn Williams, Sally-Anne Gross, Stuart Cumberland, and Ro Spankie.

I would also like to thank all the interviewees who I spoke to for some of the book's chapters for their openness and trust.

This book is dedicated to my daughter Frieda. She has shown me the miracles of this world and proved how insignificant everything is in light of the magical experience of seeing her growing up. Finally, my greatest thanks go to my wife. I am grateful for her love, wisdom, humour, strength, and for every day that I am with her.

Introduction

Psychoanalysis, Affect, and Digital Culture: Debates, Theories, and Methods

This book brings psychoanalytic theory and methodology into conversation with digital media studies in general and audience research in particular. I place a special emphasis on affect in relation to various forms of media use: watching reality television, using social media, as well as the role of big data mining and its implications for users' subjectivities online. In doing so, I am interested in finding out empirically how media users engage with media on conscious and unconscious levels as well as in shedding light on the relationship between contemporary subjectivities and digital media in a more exploratory manner. This book's chapters can be seen as case studies or detailed examples of different mediums and platforms that aim to illustrate the fruitful relationship between media and communication studies and psychoanalysis. I pay particular attention to affect and moments of affectivity between users and media texts and services. Chronologically speaking, the book begins with the 'older' medium of television in Chapter 2, featuring data from a research project on the British reality television programme *Embarrassing Bodies* (Channel 4, 2007–2015). Reality television, as some scholars have pointed out, has been *the* genre of the last two decades that shows a detailed, often obsessive and invasive, focus on the body (Kavka 2009; Bratich 2011; Ouellette 2014). *Embarrassing Bodies* was a show in which people who were portrayed as having common – as well as very rare – medical conditions and problems were diagnosed and referred for medical treatment. A great deal of time was spent commenting on, explaining, exposing, and showing the patients' bodies. Diagnoses by doctors and the medical procedures that were administered were shown as well as 'after' shots about the (mostly) improved situations of the patients (see Johanssen 2017 for a detailed discussion of the content). The programme lent itself to an audience study based on a theoretical prism of affect and psychoanalysis because of its unique graphicness. Operations were shown in great detail, and the patients regularly undressed in front of the camera. Many medical conditions considered shameful and taboo were examined by the doctors on the programme. A key concern for me was exploring how viewers make sense of their affective responses to the show in relation to their life histories.

The book's subsequent chapters then move to 'newer' media and discuss the *Embarrassing Bodies* viewers' inhibited use of Twitter in Chapter 3. Chapter 4 presents data from another research project on the affective labour on social media of individuals with facial disfigurements. Finally, Chapter 6 discusses big data and the dis/individualising process of data mining through the psychoanalytic notion of perversion.

In its theoretical orientations, the book, broadly speaking, takes an approach to media and communication which draws on the discipline of psychosocial studies. More specifically, I rely on psychoanalysis, especially Sigmund Freud and Didier Anzieu, in order to conceptualise and research the relationship between the social, affect, notions of the human subject, and media use. This chapter introduces the book's main themes and related debates.

Some academic scholarship that is psychoanalytically inflected thinks of the individual, the social, and culture as being interwoven. There is a widespread dichotomy involving the individual versus the social in academia that is particularly evident in the disciplines of psychology and sociology. An emerging field in Britain, known as psychosocial studies, explores the ways in which the two spheres of enquiry are interwoven (e.g., Hollway and Jefferson 2000, 2012; Clarke 2002; Frosh and Young 2008; Jones 2008; Clarke and Hoggett 2009; Day Sclater et al. 2009; Frosh 2010; Woodward 2015; Krüger 2017). Briefly put, in their analyses psychosocial researchers combine sociological and sometimes cultural studies ideas and theories with psychoanalytic ones. As a field, psychosocial studies has experienced sometimes heated debates with regard to the theoretical and empirical use of psychoanalysis (Frosh and Baraitser 2008; Hollway 2008; Hollway and Jefferson 2012). Importantly, the concept of the psychosocial, or, as it is sometimes spelt, the psycho-social (Hoggett 2008), seeks to move beyond the individual/social dualism. As Wendy Hollway has remarked, 'We are psycho-social' (Hollway 2006, 467) because we 'are influenced by desire and anxiety provoking situations that are affected by material and social conditions, discourses, as well as by unconscious defence mechanisms and inter-subjective relations' (Hollway 2006, 467–468). Psychosocial studies is a very useful perspective for this book because it responds to critiques which have sometimes been put to psychoanalysis in the past for being too individualising and for not taking account of the social. Many psychosocial researchers are also particularly interested in exploring the potential of psychoanalysis for empirical social research, and this book is a case in point.

In terms of its wider theoretical framework, the book specifically introduces and engages with two psychoanalysts and their ideas about affect: Sigmund Freud and Didier Anzieu. For Freud, an affective experience means a bodily experience that cannot be discursively named as a specific emotion (1981a, b, c, d, e, f, g, h, i). The subject experiences something bodily in response to an event, a thought, or a fantasy, for example. Freud names affect as a process that is subjective but also relational in response to the social and others. An affective experience is something that is primarily experienced and then made sense of in a deferred manner. As André Green (1999) stressed, it is in tension with discourse but not outside of it and therefore the subject can attempt to verbalise, explain, or question it.

Freud's ideas may be supplemented by Didier Anzieu's book *The Skin-Ego* (2016). Drawing on object-relations psychoanalysis and Wilfred Bion and D. W. Winnicott in particular, Anzieu conceptualised the beginning of a subject's life as characterised by a relational unity of mother (or caregiver) and baby (and father and others to a lesser degree). Through she is fed, held, rocked, kissed, touched, and talked to, the baby has the illusion that she shares a common skin with her mother. This (virtual) illusion is based on actual affective and sensual communication on the skin, and the relational exchanges between baby and mother. Essentially, this 'skin envelope' offers a containing and holding function that makes the baby feel secure as she matures and reaches more independence. This mode of affective communication essentially develops Freud's model into a more relational, lasting one that describes affect as something that is sensually experienced by the baby as the first form of communication between her and others.

I suggest that these virtual (Shields 2006) and material qualities of the skin ego are beneficial for thinking about the process of affectively engaging with media content, for example, a television programme or using social media, because any engagement with the media occurs on a virtual level (through the very consumption of something mediated) as well as on an affective level (through being affected by it bodily). In other words, media use relates to fantasy, thought, and utterances as well as to bodily responses that are situated at the intersections of consciousness and the unconscious. Such a framework can offer a new perspective on media and communication studies, a field which is still often dominated by rational or simplistic theories of the human subject as a media user.

Media and Psychoanalysis: A Brief Overview

Compared to in previous decades, psychoanalytic theories and methods in media and communication studies now occupy a marginalised position and have largely fallen out of fashion. As this book argues, media and communication research, audience studies in particular, can be enriched by psychoanalysis. Peter Dahlgren (2013) has suggested that there is a need for 'reactivating concerns about the subject' (2013, 73) in media studies research. He notes that media and communication studies consist of 'implicit models and assumptions about how people [...] actually function' (Dahlgren 2013, 72), particularly in relation to questions of media exposure. As a result, 'what is operative in just about all such research are *implicit* notions about the subject' (ibid., my italics). Dahlgren expresses dissatisfaction with the state of media research in general when it comes to theoretical conceptualisations and empirical research on the human subject as a media user, and he specifically suggests (Freudian and post-Freudian) psychoanalysis as a way forward. He asks a key question in this context: 'What if the subject cannot fully understand why he or she does and says all the things that he or she does?' (ibid., 81). He advocates that psychoanalytic theories can help scholars to think about the complex processes of using and making sense of media and mediums. He goes on to specifically advocate a consideration of the (Freudian) unconscious and its relation to affect:

> The Freudian view of fear, desire, and pleasure accords affect a strong and volatile position, given that the unconscious usually slyly outwits conscious awareness and its rationalism. In regard to politics and communication, this means we need to analytically pay attention to not just information and formal argument but also to symbols, imagery, rhetoric, allegory, emotional pleas, ideology, and all the other communicative modes beyond the rational; it is through these that the civic subject takes on agency.
>
> (Dahlgren 2013, 82)

It is one of this book's key aims to pay this sort of attention, which goes beyond the rational. As a discipline, psychoanalysis shifts the attention from rationality to contradictions, incoherencies, ambivalent and seemingly nonsensical subjective experiences that also find expression in cultural products such as media texts and responses towards them. This is valuable because it can add levels of complexity to research on media use. Ben Highmore (2007) defines psychoanalysis as a particular mode of 'attention' (Highmore 2007, 88) that always includes a focus on aspects of a subject's life history. Following Dahlgren (2013), one may argue that the models of audiences commonly used in media and communication studies all harbour implicit and underpinning notions of the subject in relation to media. Audience studies in particular have not managed to adequately theorise the subject and her affective, conscious, and unconscious relationships with media use.

One might ask, 'Isn't psychoanalysis a clinical discipline? How can it be taken outside the clinic and "applied" to media?' This is a fair point. Psychoanalytic explorations of culture have at times sounded overtly pathologising. Psychoanalysis is sometimes at risk of becoming a master discourse, conveying an ultimate truth about subjects and their cultural investments. In this book, I do not engage in wild analysis that seeks to psychoanalyse everything or label everything with psychoanalytic language. My approach to digital media and their audiences is influenced by psychoanalysis, among other theoretical traditions. A key value of psychoanalysis is that it presents a notion of subjectivity which includes rational, conscious elements but also includes irrational dimensions and the unconscious.

One of the fields that has made use of theoretical psychoanalytic concepts in a rigorous manner is film studies. Specifically the notions of 'identification' and 'the gaze' have been employed to conceptualise the relationship between cinematic content and the viewer. This tradition is often referred to as *Screen Theory*. Primarily articles published in the French journals *Cahiers du Cinéma* and *Communications*, and the British journal *Screen* from 1968 onwards dealt with psychoanalytically informed film theory that was also influenced by Marxism. It was psychoanalysis and Marxism that enabled ideology critique of mainstream Hollywood narrative cinema. Film scholars asked, 'What are the social and psychic functions of cinema?' (Bordwell 1996, 6). Laura Mulvey's (1975) *Visual Pleasure and Narrative Cinema* was particularly influential, and her work prompted many other scholars to explore film through a psychoanalytic lens (de Lauretis 1984; Doane 1987; Copjec 1989; Cowie 1990; Modleski 1990; Silverman 1992). Those works, which often drew on Lacan and Freud, all remained at the theoretical level and imagined audiences. They operated with essentialist categories that posited effects on spectators in the cinema. This has led to criticism within media and communication studies as well as cultural studies. During the 1970s and 1980s, a direct exchange of ideas and debate between psychoanalytic film studies and cultural studies emerged. Debates often concerned meaning and ideology in relation to the spectator (see Hall 1980; Morley 1986, 1992; Grossberg 1987) as well as, more recently, questions on methodology and how such interpretations were made without speaking to individuals (Couldry 2000; Barker 2005). While valid points about the status of psychoanalysis as a kind of master discourse uncovering hidden desires and ideologies were raised by the authors mentioned earlier, such critiques have often been rather hastily dismissive of psychoanalysis as a whole and, at times, misunderstood some of its key concepts.

However, what *Screen Theory* lacked was empirical studies of audiences. In terms of empirical audience research, it is Valerie Walkerdine's famous work (1986) on a family who watched *Rocky II* which needs to be mentioned. This study was the first to use psychoanalysis as a prism through which to conduct ethnographic research (see also Stacey 1994). Walkerdine made the crucial point that any media use, be it watching a film or television programme, listening to the radio, or something else, takes place in *already* (historically) established contexts and relational, intersubjective dynamics. These dynamics are anchored in both the social and the psyche, and their interplay. Being from a working-class background like the family, she identified with some of the fascination with and responses to the film.

There are some works within media and communication studies that make use of specific psychoanalytic concepts or at least mention them: for example, Janice Radway's work (1984) on female readers of romance novels; Ien Ang's *Dallas* study, which drew on the psychoanalytic notion of fantasy (Ang 1985); John Ellis's (2000) work on television and 'working through'; Nico Carpentier and Marit Trioen's (2010) work on fantasies of objective reporting by journalists; Carpentier's take on participation as a Lacanian fantasy (2014a,b); Martin Barker's (2005) critique of identification with regard to media research; Annette Hill's work (2007) on reality television audiences that draws on Christopher Bollas; and, as already mentioned, Peter Dahlgren's (2013) consideration of Freudian and post-Freudian psychoanalysis in relation to concepts of the subject in research on media and participation. An important media studies scholar who drew on psychoanalysis to a fuller extent was Roger Silverstone (1994) in his work on television. 'Our media, television perhaps pre-eminently, occupy the potential space released by blankets, teddy bears and breasts' (Silverstone 1994, 12–13). Television can be similar to a transitional object of the young infant (e.g., a teddy bear or blanket). It can be an emotional comforter by creating a safe space, the 'potential space' (Winnicott 2002), between the viewer and television in which the viewer can feel comforted and held. It is unconsciously used to work through feelings of loss or anxiety, for instance (Winnicott 2002). The transitional object is an important category for certain areas of media research (Harrington and Bielby 1995; Hills 2002; Sandvoss 2005; Yates 2007; Bainbridge and Yates 2010; Bainbridge 2012; Kuhn 2013; Krüger and Rustad 2017). The fan studies scholar Matt Hills (2002, 2005, 2014, 2017) has been key in introducing the transitional object into wider debates around the status of media objects for fans. Hills has argued for a biographical connection between fan objects (such as media texts) and fans' life histories that is shaped by conscious and unconscious processes. However, I do not regard the transitional object as particularly useful when theorising media users who are not fans. The transitional object may work well for that very particular category of media users. Furthermore, there are conceptual irregularities and flaws that complicate the usage of the concept for digital media research. The transitional object is, like the skin ego, of an essentially relational nature that is about creating a secure and sensual environment for the subject. For Anzieu, the skin ego comes into being in the imagined and experienced unity of baby and mother. While both concepts are about a relationality, materiality, and virtuality, it is the skin ego, I argue, that is not about omnipotence over an object (like the transitional object) but about communication and the emergence of affects and sensations in a relation. It is further Freud's notion of the ego as a protective shield that acts as a protective layer against stimuli that was taken up by Anzieu and that allows for a nuanced theorisation of media use that is about both notions of containment and ruptures in the protective shield. The overall, implicit characterisation of the transitional object by Winnicott as 'benign' (Gutwill and Hollander 2002, 268), 'cosy' (Minsky 2013, 50), and positive may not quite account for the affective and ambivalent media use processes that I discuss in this book. Drawing on the transitional object as a concept may lead in some cases 'to an idealization of the child, of fantasy, of thinking, and of creativity' (Brody 1980, 589).

The psychosocial studies scholar Jo Whitehouse-Hart (2014a), who draws on fan studies and object-relations psychoanalysis, has conducted detailed interviews with viewers about their favourite film and television texts. Like myself, she uses the notion of free association, as developed by Wendy Hollway and Tony Jefferson (2012), in her work (see also Cohen 2013). Whitehouse-Hart has argued for the (un)conscious relationship between subjects' life histories and their attachments to media texts to be considered more carefully by media researchers.

Studies into Internet-based and networked media have increasingly relied on psychoanalysis, and one could say that they have ushered in a renewed interest in psychoanalytic concepts within different fields. This is because social media platforms and smartphone apps are, compared to mass media like television, aimed at the *individual* user and their subjectivity. Sherry Turkle (1984, 1985, 2009, 2011) has been one of the most well-known scholars of psychoanalysis and technology. Her early work, drawing on the psychoanalysts Jacques Lacan and Erik Erikson, was pioneering in thinking about the relationship between virtual worlds and subjectivities. The Internet allowed for a playful creation of identities that the offline world did not allow. Over the years, Turkle's view has shifted from a cautiously optimistic one to a distinctly pessimistic one regarding the role of communication technologies in our lives. Internet-based devices have made humans more narcissistic and less relational, as Turkle argues (2011). Individuals seem to trust machines (robots or devices equipped with artificial intelligence) more than other humans when it comes to social interaction. There has been a shift, Turkle notes, in the willingness of subjects to accept machines as if they were humans.

> The robotic culture has us demanding more of technology than technology can offer. I've also found that we expect less from each other. Here, mobile communication and social media are key actors. Phones in hand, we're always distracted by the worlds on our devices, and it's become more common to go to great lengths to avoid a certain kind of conversation: those that are spontaneous and face-to-face and require our full attention, those in which people go off on a tangent and circle back in unpredictable and self-revealing ways.
> (Turkle 2014, 246)

In general, there is an unprecedented focus on subjectivity through and by digital media today. On the Internet, the individual has become the producer of content online and is herself produced and turned into data (Krüger and Johanssen 2016, 6). This has been explored by John Suler (2004), amongst others, and his work on the online disinhibition effect. Work on mobile media (Elliott and Urry 2010), gadgets (Krzych 2010), and social media and subjectivity (Balick 2014; Krüger and Johanssen 2014; Flisfeder 2015; Zajc 2015; Johanssen 2016a, 2018; Johanssen and Krüger 2016; Krüger 2016; Singh 2016) has also drawn on psychoanalytic theory. Some authors have worked with the ideas of Jacques Lacan and Slavoj Žižek (Flisfeder and Willis 2014; Flisfeder 2015). In her influential work on communicative capitalism, Jodi Dean (2009, 2010) has demonstrated how social media and the Internet more generally are governed by the (Lacanian) drive. Users endlessly circulate through such spaces without specific goals (see also Gutierrez 2016; Horbury 2016 for other, critical Lacanian accounts of networked media). The German sociologist and psychoanalyst Alfred Lorenzer's method of depth-hermeneutics (Lorenzer 1986) as a way of introspectively exploring the relationship between researchers and research material, which drew on sociology, critical theory, and psychoanalysis, has been important in the German-speaking world (e.g., Löchel 2006; Prokop 2006) and has been brought into the English context, particularly by Steffen Krüger in his work on online interaction forms (Krüger 2013, 2016, 2017).

Psychoanalysts have also written about digital media from a clinical perspective and how they shape sessions in the consulting room (Lemma 2017).

To sum up, there is clearly a growing field, which one could term 'psychoanalytic media studies', and this book makes a contribution to it by introducing the reader to and arguing for a particular focus on affect in relation to digital media and audiences. This specific focus has been largely absent from the field.

Affective (Media) Interfaces

Over the past two decades, there has been a critical response to structuralist and post-structuralist theories and their focus on representation, textuality, discourse, written texts, and language. The increasing works on affect in cultural studies, queer theory, postcolonial theory, feminism, and film and media theory, as well as to some degree in the social sciences, are about going beyond this focus and paying attention to matter, bodies, and the human subject in a different way (Hemmings 2005; Blackman and Cromby 2007; Clough 2007; Seigworth and Gregg 2010). More generally, the term 'affect' describes how particular relationships are established between bodies, matter, and other objects. It points to abrupt, excessive, raw, intersubjective moments that are difficult to make sense of through the discursive realm alone. As a concept, affect is perhaps best defined by its non-definition. It is a broad term that has been interpreted very differently by many thinkers. This opens it up to fascinating work, but it also risks making the concept an empty signifier with no shared meaning. A distinct, psychoanalytic conceptualisation of the term, which I develop in Chapter 1, is helpful when it comes to empirical research. To a degree, affect theories have also been formulated as a critical response to the individualising tendencies of psychoanalytic thinking (McLaughlan 2015, 41). However, there is some value in maintaining a psychosocial perspective on affect, one that combines the subjective perspective with that of the social angle. I also do not see a strict opposition between psychoanalytic and non-psychoanalytic affect theories. There is a common denominator between the two. Both generally understand affect as being about bodily experiences that occur in a process-like nature. For both, affect may be defined as having unfixed, abrupt, excessive, raw, and intersubjective qualities that are difficult to make sense of and put into words. While the majority of affect theories are non-psychoanalytic, some works have drawn on the Lacanian and Freudian models of affect, and I discuss these at the beginning of Chapter 1.

More generally, non-psychoanalytic affect theories are being increasingly used to theorise and think about digital media. A wide range of authors have written about this subject recently (e.g. Gibbs 2011; Karatzogianni and Kuntsman 2012; Sampson 2012; Clough 2013; Garde-Hansen and Gorton 2013; Ruckenstein 2014; Jarrett 2015; Matviyenko 2015; Paasonen et al. 2015; Papacharissi 2015; Graefer 2016; Johanssen 2016a; Krüger 2016; Handyside and Ringrose 2017; Malinowska and Miller 2017; Bore et al. 2018; Sampson et al. 2018). Often, studies on affect and the digital do not fully define what is meant by the term and how it is used. I return to some of them in more detail in Chapters 4 and 5.

Affect theories share some conceptual common ground with the notion of the interface. Just as affect is, ontologically, about a processual relationality, the interface is, broadly speaking, a facilitator or enabling moment of a state of in-betweenness. A relationality between hardware and user, software code and user, software and hardware, user and user. I implicitly return to questions about the (affective) interface character of media surfaces in today's world throughout the book's chapters.

Television and, as some have pointed out, reality television in particular is also an interface of sorts. From a relational perspective, watching television is made possible through the viewer's consuming something that is shown on screen. The television screen 'interfaces' between the viewer and the content. Linked to this, there has been a focus on the mediated body in relation to (non-psychoanalytic theories of) affect on television (Bonner 2005; Kavka 2009; Bratich 2011; Skeggs and

Wood 2012). Scholarship that addresses the conjuncture of affect and the mediated body responds to television programmes that foreground the body or bodily matters, such as *Embarrassing Bodies*. Misha Kavka has written that reality television marks 'an interface' (2009, 28) or 'affective base' (ibid., 29) that binds viewers and show contestants. Medical reality television shows in particular often depict bodies in a very graphic manner and can have an 'ability to shock – that is to produce an excess of affect' (Bonner 2005, 106) on the part of the viewer. Similarly, Moseley (2000) has described reality television as generally showcasing 'the excessiveness of the ordinary' (Moseley 2000, 314), such as close-ups of body parts that we all have. Skeggs and Wood have called reality television an 'intensification of affect' (Skeggs and Wood 2012, 38), and Kavka has named reality television a 'pornographic "excess" of too much visibility' (Kavka 2009, 164). These authors stress that reality television's intense and graphic focus on something trivial that is often invisible in 'real' life makes it stand out. Bratich has similarly defined reality television as a genre that 'combines, connects, accumulates, and programmes affects' (Bratich 2011, 63). For him, reality television embodies 'conditions for maximal affective volatility' (ibid., 64) that are about (performed) bodily relations between participants, such as crying, verbal and physical fights, undressing, changing bodily appearance, competitions between participants, judgement by experts, and so on.

Kavka (2009) writes that reality television is full of affective moments that are 'in excess of meaning-effects' (ibid., 27). She posits that viewers feel an affective connection towards the subject or subjects on screen because they have been in similar situations. There is a strong familiarity on the part of the viewers with situations, scenarios, and responses that are shown in reality shows precisely because they are about (supposedly) 'real' people and everyday challenges and situations. Viewers recognise their own feelings in the other on screen and feel that their feelings 'are not quite their own' (ibid., 28). This relationality between viewers and contestants makes reality television and the viewers' affective responses 'all the more real' (ibid.) for audiences. Affect stands for a join or cusp that traverses bodies, subject and object, self and other. Drawing on André Green (1999), Kavka maintains that affect emerges in the relational tension between two forces: for instance a television show and a viewer. This crossing or emergence of the process of affect as the result of a relation makes it a fruitful concept for thinking about reality television, Kavka argues, because it mediates between a viewer and a television show. In its process, affect's ability of mediation can be located spatially within the television screen. In this sense, the TV screen 'is not a glass barrier between illusory and real worlds; instead, the screen is a join that *amplifies* affect and connects real people on one side with the real people, in another sense, on the other side' (ibid., 36, italics in the original). While the majority of the works mentioned earlier have examined the affectivity of reality shows through content analyses, I offer a theoretical framework that helps to make sense of the affective relationships between audiences and the consumption of (reality) television programmes. I return to these aspects in the coming chapters.

Computer-based media are also defined by the interface (Farman 2011; Galloway 2012). The most commonly used interface is the graphic user interface (GUI), which enables, for example, computer software to have a graphic surface that users can easily navigate rather than having to enter code in a command line. Interfaces, as Wendy Hui Kyong Chun has put it, carry an inherent fantasy of empowerment for the user. 'The notion of interfaces as empowering is driven by a dream of individual control: of direct personal manipulation of the screen, and thus, by extension, of the system it indexes or represents' (Chun 2011, 62). The interface enables users to develop 'feelings of mastery' (ibid., 63) over the software they are using. Florian Cramer and Matthew Fuller make a similar point when they write that interfaces 'are the point of juncture between different bodies, hardware, software, users, and what they connect to or are part of. Interfaces describe, hide, and condition the asymmetry between the elements conjoined' (Cramer and Fuller 2008, 150). Branden Hookway (2014) has maintained that the interface is not so much a technological invention or characteristic but more the relationship with technology. This is most often a relationship between humans and technology, a psychosocial relationship which involves the virtual and material, the psychological and the social, coming together. Such an affective relationship is examined in Chapters 4 and 5 when it comes to affective labour on social media.

The human body is itself an interface. As I am in the world, my body is always in relation to someone or something. Even when I am alone in a room, I am still in relation to the matter around me. The body establishes a connection with the world, and vice versa. In today's media-saturated world, the body is also bombarded with and responds to many different stimuli from different sources and mediums throughout the day. We face and engage with different interfaces. Meredith Jones (2017) has argued that the projection of bodies through various technologies and images has implications for how the body, skin in particular, is experienced and shaped. '[T]he living, fleshy body and its flat image are conflated and culturally intertwined' (Jones 2017, 30). She goes on to draw a connection between skins and screens. Both are intermediaries and interfaces between subjects and the world. One of the meanings of the word 'screen' is of course to act as a divider, as in 'room screen', within a room. It acts as a protective barrier between different spaces within a room. 'Skins and screens are surfaces that hide and contain even as they also show and communicate' (ibid., 32). They show and conceal messages and impressions. Screens and skins are also affective or rather capable of transporting/initiating affect between subjects and objects (see also Hansen 2006). Like Kavka (2009), Jones argues that

> the screen operates as both separating membrane and connecting facilitator between sensing body and image and so confounds the real and the represented, the seen and the felt.
>
> (Jones 2017, 33)

The same goes for the skin. Skins and screens are both media in their own rights. Using the case of the 'designer vagina', Jones notes that we often compare our bodies to bodies we see on various screens in the hope of having different bodies. This is facilitated by digital media: reality television in particular but also social media. In that sense, the skin which is subject to cosmetic surgery, for example, becomes a bearer of culturally constructed meanings of what it means to be beautiful, normal, and desirable, meanings which are transported and affectively responded to through screens and skins. The 'relations between skins and screens are affective, expressive, and intertwined' (Jones 2017, 44).

As a discipline, psychoanalysis is particularly suited for exploring such ideas further. I do so through Sigmund Freud's conceptualisation of affect as well as through post-Freudian psychoanalysis. The French psychoanalyst Didier Anzieu's book *The Skin-Ego* (2016) is very useful in this respect, and I return to these notions in Chapter 1 in more detail. Anzieu has been scarcely used within the humanities and social sciences. He has been applied recently in psychosocial studies (Diamond 2013a) and cultural and media studies (Hansen 2006; Pile 2009, 2011; Segal 2009; Cavanagh et al. 2013). The philosopher Mark B. Hansen (2006) has discussed Anzieu particularly in relation to digital media art. I return to Hansen's stimulating and useful work in the book's Conclusion. Before ending this chapter with a summary of the book's other chapters, some discussion on methodology is necessary.

Free Association and Qualitative Interviews

Chapters 2, 3, and 5 feature data from qualitative interviews. Tony Hollway and Wendy Jefferson have pointed to the widespread rationality within social research. They write that there are

> widespread assumptions in the tradition, by ethnographers, participant observers and interviewers alike, that their participants are 'telling it like it is', that participants know who they are and what makes them tick - what we might call the 'transparent self problem' - and are willing and able to 'tell' this to a stranger interviewer - what we might call the 'transparent account problem'.
>
> (Hollway and Jefferson 2000, 3)

Embracing the limits of social research and the messiness of data, as well as the admission on the part of researchers that we are not able to know/understand everything about a participant, for example, is an important paradigm. One way of taking it into account is through the psychoanalytic notion of free association. The psychosocial studies scholars Wendy Hollway and Tony Jefferson have used the notion of free association in their work (Hollway and Jefferson 2000, 2012).[1] They note that they think of a research participant as someone 'whose inner world is not simply a reflection of the outer world, nor a cognitively driven rational accommodation to it' (Hollway and Jefferson 2000, 4). '[U]nconscious processes infiltrate the narrative accounts given by research participants' (Frosh 2010, 200). Hollway and Jefferson stress that social research should generate rich, personal accounts about people's lives. One way of achieving this is through free associative interviewing. A participant should talk about anything that comes to mind. In that way the interview is not structured according to a formalist, conscious logic but according to an unconscious one: 'the associations follow pathways defined by emotional motivations, rather than rational intentions' (ibid., 37). In addressing the subject in a more complex way, I opened up ways of responding in a less restricted and conscious manner than in traditional interviews. In this way, one may be able to 'secure access to a person's concerns which would probably not be visible using a more traditional method' (ibid., 37). The emphasis here is less on coherence and consciousness than it is in traditional social research.

Freud himself spoke of psychoanalysis as a 'method'. Similarly, George Devereux (1967) was one of the first to stress that 'the most novel thing about psychoanalysis is not psychoanalytic theory, but the methodological position' (Devereux 1967, 3) it offers. How then does this mode of attention translate into an empirical method? This methodological position, Ben Highmore (2007) argues, is precisely structured by the idea of free association. If we follow the idea that psychoanalysis offers the researcher a 'form of attention' (ibid., 93) as well as theoretical concepts, it offers the chance to speak, and perhaps listen, differently. This mode of attention comes in the form of free association. The idea of free association is one of the core principles of psychoanalysis. Sigmund Freud encouraged his patients to freely associate because he believed this would allow unconscious moments to come to the surface. It is precisely by asking the patient to freely associate that 'nothing can occur to him which is not in an indirect fashion dependent on the complex we are in search of' (Freud 1978, 32). In that sense, free associations are never completely 'free'. They are not free of personal significance for the associating individual; they are neither, from a psychosocial perspective, free of sociocultural, sociopolitical significance (in that individual practice always feeds into the constitution of social practices). At the same time, they are free in that the practice of free association – that is, lying on a couch, not facing the analyst, and saying whatever comes to mind – enables a flow of utterances that, according to Freud, is not entirely subject to conscious censorship. Repressed, forgotten, or negated fragments could thus come to the surface. The psychoanalyst should remain in a mode of 'evenly-suspended-attention' (Freud 1981e, 111). Freud supplied a vivid image that underpins this idea: The psychoanalyst turns their unconscious 'like a receptive organ' (Freud 1981e, 115) towards the patient; they are angled towards each other, just like 'the telephone receiver is adjusted to the transmitting microphone' (ibid., 116). For Freud, silences often occur not because the patient has finished talking but because they hold back an idea that has come into their mind in a resistant manner. To the patient's mind, that idea or thought might seem of no importance. This kind of self-censorship has to be broken down in the analysis by gently but firmly assuring the patient that, potentially, everything is relevant (Freud 1978, 31). It is these side effects that psychoanalysis puts centre stage. The seemingly irrelevant becomes relevant. While I do not claim to uncover a research participant's repressed memories, it is the methodological framework that free association offers that I follow here.

Psychoanalysis and Life History

It is a key belief of psychoanalysis that early experiences and experiences of growing up are key to shaping a subject and how they experience themselves, the world, and others: 'No one calls in question the fact that the experiences of the earliest years of our childhood leave ineradicable traces in the depths of our minds' (Freud 1981c, 303). If one follows psychoanalysis as an epistemology, one will always ask an interviewee about their biography and how they would give an account of it. Thus, the first thing I did in each interview was ask the interviewee to tell me about their life story and share anything they wanted to share about it. Related to this, it was not the case that I, as a researcher, simply sat in front of an interviewee and asked him or her to speak, and he or she did so. An interview is more than just a question followed by an answer. I was consciously and unconsciously receptive of whatever would emerge from a participant, and they unconsciously (and consciously) responded to my receptiveness by speaking and (at times) associating freely. The fact that some of the things I heard and responded to in the interviews were of such an intimate nature may be explained by two things. First, it seemed to be of value to all interviewees to talk to someone about the whole complex of themselves and their media use (be that using social media or watching a reality show). Second, I suggest that interviewees felt that they were in a secure environment with me in terms of talking about some of the things they spoke about. It was my ability to listen to the participants that undoubtedly allowed for an emergence of these narratives. Additionally, it was my open declaration of my own vulnerability and narratives of my own body that possibly led to rapport and a sense of trust between me and the interviewees. Before the interview commenced, I talked about my visual impairment and explained to each interviewee that it might look like I was not looking them in the eye. I believe that it is this sharing of my own vulnerability and disability that possibly had an impact on creating an atmosphere in which I was not merely an anonymous university researcher but someone with a body and a life history of my own. In that sense, my disability opened up the interviewees' abilities to speak about their own bodies in relation to their media use. So, by having established a more equal relationship before an actual interview would begin, I argue that interviewees consciously – but more importantly, unconsciously – opened up, and this was further helped by my letting them freely associate. This not only led to more transparency on my part but allowed for complex narratives to emerge that, had I adopted a conventional method of simply asking questions without having a sense of the form of attention that psychoanalysis offers, may not have emerged.

Analysing Data Psychoanalytically: From Common Themes to Cases

Clinical psychoanalysis works mostly with individual cases. Given the theoretical and empirical weighting psychoanalysis has in this book, I focussed on individual case studies, which are supplemented with additional interview data, in Chapters 2, 3, and 5.

As a result of my approach to data analysis, I treated each case as a whole and focussed specifically on how the text resonated (consciously and unconsciously) in my reading of it to identify moments that pointed to the unconscious of the interviewee and my own. I was of course equally interested in utterances that were of a very conscious nature. Bereswill et al. (2010) suggest that such moments in which something unconscious is rendered conscious through free association are

> often signalled [sic] by gaps, inconsistencies, unusual or disjointed language, narrative leaps and abrupt changes of subject; but they are also to be found in episodes or remarks whose emotional tone or resonance feels in some way distinctive. For example, they may be troubling, cause confusion, provoke irritation or seem oddly affectless.
>
> (Bereswill et al. 2010, 239)

Hollway and Jefferson (2005) talk similarly about analysing data from a psychosocial perspective. There are different sources of information in one text and sources that are of a more implicit nature. These sources are identified as evoking conflicting feelings that point to the unconscious of a research participant:

> In other words, the multiple mediations that produce the narrative through memory (intra- and inter-psychic processes as well as

discursive positioning) are sources of information available in the text. Thus, in addition to typical thematic and narrative analytic procedures, we paid particular attention to the link (free associations) between textual elements and to behaviours that signalled conflicting feelings about the material; for example, changes in emotional tone, long pauses or avoidances.

(Hollway and Jefferson 2005, 151)

It is these, what could also be called *irritations* on the part of the researcher, that point to utterances that are rendered conscious through expression in each interview. They can potentially point to incoherences, or rather complexities, in a person's narrative. It is these incoherences and complexities that underline a break in the self-censorship of the narrative that is interesting. They point to unconscious ideas, fantasies, or affects. They make ideas of motives or rationally chosen media content more complex, if not problematic. They point to the unconscious that often governs how and why we do or do not do something. This focus on the unconscious does not exclude conscious agency and consciously uttered narratives. I am interested in both and how they relate to one another.

Chapter Overviews

Chapter 1 provides a detailed introduction to and discussion of the theoretical foundations of this book which were briefly mentioned earlier. It focusses on a psychoanalytic conceptualisation of affect by drawing on Sigmund Freud and Didier Anzieu (as well as André Green and Ruth Stein), which is used in particular in Chapters 2, 3, 4, and 5.

Chapters 2 and 3 discuss research data from a research project on audiences of the reality show *Embarrassing Bodies* that I carried out. As pointed out earlier, the programme was unique at the time of its first airing in terms of its graphic display of bodies. The show has had a strong presence on social media and its own website and smartphone apps. The aim was to explore the extent to which *Embarrassing Bodies* related to the interviewees' own biographies and feelings about their bodies. I argue in the chapters that aspects of the show that are described as 'shocking', 'exciting', or 'entertaining' by the interviewees link to the processes of affective experiences discussed by Freud. The interviewees' narratives suggest that the show and its graphic content tap into experiences of fear and uncertainty about the body, yet the programme also creates a sense of containment (as defined by Bion and Anzieu). At the level of fantasy, *Embarrassing Bodies*, following Anzieu, may be seen as a kind of skin ego that enwraps, holds, and contains the interviewees in a safe space. This is largely due to the doctors on the programme, who provide a sense of reassurance for the viewers that there is always a (medical) solution for everything. Such findings have implications on the value of reality television for viewers, a relationship that is often discussed in critical terms by scholars. Critical analyses of neo-liberalism and reality television along with a focus on class and gender are common in media and communication studies. In the past, the notions and concepts of class, gender, and neo-liberalism have been applied by scholars via Foucauldian, feminist, or critical content analyses of reality programmes (e.g. Ouellette 2004; Bratich 2007; McCarthy 2007; Ouellette and Hay 2008a,b; Sherman 2008; Weber 2009). The general argument of such research is that reality genres present ideological narratives on how to become a 'better' citizen. While *Embarrassing Bodies* was a distinctly commercial product of our current neo-liberal age, it was not primarily about ideological or heteronormative questions in relation to class, gender, or ethnicity. Instead, the programme showed diversity in the age, gender, and ethnicity of its patients.

Chapter 3 presents data on users' Twitter behaviour and introduces the Freudian concept of inhibition into that context. It features more data analysis from the research project on *Embarrassing Bodies* audiences. Following from the previous chapter, I argue that the programme resulted in such affective responses to the show in the interviewees that they may have been unable to engage with it on social media. *Embarrassing Bodies* has a strong Twitter presence (through an official profile and the doctors'/hosts' individual Twitter profiles), but the interviewees in my research project all expressed how inactive they were on Twitter about the show. Yet they were using the platform for other purposes and actively tweeted about other things. I situate such narratives in relation to the notion of 'sharing' and how it is mobilised by social media companies. It seemed that there was a discrepancy between the interviewee's active Twitter use and their conscious (and unconscious) exclusion of tweets on *Embarrassing Bodies*. I explore this further through Freud's notion of 'inhibition' (Freud 1949), which refers to a self-selected restriction of a situation in order to avert the affective experience of anxiety. Inhibition may be regarded as a subjective state that protects against unintended or undesired encounters, ideas, or actions. On the surface, it may appear that interviewees chose not to tweet about the show because such tweets might be considered embarrassing because of the show's trashiness or vulgarity. However, as discussed in Chapter 2, *Embarrassing Bodies* affected the respondents in such powerful manners that they had difficulty in explaining discursively. The interviewees were also not really able to say why they did not tweet about the programme. I therefore suggest that the programme facilitates an unconscious connection between aspects of their biographies that relate to their bodies (anxiety, trauma, uncertainties), but this connection was not made by the respondents. Many respondents talked to me about aspects of their bodies and how they felt about them (this often related to anxieties, uncertainties, or traumatic bodily experiences), but this was not in relation to their consumption of the programme. I therefore suggest that such experiences were facilitated through the viewing of the programme but that the respondents were not aware of such a connection. This is amplified through their inhibition to share anything about the programme on Twitter. As a result, we could argue that the falling silent on Twitter is an unconscious act of resisting the very idea behind social media: that we should share everything about us and others. Not tweeting about the programme is thus an act of protection on the part of the users in order not to publicly engage with aspects of their bodies.

Chapters 4 and 5 focus on social media and discuss the notions of digital and affective labour (Fuchs 2014). I draw on Kylie Jarrett's (2015) critique of Autonomist Marxism and her argument that feminist work on unpaid labour can be beneficial for the digital labour debate. I specifically engage with Michael Hardt and Antonio Negri's immaterial labour concept (2000, 2004, 2009) and argue that it can be enriched by drawing on Freud's affect model. Hardt and Negri remain too vague when it comes to the specifically affective characteristics of immaterial labour. There is an implicit Cartesian dualism evident in their concept which frames affective labour as being about mental rather than fully embodied kinds of labour. However, all labour is always embodied. Critical political economists have argued that the use of commercial social media, such as Facebook, Twitter, and Instagram, is a form of unpaid labour because it contributes to the profit maximisation for those platforms by selling user data to advertising clients. I outline the field of digital labour studies and focus on how the notion of affective labour, based on Hardt and Negri, has been taken up by scholars. Kylie Jarrett (2015, 2018) and others (Coté and Pybus 2011; Pybus, 2013, 2015; Elerding and Risam 2018) have argued that it is user activity on social media as distinctly affective that is exploited. Chapter 4 also makes the argument that the notion of digital labour which is often discussed from a structural perspective in critical political economy can be enriched by a focus on the inherent characteristics of such labour (Jarrett 2015). I focus on this in Chapter 5, where I analyse interview data from a research project with individuals with facial disfigurements and their use of social media. Both chapters advance the Freudian affect model as I seek to move away from a sole focus on the affective discharge, which I discuss in Chapters 2 and 3, towards a multiphasic model of affect which maintains Freud's 'affect' and 'idea' relation. The narratives of the interviewees in Chapter 4 were about their use of social media to raise awareness of facial disfigurements and bodily differences in order to critique hegemonic ideas (such as ableism or sexism). I show how the interviewees struggled with their affective labour as they were keen to create good enough affective atmospheres online which were often in danger of being disrupted through trolling or toxic communication. Many interviewees spoke of themselves as (desiring to be) entrepreneurial subjects and (unconsciously) reproduced ideological notions (success, productivity, beauty) which they also critiqued at the same time. I introduce Jacques Lacan's notion of lack (2002) and André Green's term 'negative hallucination' (1999) to make sense of such narratives. Subjects with bodily differences are made lacking through ableist discourses and practices, and this lack was simultaneously embraced and glossed over by the interviewees. Users wished to go beyond their bodily differences and at the same time actively used them in their affective labour on social media. They spoke of themselves in agentic terms and at the same time were carefully crafting their acts of self-representation to maintain a good enough affective atmosphere online so as to avoid negative responses.

Chapter 6 shifts the focus to a more exploratory terrain. I think about the increasing attention that big data and algorithms have received, and focus on data mining practices on social media and Netflix. I argue that such practices are dis/individualising users through a perverse logic which reveals a simplistic understanding of human subjectivity. Data mining practices are expressions of both making the use of digital media more individualised – by promising a bespoke user experience which values the *individual* subject – and disindividualising by using mined user data in order to construct user profiles and merge users into large data sets. Drawing on the psychoanalytic notion of perversion, I outline how users are at once both loved and abused by contemporary tech companies. Up until the recent revelations about Cambridge Analytica's role in the 2016 US election and the European Union Referendum in the United Kingdom, users knew virtually nothing about what happens to their data online. I use the infamous *Christmas Prince* tweet by Netflix, which revealed some of Netflix's data mining practices, to illustrate the perverse relationship between users and digital media services. It is a rare instance which showed a company revealing something about their use of user data and how users responded to it. I also return to affect in this discussion to explore the level of complicity that users have in this relationship.

The Conclusion returns to Freud and Anzieu in more detail, and I present further thoughts on digital media and affect. I also outline some common themes of the book that connect the different chapters with each other.

Note

1 Drawing on Melanie Klein, Hollway and Jefferson (2000, 2012) have put forward the notion of the *defended subject*. They argue that there is a 'dynamic unconscious which defends against anxiety and significantly influences people's actions, lives and relations' (2000, 19). I do not apply the model of the defended subject because I feel it would be problematic to uphold the idea that participants automatically defend against a particular media text, for example. I feel it would have been problematic to posit the notion of the defended subject in this particular project. A more nuanced and context-specific theorising is more helpful.

1 Audiences, Affect, and the Unconscious

This chapter provides a detailed engagement with the works of Sigmund Freud and Didier Anzieu. It lays the groundwork for much of the theoretical framework of this book. I present and develop two main topics: Freud's theory of affect and Anzieu's theory of the skin ego. First, specific points of Freud's work (Freud 1981a, b, c, d, e, f, g, h, i, k) [1895, 1892, 1894, 1900, 1912, 1915, 1933, 1925, 1927] and how André Green (1999) and Ruth Stein (1999) developed his notion of affect are outlined. Second, I introduce the notion of the *skin ego* as proposed by Didier Anzieu (2016) [1985].

I argue that by drawing on the Freudian definition of affect, bodily responses to media use (and, e.g., their verbalisations in interviews) can be theorised in a manner that takes the unconscious and conscious into account. As will be discussed, for Freud, an affective state can (but does not have to) be a response to an external situation (Freud 1981a,b). It is his model that is important for the wider theoretical framework of this book because it allows me to theorise the affective experiences of media use that occur in a rhythmic manner. I then draw on Lisa Cartwright (2008) and Misha Kavka (2009) and their use of Freudian affect when analysing film and reality television. Cartwright regards affect as something that always needs to be seen *in relation* to representation. In engaging with a Freudian conception of affect, I am able to map out its complex relationship to the conscious and unconscious, to language, the body, the subject and the social – and most importantly to media use.

Furthermore, Freud's emphasis on affects as sensual experiences is a key reference point when understanding Anzieu (2016) and the interactions through skin between the mother and baby. Following on from the discussion of Freudian affect, the sections 'Freud and Affect' and 'Affect and Audio-Visual Representation: The *Project* as a Scene of Earliest Communication' discuss the Freudian ego as a protective shield (Freud 1991a,b) [1920, 1923] and examine how Didier Anzieu (2016) took up this notion in his book *The Skin Ego*. André Green (1999) suggested that the Freudian theory of affect may sound too metapsychological and abstract at times. A more nuanced and palpable account of the nature of relational, affective experiences is beneficial (see also Stein 1999, 132). Additionally, I argue that the Freudian notion of affect does not adequately take into account the social world and the relational dimensions of interpersonal encounters. It is too narrowly focussed on the individual subject (Diamond 2013a). I outline the developmental and process-like nature of affect by shifting the focus to its social and relational dimensions by drawing on Anzieu (2016) and his more phenomenological discussion of the role of the skin in affective-sensual communication between baby and mother/ father and others (Segal 2009; Diamond 2013a).

Anzieu argued that the baby forms an image of sharing a common skin with the mother that is rooted in the material, sensual experiences of being touched, kissed, held, rocked, and so on. The skin ego prefigures the ego and its capacity for reflexivity. Affective communication plays an important role in this concept. Anzieu makes it clear that the common skin is based on the illusion that the mother and baby's skin are the same. This is a soothing illusion that, I argue, media may offer to subjects in a related manner. One could say that media use often 'envelops' the viewer in a safe space. Yet the skin ego is not fully closed but is permeable and the skin also consists of orifices. Disruptive experiences of the skin/ego as other, as being broken and damaged, may also be evoked in viewers. In particular, the close-ups of surgery, torn and irritated flesh, and skin eruptions may remind the viewers of problems with their bodies, and it is in such moments that viewers experience a flooding of affect, leading them to react bodily.

Psychoanalysis and Affect

Since the publication and translation of two key books on psychoanalytic theories of affect by André Green (1999) and Ruth Stein (1999), there has been an increased interest in the subject in psychoanalytic circles. Green argued that it had been more or less neglected by post-Freudian analysts, and his efforts can be seen as important in revitalising interests in affect. Famous analysts such as Winnicott, Klein, or Bion showed little interest in affect. Jacques Lacan had similarly neglected affect (Green 1999, 99; Stein 1999, 133). A similar criticism of Lacan was put forward by Jean Laplanche (1999, 18). Collette Soler (2016) has argued in her recent book *Lacanian Affects* that Lacan did in fact consider affects. It is Lacan's *Seminar X* on anxiety that puts affect on the agenda (Lacan 2014). Lacan has indeed emphasised the affective dimensions of anxiety and this remains an impressive development. A more holistic treatment of affects, however, is difficult to find within Lacan's texts. Soler writes that, for Lacan, the first instance of being affected is when the subject enters the symbolic order via the mirror stage. The signifier 'affects the bodily individual that is thereby made into a subject' (Soler 2016, 53).

Soler places an emphasis on the relationship between affect and language when she writes that

> Language is the affecting party that passes over to the real by latching onto the bodily jouissance that it affects. The subject produced as an effect is affected by the status of this jouissance.
>
> (Soler 2016, 59)

This establishes a relationality between language and the subject who is affected by it, but the specific role of affect is left unexplained here. I also do not think that the notion of *jouissance* is particularly helpful when it comes to thinking about affect. Soler then goes on to comment on, what she calls 'Lacanian affects' (ibid., 68), namely anxiety (or anguish), sadness, joyful knowledge, boredom, anger, and shame. While she describes affect as something 'formless, unspeakable, and, furthermore, highly personal' (ibid., 5), there is nonetheless a strong anchoring in the discursive, as indicated by the various terms that designate affective states. There is some similarity between her discussion of affects, as bodily experiences that are then attempted to be signified by the subject, and the Freudian affect model, but I argue that returning to Freud helps us to find more comprehensive ideas on affect than Lacan's. Freud and Anzieu also allow for a more phenomenological conceptualisation of affect than Lacan's structuralist models that place such a strong emphasis on language and the role of the signifier.

The psychologist Silvan S. Tomkins has also been influential for scholars in the social sciences and humanities (e.g., Sedgwick 2003; Gibbs 2011). Drawing partly on Freud, he (1962) defined affect as referring to nine specific physiological reactions which are present from birth, such as enjoyment/joy, interest/excitement, surprise/startle, distress/anguish, anger/rage, disgust/contempt, shame/humiliation, and fear/terror. Tomkins saw emotions as the products of affects coupled with memories of previous experiences or thoughts of that affective experience. Affective experiences are similar to drives, in so far as both are activated and reduced by stimuli and responses. He regarded affects as sets of neurological, facial, and physiological responses to experiences that originate outside or inside the body. For him, affects are always psychosocial because they are experienced by an individual as a bodily state that is communicated outwards to the social world at the same time: for example, through screaming, lowering the gaze, or blushing (Gibbs 2011, 255). This model limits affects to hard wired states. As we shall see, the Freudian model is more open in that respect.

While, as mentioned in the Introduction, application of psychoanalytic affect theories in media and cultural studies has been relatively limited compared to non-psychoanalytic affect theories, there are some scholars who have drawn on the Freudian model. These can be broadly, if crudely, grouped according to common interests and attentions.

One author may of course belong to more than one group and spill over into another category. This, by no means exhaustive, list is merely drawn up as a way of orientation. There are, to begin with, *clinical-theoretical* works on (Freudian) psychoanalysis and affect: Mikkel Borch-Jacobsen (1993) offers a critical discussion of affect and of Freudian psychoanalysis as a whole. Many authors (e.g., Rapaport 1953; Basch 1976; Green 1999; Stein 1999; Esteban Muñoz 2009; Spezzano 2013) have offered meta-commentaries on the role of affect within psychoanalysis. I return to Green's and Stein's discussions at numerous times throughout this book.

There are also *theoretical works on affect, or the nature of affect as a category*: In her extensive engagement with (and critique of some) affect theories, Margaret Wetherell (2012, Chapter 6), has commented on and reworked Feud's notion of affect. While she is critical of the Freudian unconscious and his theory of repression, her notion of 'affective-discursive practice[s]' (Wetherell 2012, 83) is very useful in combination with Freud. I return to it later in this chapter. I also agree with her emphasis on conceptualising affect as something subjective yet social. As mentioned in the Introduction, one of the most important critiques and productive development of psychoanalysis and affect theory has been articulated by Gilles Deleuze and Felix Guattari (1983, 1987). Guattari has also written about affect elsewhere (e.g., 1990, 2005). Adrian Johnston and Catherine Malabou's (2013) *Self and Emotional Life* can be named here too. In this impressive work, they engage with questions on the unconscious nature of affects for Freud as well as on wider issues around the relationship between philosophy, neuroscience, and psychoanalysis. Karyn Ball (Ball 2015) has related Freud's ideas on affect to Marx's theory of labour and discusses the economics, as their energetic foundations, of both (see also the edited collection by Ball 2007). Ranjana Khanna (2012) has drawn on Freud and deconstructionism to argue that affect functions as an interface between the subject and something beyond it. I return to this notion when discussing Anzieu's skin ego interface later in the chapter.

There are works on *affect, the representational and (media) technologies*: Marie-Luise Angerer (2015) has drawn on Freud, amongst other affect theorists, to explore the changing ontological status of sexuality in (relation to) contemporary digital cultures. Patricia Ticineto Clough's work makes numerous references to Freud (e.g., Clough 2000a,b, 2008, 2009). She, similar to Massumi (2002) and other affect theorists, argues that affect is something beyond the subject and discourse and essentially moves through subjects and is only subsequently registered. Clough has a particular interest in technologies. Her early work (2000) presented an interest in but also critique of Freudian psychoanalysis when she identified the need to move away from the notion of the Freudian unconscious in favour of the reworking of psychoanalysis by Deleuze and Guattari. Writing about television, she argued that it 'operates on the unconscious of the circuit, befitting the notion of the machinic assemblage. Television gives the thought of an unconscious that is irreducible to human subjectivity' (Clough 2000a, 71). For her, contemporary societies are structured by affectivity as a force that operates through biopolitics and code, thereby modulating populations (Clough 2013). I return to some of these questions and their implications for subjectivities in the book's Conclusion. Other works in this category have used Freud for thinking about the representational realm (e.g., Cronan 2013) or technologies such as artificial intelligence (Wilson 2010) or tracking apps (Gutierrez 2016).

Scholarship on *cultural texts, literature and literary criticism*: Most notably, Sara Ahmed (2004, 2014) has specifically drawn on Freud in her work on different emotions and their cultural politics as well as affect/emotion as a form of capital. While she rejects the 'inside-outside model of emotions' (Ahmed 2014, 6) and is thereby also in a way rejecting the Freudian discharge model of affect without saying so, her work nonetheless shows the value of the Freudian affect/idea distinction when analysing affectivity within texts and their cultural implications. Sianne Ngai's *Ugly Feelings* (2005) teases out negative affects and their expressions in literature, film, and theoretical works (see also Sedgwick and Frank's (2007) work on shame as well as Wilson 2004). Dina Georgis (2013) uses a Freudian lens (along with queer theory) to think about the use of collective stories and storytelling as responses to trauma, war, and genocide. Her book places a focus on emotion and affect through close readings of texts. Eugenie Brinkema (2014) also connects affect to the representational realm (cinematic and literary texts). In her book, she refers to Freud's writings on emotion, mourning, the uncanny, and anxiety, but not specifically to his ideas on affect. Christopher Breu (2014) theorises materiality and the body in relation to biopolitics through literature. This is done by drawing on Freud, Lacan, and other thinkers. Robbie McLaughlan (2015) has connected Freud's thinking on affect to that of Deleuze and Guattari. He relates it to Proust and how the death drive can be found within literature. Greg Seigworth (2003, see also Seigworth and Gregg, 2010) has discussed the Freudian notion of affect in relation to Deleuze and Guattari (1983, 1987). He considers affect as an intersubjective space and modality between individuals. It is worth quoting the following, beautiful passage at length:

> In an encounter with either [music or infants], there are moments of unspeakable, unlocatable sensation that regularly occur: something outside of (beyond, alongside, before, between, etc.) words. For instance, what is it that transpires in the flash of your baby's smile as you walk through the door, exhausted, at the end of the day? What is it that instantaneously evaporates and what happens as something else takes its place?
>
> (Seigworth 2003, 85)

This idea of affect as an intersubjective modality and space is picked up again when discussing Anzieu later in this chapter.

While the authors cited earlier have all engaged with Freud and his conceptualisation of affect to varying degrees, a detailed discussion of his ideas is missing from such works. I shall do so in the next section. Freudian affect has also not really been used in empirical research which would be more closely linked to the social sciences than the humanities.

Freud and Affect

Sigmund Freud used the term 'affect' (Freud 1981a) [1895] early in his works when describing a subjective bodily state. Freud's early, so-called 'discharge model' marks the beginning of his affect theory (Green 1999, 21), and this chapter (chronologically) discusses other notions that subsequently informed the developments of his thinking.

For Freud, affects are subjective bodily states. In particular, his early theory of the mind was based partly on a model of energy (entropy). His work on hysteria [1883] focussed on an *excess* form of energy in the patient that demonstrated itself in hysterical symptoms. In that work, affect was initially understood as a quantitative 'sum of excitation' (Freud 1981a, 153) that had no outlet and consequently led to hysteria. Freud discovered that when his patients talked to him about traumatic events whose repression had led to hysteria that excess quantity of 'affect' (as he called it) was allowed to be discharged, to leave the body.

The Project for a Scientific Psychology

One of Freud's most important theorisations of affect (following on from his earliest in *Studies on Hysteria* [1893–1895]) can be found in the *Project for a Scientific Psychology* (1981a) [1895] (henceforth the *Project*). It laid the ground for his understanding of the term. Freud attempted to describe the very functioning of the brain, to be more precise cognition and perception.[1] After all, affect occupies a central position in the *Project*.

Early in this text, Freud defines the general nature of the nervous system as that of responding to and having to discharge stimuli from the outside and inside. It has two main functions: 'the reception of stimuli *from outside* and the discharge of excitations of *endogenous* origin [...]' (303, italics in the original). The quantities of either external or internal energies 'impinge on sensory neurons' (Schore 1997, 810) and need to be discharged. Freud was implicitly – and over the course of his text more explicitly – referring to affect here, as has been pointed out by some scholars (Schore 1997; Green 1999): 'Affect is brought about by a sudden discharge of previously stored excitation' (Schore 1997, 810). Stimuli from the outside are discharged by the neuronic system in so far as it 'employs the quantity of energy it acquires from outside in order to get rid of it' (Hansen 2000, 159). In the case of endogenous stimuli, the organism 'cannot withdraw' (Freud 1981a, 297) from stimuli from the inside. They can only be discharged through a quantitative amount of energy that is stored up in the nervous system for such a task. Freud then posited that there are two classes of neurones. One class allows stimuli to pass through and one only permits partial quantitative amounts of stimuli to pass through (ibid., 299). In Freud's words, 'Thus there are permeable neurones (offering no resistance and retaining nothing), which serve for perception, and impermeable ones (loaded with resistance [...]), which are the vehicles of memory and so probably of psychical processes in general' (Freud 1981a, 299–300). The notion of discharge was, for Freud, a general characterisation of mental functioning as far as perception and memory are concerned. However, it also acquires a central role in his affect theory. We will return to his definition of memory in a short while.

Up to this point in the *Project*, Freud provided a quantitative and universal theory of the human brain that describes the aforementioned processes as occurring unnoticed (one is not aware of neuronal processes as such). However, Freud then went on to add a qualitative/subjective dimension that he equated with conscious perception. It is this combination of quantity and quality that is also of importance for Freudian affect theory. Freud consequently defined consciousness as 'the subjective side of one part of the physical processes in the nervous system' (ibid., 11). As a result, the nervous system thereby consists of a system of turning quantity into quality: 'This system is linked with perception, and when it discharges energy, it produces consciousness by allowing the neuronal apparatus to perceive quality of impressions coming from the external world' (Stein 1999, 13). Before we can turn to Freudian affect theory in more detail, Freud's understanding of memory will be sketched here.

Affect and Memory

There are two key texts by Freud about memory – the *Project* [1895] and the *Note on the Mystic Writing Pad* [1925] (1981i). In its emphasis on resistance, receptivity, storage, and retrieval, the *Project* already alluded to notions that Freud would discuss more specifically 30 years later. He described the process of memory that is about storing and transmitting in his reference to the so-called 'mystic writing pad' (1981i). The writing pad is covered by a thin cellophane, a skin-like layer that protects the surface it covers from damage. By pressing upon the surface with a pen, one can write on it. It is the pen that leaves traces on the skin that can then be felt on the surface of the pad. These notions about storage and retrieval bear a striking similarity to contemporary digital media. It is thus, as Thomas Elsaesser (2009) argued, Sigmund Freud who is the first media theorist of our modern world.

To Freud, the psyche has the same capacity to store and retrieve data. It is the system of consciousness that receives but does not store data or perceptions while the unconscious stores excitations that are retained as mnemic traces. In that sense, all memories are unconscious at first. The system of consciousness excites what Freud called the memory system (Freud 1981a) and the mnemic trace is discharged and thus becomes conscious to the subject. As presented earlier, Freud conceptualised 'consciousness' in terms of what he would later refer to as the 'ego', that is, it works as a protective shield against 'sensory overload' that prevents 'perceptual overstimulation' (Elsaesser 2009, 104). The mnemic trace (or memory trace) that has crossed the protective shield is produced from unconscious perception and is thus rendered conscious or remembered (Freud 1981a,b,c).

This notion of memory is crucial for contextualising Freud's affect theory. The memory trace itself 'is a representation of an absent object, accompanied by affects' (Richard 2005, 1063). In that sense, the act of remembering is always accompanied by affects. As soon as a certain memory trace 'is touched, it springs into life again and shows itself cathected with excitation' (Freud 1981d, 578). All memories are stored or recorded, but their recollection depends on their cathexis. Affect comes into play here in so far as it is

> capable of increase, diminution, displacement and discharge, and [...] spread over the memory-traces of ideas somewhat as an electric charge is spread over the surface of a body.
>
> (Freud 1981c, 60)

It is the affect-as-process that is capable of discharging the memory trace into consciousness, so to speak. It is not a coincidence that Freud invokes the image of the skin surface that is hit by lasting impressions here. I return to this when discussing Anzieu. Memory traces, we could say, always bear tracks or swathes in which affect can fit in so that they are pushed into conscious awareness. In turn, a memory trace is stored in the form of *moving images*. I shall further outline this aspect in the section 'Affect and Audio-Visual Representation: The *Project* as a Scene of Earliest Communication'. As I have just discussed, the act of remembering is accompanied by affect. Yet this does not mean that in an affective experience something is necessarily remembered. Affective experiences can occur without conscious memory. Indeed, there is a significant amount of memory that lies outside our conscious awareness.

I have spent some time discussing Freud's early model of the mind because it harbours notions (quantity, quality, discharge, memory) that form the basis of his early affect theory (Green 1999, 22). This exposition was carried out in order to map and contextualise Freud's ideas that implicitly allude to affect. They will be unpacked further in the remaining sections and I will link them to watching media content more specifically. I will also return to a key passage in the *Project* later in this chapter. However, I now turn briefly to the relationship between Freud's theory of affect and the unconscious.

Affect and the Unconscious

Over the course of many years, Freud diverted more and more from a focus on conscious perception outlined in the early pages of the *Project* and devoted increasing effort to writing about the unconscious. This resulted in major shifts in his thinking. Briefly, he believed that subjects are influenced by unconscious processes and mental conflicts to a significant extent. These are often rooted in childhood experiences (accompanied by affects) that are too embarrassing, traumatic, or painful to be remembered. As a result, they are repressed by the individual and remain unconscious. This act of repression has given rise to the unconscious as such. The aim of repression is 'affective neutralization' (Green 1999, 49), a state in which the idea[2] and its affect are eradicated. Freud made a crucial distinction between 'affect' and 'idea' or 'representation' (Green 1999). Briefly put, he understood 'idea' or 'representation' as content of thought (*Vorstellung* in German), as something that is perceived. Of course, for Freud, something external is not simply perceived and processed or remembered, but, for example, ideas can be unconscious as a result of repression. Representation essentially refers to an inner and mental act. In his paper *Repression*, Freud (1981g) [1915] said that if an idea is repressed, there can be a residue – a 'quota of affect' (Freud 1981a, 170) – that makes the repression incomplete or failed. The ideational part of the repression may have succeeded but there are still 'feelings of unpleasure or anxiety' (1981e, 153) that can arise. This quota of affect is thus uncoupled from the idea and exists independently and finds expression in affective states that are experienced bodily. The quota is of quantity in so far as it can be experienced at different energy levels.

In *Fetishism* (1981k) [1927], Freud advanced the idea of repression and wrote that in the act of repression what is primarily targeted is the affect, only to be followed by the representational idea. While affects themselves can be repressed, this is an uncertain endeavour that leads to a conflict between the conscious and the unconscious. Repressed affects are either exchanged for diffuse feelings of anxiety or are in an idle state, waiting to attach themselves to a new, substitute idea: 'Thus the affect is always in an intermediary position. It is caught between its annihilation (reduction to zero) through discharge and its necessary supersession [...]' (Green 1999, 52). Affects may be repressed, but they may equally be discharged. Freud also regarded affects as consciously experienceable: 'The affect is a moving quantity, accompanied by a subjective tonality. It is through discharge that it becomes conscious [...]' (Green 1999, 70). If we regard the occurrence of affects as movement, it is only the last step in the sequence that is consciously experienced by the subject: 'Freud sees affect as consisting of an increase in psychic energy within the memory system; it is the cathecting of that system. The perception of an affect is effected through the excitation of a third system, consciousness [...]' (Stein 1999, 12). I have included Freud's conceptualisations of the relation between affect and repression here because they are an important aspect of his affect theory. They further illustrate the usefulness of his distinction between 'affect' and 'idea' for this book. An affective response to a scene from *Embarrassing Bodies*, or to a particular post on social media, for example, may be understood as a process whereby an idea (the show/the post's content) is cathected with specific affect. In my analyses of interview data, I do not go as far as to claim that interviewees had repressed ideas that return in the viewing process. Yet there seemed to be a relationship between aspects of their biographies, memory, and media use (see Chapters 2, 3, and 5). There appear to be certain affective responses that occur suddenly without an ideational referent that could deliver an explanation as to why they happen to the interviewees and myself. Ruth Stein (1999) has noted, contra Freud, that affective experiences that occur without context or are perceived as unpleasurable (such as the ones the interviewees spoke of) do not necessarily have to relate to repressed memories or ideas. Instead, the affect is 'excluded' (Stein 1999, 181) from the subject's body and attributed to other objects (such as the *Embarrassing Bodies* content). This act of exclusion may also be done through subjects' narratives.

The origins of affective experiences that occur suddenly, in the process of seeing something on *Embarrassing Bodies* for instance, may thus lie in the unconscious. According to Marjorie Brierley (1937, 259), 'Affects which appear to arise spontaneously always have unconscious stimuli [...]' that triggered them. Therefore, it may be highly difficult for the subject to speak about or to put affective moments into words (Green, 1999).

An affective experience may thus be 'aroused either by external perception [...], or by representation (evocation of a phantasy constructed in the psyche)' (ibid., 56), as Green highlights. For Freud, affective states do not exist in isolation. They are triggered by memory or an idea/representation. Alternatively, the (repressed) affect that has been uncoupled from the idea can also be in search of a new idea in order to be triggered off (Green 1999, 70). An idea/representation can be fantasy or language or even a film/television series being watched (Cartwright 2008; Kavka 2009) or a social media platform. The term, 'representation' does not refer to an external object or image as such, but rather to the processing work undertaken when we form and develop a perception of something. This notion of the connection between representation and affect is of relevance because of the affective reactions that were recounted by the interviewees.

In summary, affects are bodily sensations that are experienced and brought into consciousness or can be repressed altogether. In his early discharge model, Freud regarded affects not as energy itself but as 'processes of discharge of that energy' (Stein 1999, 7) that can be successful (neutralised or repressed) or not. They further relate to memory. An act of remembering is accompanied by an affective experience. Alternatively, an affective experience may result in remembering, or, lastly, it may occur suddenly without an origin or explanation and may therefore have unconscious origins (such as unconscious memories or ideas). But what exactly is an affect as an experience and how is it felt? I shall return to this question in a moment.

Freud failed, as André Green notes, to offer a conclusive definition of the term. However, he did outline an important definition in the *Introductory Lectures* (1981h) [1917]:

> And what is affect in the dynamic sense? It is in any case something highly composite. An affect includes in the first place particular motor innervations or discharges and secondly certain feelings; the latter are of two kinds—perceptions of the motor actions that have occurred and the direct feelings of pleasure and unpleasure which, as we say, give the affect its keynote.
>
> (Freud 1981h, 395)

This point about discharges and feelings has been often overlooked in discussions on Freud (Green 1999). It presents a development in his thinking that renders the notion of affect more complex. The affective experience that was triggered for whatever conscious or unconscious reason is characterised by two things: discharges (in the physiological sense) and feelings. These feelings (that are of two kinds themselves) consist of a perception by the subject that the affective experience has occurred (e.g., the feeling of sweat beads on my skin when I am frightened) and, second, feelings of pleasure or unpleasure or a wishful or fantasmatic nature that are tied to the affect, not the idea (e.g., a feeling that could be characterised as unpleasure because of the fright). In other words, 'Affect is regarded as both a bodily and a psychological experience, the former being the condition for the latter' (Stein 1999, 126). The affect itself has thus a *sensation* and a *quality* to it. André Green has summarised this in a rather reductive but nonetheless helpful way, and he provides an overview of what an affect essentially consists of for Freud:

The affect is split into two sides:

1 A corporal, above all visceral side;
2 A psychical side, itself split into two:

    a   Perception of corporal movements;
    b   Sensations of pleasure – unpleasure.

(Green 1999, 159)

We can see here once again how, for Freud, the affective discharge as a movement moves from a physiological-neurological dimension to a psychical one. The moment of discharge 'snatches the body from silence' (Green 1999, 160) and makes the subject feel alive and bodily.

Affect and Language

In this book substantial emphasis is placed on language in the form of transcribed interviews. Transcription is itself a way of turning speech into written text. This speech may refer to bodily feelings: for example, experiences of watching *Embarrassing Bodies* or using social media. For that reason, the issue of affect and language has to be addressed. This will be outlined in this section before I can proceed to making a link between affect and media representation. As I was not with the interviewees when they watched *Embarrassing Bodies* or used Twitter or Instagram and did not witness their affective reactions first-hand but only as attempts to verbalise them, the question of affect and language is quite important. For Freud, affect is not outside or excluded from language (that is, words and speech) but in tension with it: 'Affect may allow itself to be expressed by language, but it is essentially outside it' (Green 1999, 48). This sentence does not mean that the affective experience cannot be verbalised *a postiori*. If we recall in the description of perception in the *Project*, the mechanisms Freud described occur in the brain and are not felt in their process-like nature. I cannot feel the act of a neuronal process in my brain as such, but I can feel its results: for example, in the act of remembering something. Similarly, affective states may 'short-circuit' (ibid., 47) language, as Green says, and I would posit that in the first instance, they always do so. I might feel a particular sensation when using media and, second, I might verbalise it. Here, one could argue that there is no opposition between affect and language but a fundamental tension.[3] Green has drawn on Freud's model to elaborate this point. Freud remained relatively silent on the matter of affect and language. For Green, one can essentially not say anything about the affect as such: '[H]aving reached the essential of the experience of the affect, I can say nothing more about it: it is pleasant or unpleasant' (ibid., 160). It is helpful to illustrate this point with a short quotation from an interview (see Chapter 2 for a detailed analysis):

> Erm, not very good at watching needles go in, don't know why, I have to look away at that point. Don't like, can't watch things with eyes that freaks me out and can't watch anything that involves boobs being pulled around. Breast augmentation just makes me feel ill and liposuction because I don't know why.
>
> (I2, 491–494)

The interviewee was able to comment on the unpleasant quality of her affective experiences but she could not say anything about the nature of them. One could interpret the quote, following Stein (1999, 81), as a narrative about unpleasurable affect that is solely attributed to the content of the show, thereby expelling it from the speaker's body. I suggest that there may be a kind of circular movement at stake here by which the affective experience relates *both* to the perceived content and to the interviewees' life history and bodily experiences: 'Through the affect, the unconscious is manifested as that which seizes the ego, questions it, subjugates it' (Green 1999, 162). This abrupt and visceral seizure does not, however, necessarily lead to knowledge about the nature of the affective experience or the reasons that lay behind it. Affect is structured by an 'energic upsurge that invades language and may destructure it to the point that it becomes unintelligible and refers, on the analysand's admission, to the unsayable' (ibid., 174). Later in his book, Green stresses this again when he says that 'affect appears only when the other parts of speech have exhausted their possibility of speech, hence my difficulty in speaking about it' (ibid., 251). Again, there is 'difficulty' but no impossibility in speaking about affective experiences. As affects can be consciously experienced, the ego (possibly) reflects on them. Affects 'are palpable as they can dynamically infuse the space between the conscious and nonconscious aspects of human experience' (Ellis et al. 2013, 719). Ruth Stein has elaborated on a similar point when discussing the Freudian affect:

> In this sense, affect is reflexive and even reflective. It reflects on what has been experienced in a delayed manner [...]. Hence, the moment of experience and the moment of meaning or signification never coincide, the latter always being retroactive.
>
> (Stein 1999, 132)

It is this delayed bringing into consciousness of affect that was discussed by some of the interviewees during the interviews. In speaking about their watching of *Embarrassing Bodies* they reflected on moments of 'excitement', 'shock', turning away from the screen, or 'relief' as experienced at different points in time. These words suggest descriptions of experiences that precisely escape accurate language description and do not refer to clear emotions but affective states that are harder to pinpoint and explain.

Affect and Audio-Visual Representation: The *Project* as a Scene of Earliest Communication

Lisa Cartwright (2008) draws on Sigmund Freud and André Green (1999) and the Freudian notion of affect.[4] Cartwright argues that we may be particularly affected by media in a way that is felt by the body.

As discussed earlier, affect is tied to representation and mnemic traces. It is either coupled or uncoupled from a mnemic trace but has a life of its own with a qualitative tonality. In order to develop this theme, it is helpful to return to Freud again here in more detail.

In the *Project for a Scientific Psychology* (1981a), Freud outlined (among other things discussed earlier) how affect is experienced by the baby in an early situation that is marked by the experience of satisfaction. For example, a baby is hungry and feels this internally and begins to cry.

Satisfaction is only made possible, through the other (e.g., mother or father) responding to the cries and providing food. The cries are of an affective nature that seek to discharge the feeling of unpleasure. The discharge is completed in that sense by the reaction of the mother or father who provides food. 'In this way this path of discharge acquires a secondary function of the highest importance, that of *communication* [...]', writes Freud (1981a, 318, italics in the original). Here affect is simultaneously discharge and a form of social communication (that is not of a linguistic nature of course) towards an other. As Diamond says,

> The caretaker introduces a response which conveys affect and meaning, which in turn indelibly colours somatic experience, giving rise to somatic–affective–evaluative states.
>
> (Diamond 2013a, 84)

It is the totality of the event with its different moments, sequences, and rhythmic movements that constitutes the experience of satisfaction for the baby. Green argues,

> [F]rom now on satisfaction will be associated with the image of the object that first aroused it [e.g. the breast, JJ] and the moving image of the reflex movement that allowed its discharge [e.g. crying].
>
> (Green 1999, 23)

Green says that, on the one hand, affect is consequently linked 'to the function of communication and therefore to language, and, on the other, to bodily experience through the moving image of discharge' (ibid.). These bodily experiences can be viewed as discharges and are remembered as moving images (e.g., crying-as-discharge) that are stored as memory traces (that are themselves subject to variation and change) in the baby's memory. They are, as discussed earlier, unconscious. The memory traces and how they came into existence are relational in nature. They are formed as part of 'a relationship where a memory is acquired and the "pathway of discharge", the "neuronal pathways", are forged from memory of past experience, from a communication that leaves its indelible mark' in the subject (Diamond 2013a, 86). Any subsequent affective experience, then, marks 'the re-emergence of a memory accompanied by body sensations' (Stein 1999, 13). As noted earlier, affect always has a psycho-biographical element to it and so affective experiences always need to be seen in relation to a subject's conscious and unconscious history. Of course, the memory as such is not re-emerging, for memory is always subject to variation and change. The memory trace that is (unconsciously) re-emerging within the affect is either of a pleasurable or unpleasurable nature. It can also be associated with fantasies or wishes. Affects, even though Freud tended to change this in his work that followed the *Project*, are thus more than mere drives (Stein 1999). This is an important insight. I will argue in later chapters that from a Freudian perspective, the affective experiences of the interviewees may have emerged because they were triggered as a result of (unconscious) memories.

As Green (1999, 205) notes, 'No notion is more directly linked to the historical dimension [of the subject] than the affect'. I shall return to this point in my discussion of Didier Anzieu. However, to put it somewhat crudely for now, in the beginning of a subject's life is the affective relation between herself and her mother and father as well as her siblings and other members of the primary group. The baby is also born in a particular social and cultural context. The very first page in a subject's biography consists of affect and the senses (Stein 1999). From a developmental perspective, psychoanalysis regards the early months and years in the infant's development as (ideally) made up of 'increasing affective maturity' (Green 1999, 70). This does not mean that affects will seize to exist at a certain point in time but rather that the baby and infant achieve a kind of control over an overwhelming dominance of those affects that they are initially confronted with. This is done in a *relational* manner, as Didier Anzieu (2016) and many of the object-relations school (e.g., Bion 1963; Klein 1988a,b; Winnicott 2002) have shown. I shall return to this point in a moment.

The notion of a relation between affect and development marks a crucial addition to affect theory that neither Freud nor Green managed to explore adequately. Green, in fact, strongly rejects a developmental approach to affect that takes account of a subject's history (Green 1999, 288). Instead he develops a structural model that ignores a subject's history given its universal approach. I differ from Green in that respect.

To return to Cartwright (2008) and to make the link between affect and visual representation, she argues that these early experiences of affects – that are not always satisfied of course – have an impact on the subject's very ability to relate to something on screen. Any affective experience to a representation on screen relates to early affective experiences and moving images as memory traces. These early experiences can be reproduced on screen 'in a form that brings together the inward, inner movement of affect as tension and discharge in and through the subject's body with the perception of, and also communication toward' (Cartwright 2008, 41) the subject on screen. As noted earlier, in any affective experience 'the old background of childhood' (Green 1999, 212) is reborn – consciously or unconsciously. For Cartwright, this is affect's fundamental capability to potentially *move* the viewer: the 'object of affect (which may be a person, an image, a material artefact) is always subject to projection' (ibid., 47) by the viewer. However, this is not the viewer alone but instead the viewer in union with the object; together they have animated the object of affect that has resulted in affective reactions on the part of the viewer. The viewer has given it 'the power "to make me feel"' (ibid., 47). This is crucial because we see a relational model of media reception being outlined here. It is not the image that affects the viewer but the viewer who has brought the image alive to let him/herself be affected by it in a kind of circular movement. This act may not always be of a conscious nature. A similar argument has been proposed by Misha Kavka (2009) in her discussion of affect and reality television. While her work is not distinctly psychoanalytic, she briefly touches on the *Project*. For Kavka, affect is closely related to the '*technology* of the moving image' (ibid., 5, italics in the original), as with cinema or television. She argues that Freud's notion of the moving image of discharge that is stored as a mnemic trace in the baby lays the groundwork for a subject's ability to be affected by technologically produced, moving images. This is why affect has such a resonance with moving media images: It is itself distinctly *technological* and *sequential*. I return to this idea in more depth in the book's Conclusion.

Both Kavka's and Cartwright's works enable one to draw on a complex and psychoanalytic theory of affect in relation to media. If for Green (and Freud), affect is 'a psychical event linked to a movement awaiting a form' (Green 1999, 65), then this movement, for Cartwright, can also be found in the media text. The text can be 'traced for the material routes by which it elicits feelings' (Cartwright 2008, 35) or affective reactions in subjects who consume it.

Skin, the Body, and Trauma: Putting the Senses and the Social into Freudian Affect

So far, I have discussed Freud's affect theory and accompanying concepts that show the complexity and conception of an intersubjective, corporeally based subjectivity that are at stake in his model. While I have shown the relationality of his model, particularly by describing the scene in the *Project*, it still remains centred on affect that is experienced by the *individual* subject. However, an affective experience designates an act of communication towards the social, towards the other, and an already existing relation with the other, a myself-other matrix in which the affective experience occurred. If I scream 'eurgh', cover my eyes, or my body is moved, I am involuntarily communicating the discharge of the affective experience.

Affect's relationship with the social can be unpacked some more. Not only are bodies always situated within social worlds, but Freud's model lacks a more concrete, phenomenological, sensual account of what an affect essentially is or how it can be experienced in its different ways (Anzieu 2016). This point can be addressed by drawing on Didier Anzieu and his writings on the communication between baby and mother, father and others that is both relational and affective. Anzieu has also underscored the developmental aspect of affect that was briefly discussed by drawing on Cartwright (2008). As I argue in Chapters 2 and 3, the affective viewing experiences of some of the interviewees may be interpreted as being related to both their biographies and the programme. Their ability to be affected by it may thus be seen in relation to aspects of their biographies and particularly affective experiences of the body that they have had while growing up. It is related to the programme in so far as specific scenes that the interviewees talked about evoke these affective experiences. I make a similar point about social media use in Chapter 5. To sum up, affect is thus both social and psycho-biographical. Before turning to Anzieu, his indebtedness to the Freudian idea of the bodily ego will be briefly reviewed.

The Bodily Ego and Trauma

In *The Ego and the Id*, Freud (1991b) [1923] defined the ego as fundamentally bodily in nature:

> A person's own body and above all its surface, is a place from which both external and internal perceptions may spring. [...] Pain, too, seems to play a part in the process, and the way in which we gain new knowledge of our organs during painful illnesses is perhaps a model of the way by which in general we arrive at the idea of our body. The ego is first and foremost a bodily ego.
>
> (Freud 1991b, 451)

Pile suggests that there are three aspects to be drawn from the idea of the ego being a bodily ego: 'first and foremost, it is bodily; second, it is a surface entity; and, third, it is a mental projection of a surface' (Pile 2011, 60). The ego is a mental skin-image and is thus similar, or equal, in function and shape to actual skin covering the body. The ego is established in the first place through sensual experiences on and through the skin itself (ibid.). As Pile points out, the ego is not just a projection of a surface. The ego is in its form like a body, body-shaped, in the sense that it has spatiality, surface, depth, and interiority and exteriority (ibid., 63). As will be explored in a moment, it also has the qualities of an envelope, of filtering, protecting, holding, sensing – in other words, the qualities that physical skin has. It is the corporeal and sensual nature of the skin that gives rise to the ego.

In returning to the previous quote, sensations of suffering and pain act as reference points for experiencing and understanding the body. When being in pain that pain becomes the body as a whole. We take our body as the painful body. As we shall see, skin – or what Freud calls the 'surface' – plays a very important role here. The skin is, as Diamond (2013a) points out, experienced as being inside and outside simultaneously. The sensations experienced from within refer to the skin surface, which is directly exposed to the gaze and touch of others. For Anzieu and Freud, the skin, like the ego, protects against outer stimuli while being angled towards the inner world, the interior of the body.

Already in the *Project*, Freud described one of the functions of the nervous system, the cortical layer more precisely (he refers to this as the 'protective shield' in *Beyond the Pleasure Principle*), to protect against too many stimuli. Perception as such is here understood

> as a mechanism for psychic defense: the information it yields helps the psyche determine how great a store of cathected energy it will need to master incoming stimuli and thus preserve its equilibrium against the threat of trauma.
>
> (Hansen 2000, 156)

This idea was to be developed further by Freud. In *Beyond the Pleasure Principle* (1991a), written in 1920, Freud gives a biological yet vivid and affective account of trauma that emphasises the bodily nature of trauma:

> We describe as 'traumatic' any excitations from outside which are powerful enough to break through the protective shield. It seems to me that the concept of trauma necessarily implies a connection of this kind with a breach in an otherwise efficacious barrier against stimuli.
>
> (Freud 1991a, 301)

We can see a parallel here with the brief sketch of the nervous system of the *Project* reproduced earlier. For Freud, perception and memory are characterised by a layer of contact-barriers that filter stimuli and allow some to pass through easily, partially or with more difficulty. This is similar to the shield of the surface ego – that Freud discussed in *The Ego and the Id* – that protects itself against being overwhelmed by stimuli. This function can break down in the case of trauma or break down momentarily as in the case of affect.

The two previous quotations from *The Ego and the Id* and *Beyond the Pleasure Principle* are very significant. They foreground the ego as bodily ego and show the significance of the skin surface. They exemplify psychoanalysis' preoccupation with the body and bodily matters. As developed by Anzieu (2016), it is this Freudian definition of the skin as a material and virtual phenomenon that is of affective significance for the protection and development of the ego that I follow here.[5] Furthermore, Freud's idea of the protective shield needs to be discussed as it is the central reference point for Anzieu's (2016) approach to the body. For Freud, the protective shield 'functions as a special envelope or membrane resistant to stimuli' (Freud 1991a, 21). This envelope enwraps the psyche and is simultaneously the skin on someone's body. It is at once virtual and material. Freud thus implicitly paved the way for a more sensual model of relational communication that is structured by touch, affect, and a subject in relation to the other as well as the virtual and fantasy.

The Skin Ego

These ideas have been taken up and developed further by Didier Anzieu. In *The Skin Ego* (2016), he argues that the skin is a complex organ that can be regarded as prefiguring 'the complexity of the Ego' (Anzieu 2016, 15). The skin – which is capable of perceiving touch, heat, pressure and pain – is closely related to the other sense organs and to a person's sense and awareness of movement and balance (ibid., 15). The skin has, of course, a highly affective dimension to it. If something 'gets under our skin', we are moved or affected by someone or something and can feel it on the outer layer of our skin (Diamond 2013a). Skin appears on the embryo before all other senses are formed (Segal 2009, 44), and it is the mother who gives the skin to the baby through her cells. Early skin contact, bodily contact between mother and child, is essential for the child's development. Anzieu, drawing on Freud, proposes the notion of the 'skin- ego' (ibid., 60) (henceforth skin ego) and regards the skin as double layered, an envelope that consists of the experiences a baby has through, for example, feeding, bathing, touching, care, and so on but also through hearing while at the same time functioning as a border that keeps other experiences at bay, such as aggression. The skin ego, even though Anzieu emphasises the idea of the surface, is three dimensional and spatial (Pile 2011). The skin is an inscribing surface that is used for communicating with others as they leave their (implicit or explicit) marks and traces on the baby's skin: 'Messages in this context are gestural and tactile, affective, multisensory and accompanied by others mirroring the child's body' (Diamond 2013a, 155). The baby achieves a sense of self *through* and with the other. Most importantly, the skin ego is also a *mental and metaphorical image* (Houzel 1990).

Based on surface experiences the baby *creates* the skin ego 'to represent itself as an Ego' (Anzieu 2016, 43). The skin ego serves a narcissistic and protective purpose in order for the baby to feel within a secure boundary. Anzieu's notion makes explicit the relationality of the body in general and the skin in particular. Touch – and thus skin – is the first experience of relationality in the baby. When the baby touches their skin, they experience skin (a finger) that is touching as well as skin (on the body) that is being touched. The mother surrounds the baby in the outer layer of the skin envelope through care, touch, communication, and so on, and the baby's body, their skin, marks the inner envelope (ibid., 63) that receives and responds to the mother (or father). We can think of the image of a mother holding a baby with her hands that form a protective shield against the outside (stimuli, heat, cold, etc.). In that sense, the mother has not only acted as a container for the embryo inside her while the foetus was growing but once the baby is born this function of a container continues (ibid., 85). This physical container is mirrored in the baby's mind as an imaginary container that enwraps her psyche and allows an ego to emerge (Diamond 2013a, 142).

The baby has the fantasy of sharing a *common skin* with the mother, 'an interface' (Anzieu 2016, 64) that binds them together. These experiences are fundamental: 'to be an Ego is to feel one has the capacity to send out signals that are received by others' (Anzieu 1989, 62). Of course, before the baby touches herself, she is *always* already touched by the other. She is mirrored and responded to through bodily contact by others in the form of touch, holding, kissing, rocking, and so on. The skin functions as an 'interface' (Anzieu 2016, 67) that binds mother and child to each other. The skin ego is a 'screen' (ibid., 67) that mirrors the baby and mother. The baby thinks of herself and feels as a subject through the eyes and touch of the other. The illusion of a shared skin also acts as a container for the baby's actions. Her actions are contained by the mother in so far as she responds to them adequately. This process is crucial for the child's development. The mother acts as a containing and filtering skin for her child:

> Thinking develops by the mother helping her child contain multiple sensations; she aids their articulation by interpreting and differentiating between experiences. Mother binds the sensory experiences so that the child can take them back in a digestible form.
>
> (Diamond 2013a, 142)

In returning to the Freudian idea of 'affect as discharge', we can see how, for example, the mother aids the baby in responding to the internal affective states (e.g., hunger) by offering the breast. In reading the scene from the *Project* (that was described in 'The *Project for a Scientific Psychology*') with Anzieu we can think about it further in relation to its sensual and virtual qualities. It is the act of offering the breast that provides nourishment for the baby but also a *discharge* of the feeling of hunger. Importantly, it is an act of sensual exchange, deep connection, and skin contact. It is also an act of affective communication between mother and baby. A surplus state of excitation, we could say, is perceived by the mother (e.g., through the baby crying or licking of the lips), responded to and thus allowed to be discharged. These dynamics are very much structured by affect: Affect is a kind of blank canvas or surface shared between infant and mother onto which different tonalities and colours can be drawn. It 'lends the color, the nuances, and the modulations to the verbal sign' (Stein 1999, 134). 'Affect acts as the supra-modal currency into which stimulation in any modality can be translated' (Stern 1998, 53), as Daniel Stern has noted in relation to the mother-infant relationship.[6] Affect is a kind of blank canvas or surface shared between infant and mother onto and through which different tonalities and colours can be drawn.

Affect, then, is *central* in the phenomenological modalities of communication between mother and baby. It is an underlying phenomenon in the rhythmic relations between the baby and others. Skin and the skin ego hold a central role in this affective communication between them. I return to it in more detail later.

Anzieu lists eight functions of the skin ego. The first function is *holding*. The baby forms a mental image of the mother's (and/or father's) touch that both in fantasy and reality creates a sense of security. We can think of a baby that cries as soon as she is put down and is soothed immediately once picked up, carried, touched, and held by the parents (Anzieu 2016, 106). The second function is *containing*.[7] Touch but also sound (the voice) lead to a mental envelope that enwrap the baby and, again, give a sense of security, or anxiety if absent. The mother and father provide a passive container that contains the child's 'sensations/images/affects' (ibid., 109) and at the same time active responses that process and digest the child's sensations, images, or affects so that they become bearable (ibid., 109–110). The third function is to *protect against stimuli*. We should recall here what was noted earlier in relation to Freud and the skin as a protective shield. The fourth function of the skin ego is to *individuate* the self, giving the baby a sense of their complete uniqueness (ibid., 112). The fifth function is *intersensoriality* or 'consensuality' (Segal 2009, 48). The skin is affected by sensations, and these are registered by the ego. A 'common sense' (Anzieu 2016, 112) is formed that always has the sense of touch as a reference point. The skin – and this needs to be stressed – simultaneously shows itself to be in a mental representation. The sixth function is *supporting sexual excitation*. The baby has many skin experiences that are of a pleasurable nature, for example, touching, kissing, bathing, and feeding, and this capacity to experience something as pleasurable will later enable sexuality to come into being (ibid., 112–113). The seventh function is that of *libidinal recharging*. It means that internal – affective – tensions and energies are maintained in a balance. The eighth function is to *register traces.* The skin provides 'direct information about the external world' (Anzieu 2016, 113) in terms of registering stimuli: for example, heat or cold or someone's touch. As Anzieu points out, 'An early form of anxiety related to this function is the fear of being marked all over the surface of one's body and Ego by indelible and shameful inscriptions derived from the Superego—blushes, rashes, eczema' (ibid., 114).

As the baby develops, the experiences of a common skin and separation from the mother simultaneously emerge. The common interface is slowly and often painfully separated into two bodies/egos/skins. The baby learns that there are two bodies and forms her own ego, what Anzieu calls the 'thinking ego' (ibid., 150). The skin and with it tactility are crucial for human beings. It provides a 'mental background' (ibid., 90) to the psyche, as Anzieu maintains. He quotes an added passage to Freud's *Standard Edition, Volume XIX:*

> i.e. the ego is ultimately derived from bodily sensations, chiefly from those springing from the surface of the body. It may thus be regarded as a mental projection of the surface of the body, besides, as we have seen above, representing the superficies of the mental apparatus.
> (Freud 1981i, 26, quoted in Anzieu 2016, 91)

Sensual and corporeal experiences are the basis of a reflexive development of the ego. Marjorie Brierley underscored this point vividly:

> The child must sense the breast, for instance, before it begins to perceive (i.e. recognize) it, and it must feel its sucking sensations before it recognizes its own mouth. It will develop recognition wherever there is a basis for it in sensory experience.
> (Brierley 1937, 261–262)

These acts of sensing are very much done through the tongue and the hands/skin in relation to the breast or mother that are the other. To reiterate, before the baby *knows* of any objects (e.g., the breast) or has a whole, coherent, conscious idea of a self, they are sensed and leave, literally, impressions on her. The skin ego holds the different parts of the baby's body together, for the baby is not yet able to think of herself as one and as a body with boundaries. The ego and with it the self-conscious human subject has arisen from touch and skin. We can see that skin is of fundamental importance to any human being. It is important to hold the notion of the relational skin and body in mind, for the body (and skin) is always relational and part of the other, especially before the baby experiences her body as her own. The body and the skin continue to be of a relational nature throughout a person's life. Skin and with it the skin ego are thus psychosocial phenomena, situated at the intersection, or rather bringing together the dialectic of the inner and outer world. As Pile has observed, 'Anzieu stresses that the skin ego is an interface, boundary, frontier or layer between the inside and outside, between the individual and the world' (Pile 2011, 64).

Conclusion

This chapter has brought together works by Freud, Green, and Stein on the Freudian notion of affect with the idea of the skin ego as proposed by Anzieu. I argue that Freud's emphasis on affect being about the body and partially non-discursive ways of experience is also a characteristic of the assertions of many affect theorists. Freudian affect theory and other affect theories conceptualise affect as an abrupt, sudden, excessive, less fixed, raw, less modulated, and fluid mode of experience. However, the emphasis by Freud on the individual experience of affect and on the tension that exists between affect, language, and representation makes him stand out against current traditions of affect theory and, so I argue, his affect theories are of value to this project. Freud's theorisation of affect is distinctly related to the subject and modes of expression that are in tension with language as discourse. I have underscored this point by drawing on Green (1999) who has written extensively about this tension.

Several media scholars (Bonner 2005; Kavka 2009; Bratich 2011; Gibbs 2011; Sender 2012; Skeggs and Wood 2012) have described reality and makeover television as particularly laden with affect and scenes that can lead to affective responses on the part of viewers. I draw on the connection between affect and contemporary reality television in Chapters 2 and 3, and think through the interviewees' affective responses to some of the scenes on *Embarrassing Bodies*. Even though these scholars' conceptions of affect are not – or only vaguely – psychoanalytic, they still offer a starting point for thinking about a psychoanalytic model of affect in relation to media.

By drawing on Freud, Green, and Stein, I have provided a detailed overview of the Freudian definition of affect and how it evolved from the *Project for a Scientific Psychology* up to his later works. I showed that for Freud affect was a key concept and he returned to it many times in his writing. The *Project* essentially claims that the nervous system consists of a protective shield (or cortical layer) that allows stimuli to pass through. The idea of discharge is already present here. It is a general function of memory and perception. The protective shield limits the amount of stimuli that enter so that no overload can take place. Freud's take on affect is noteworthy because he establishes a connection between affect and the unconscious and affect and a subject's biography.

As I discuss in Chapters 2, 3, and 5 of this book, looking at interview data from a psychoanalytic standpoint suggests that there may be an unconscious connection between the affective experiences of some of the interviewees and aspects of their biographies that are tied to bodily experiences (such as illnesses or a body refusing to function as desired).

It is the sequential and process-like nature of the Freudian model that allows one to think about an embodied viewing experience that is partially marked by affective experiences that are discharged.

I have followed Cartwright (2008) and Kavka (2009), who make a connection between media content and the Freudian affect model. Freud highlighted that affect itself is the earliest form of communication and associated with mnemic traces that are remembered as moving images. Affect is thus present in a subject's biography from birth onwards. Both Cartwright and Kavka argue that this earliest form of affective communication (and its wider psychodynamics) is of importance for a viewer's ability and ways of relating to something seen on screen. She emphasises the relationality between the viewing subject and the content that is watched. It is the viewer, and often their unconscious, that has animated a scene in order to be affected by it. It is not the image or scene that has a kind of autonomous power over the viewer, but the viewer's investment into a scene that has brought the scene alive. This *generative* movement of bringing it alive is felt by the body in an affective response that is discharged. As I discuss in Chapter 2, this circuit model of media reception is a fruitful one as it makes space for biographically inspired, relational, embodied, and often unconscious modes of media use that characterise, for example, watching television as a process.

It was the task of the second part of this chapter to make affect as a concept for analysis more concrete and grounded in the living and phenomenological body. The body is also a social body and thus always psychosocially marked by subjective and social aspects and the relationship to other subjects and objects. The challenge posed by Freud's ideas is that the actual experiential qualities of affect are not touched upon. Freud's model is very useful in thinking about bodily reactions to reality television shows, such as *Embarrassing Bodies*, but one is left with insufficient concepts to grasp the relational, social, phenomenological, and ontological aspects of an affective experience. Didier Anzieu's work on the skin ego is a vital addition at this point.

Anzieu takes Freud's notion of the protective shield that is both resistant as well as permeable to stimuli as a starting point. He emphasises that we communicate through and with the skin. The skin is the fundamental, pre-linguistic sign of our bodies that puts us in *relation* to each other. Before we touch our own bodies and form images and ideas about them, we are touched by others. Thinking about one's own body thus always implies a dual body; a thinking about another by another (Diamond 2013a, 152). It is this idea of sharing the skin that presents a further development in Anzieu's work. The skin ego is both virtual and sensual-material and exists in relation to myself as a kind of outsider to my own body and also in relation to the other. As well as protecting the psyche, the skin is a medium that is left with impressions and traces by both mother and baby. This affective communication is marked by touch and the senses that ultimately give rise to the ability to think and fantasise.

While both Freud and Anzieu conceptualise affective experiences and communication as rhythmic modes of discharge that are seen in response and relation to something (another human being or a perception, for example), this has been met with some critique by psychoanalysts (Diamond 2013a). Some argue that the subject is conceptualised as too passive and as only being reactive to internal or external states. While this model and my discussion of it works very well in thinking about affective responses to television viewing, I seek to develop the discharge model in Chapters 4 and 5 towards a more active model that relates affect in the psychoanalytic sense to discussions of affective labour.

As we shall see, the discussion of the skin and the skin ego has also served another purpose. In contrast to much of communication/media and cultural studies' conceptions of communication and the subject that emphasises (technological) screens, interfaces, audiences, responses, and interactivity, it is in fact the skin that acts as the very first medium humans engage with. The skin and skin relations mark the very beginning of any subjective communications. They are what Anzieu calls the 'backcloth' (Anzieu 2016, 164) to sensory communication and indeed to any communication. This has implications for how we should think about the media, mediums, and communication more generally. These points will be addressed in the next chapters.

Notes

1 I cannot engage with the neuroscientific evidence behind Freud's theorisations in this book. I follow his model as a theoretical idea in order to interpret data gathered through interviews (see later chapters). Many neuroscientists have described the prophetic vision of Freud (see Schore 1997 or Centonze et al. 2004 for an overview). In order to reduce complexity, as most readers of this book might not be familiar with neurology, I have omitted a detailed summary of the *Project* here. This includes Freud's detailed description (and terms) for different neurons and quantities. It also has to be noted that Freud extensively revised and changed certain aspects outlined in the *Project,* including, among other issues, concerns regarding his affect theory and the discharge model. I outline in 'The *Project for a Scientific Psychology*' why I take the basic premise of the discharge model as a part of the theoretical framework. The model is complemented by other aspects of Freud's later works, as discussed in this chapter.

2 Another key Freudian term is closely related to this: 'cathexis'. It signifies the act of attributing psychic energy to an idea, to a body part or an object (Laplanche and Pontalis 1973, 63). To give an example,

> a subject can evoke an important event in his own history with indifference, while the unpleasant or intolerable nature of an experience may be associated with a harmless event rather than with the one which originally brought about the unpleasure.

> (ibid., 63)

An idea was thus cathected with energy and regarded as harmless.

3 See Wetherell (2012) and Ellis et al. (2013) for a similar argument.

4 Misha Kavka (2009) also briefly discusses Green in her work on reality television and affect.

5 We can, of course, define skin from a biological or more cultural point of view. Steven Connor (2009) discusses how skin is thought of in different disciplines and by different thinkers. Segal (2009, 46) points out that skin has been discussed by other psychoanalytic thinkers but no one has put it centre stage as Anzieu has done.

6 Elsewhere in his book, Stern captures his understanding of affect beautifully when he writes, 'These elusive qualities [of affect] are better captured by dynamic, kinetic terms, such as "surging," "fading away," "fleeting," "explosive," "crescendo," "decrescendo," "bursting," "drawn out," and so on' (Stern 1998, 54).

7 Anzieu primarily draws on Bion's 'container/contained' model (Bion 1963) here. In broad strokes, Bion's container/contained model consists of someone (the infant or the patient) who experiences something (e.g., pain or dissatisfaction) and is in search of and being found by the mother's breast. The mother can sense the infant's feelings (e.g., distress when she is hungry) and reacts to them and feeds the baby. The baby realises that she is dependent on the mother and develops a sense of recognition as well as a sense of how to deal with affective experiences and distress (through crying, for example). In this dynamic model there is simultaneously a 'searching' and a 'being found/responding'. The model is thus about a dual process of how 'lived experience' (Ogden 2004, 1345) is processed. It is implicitly and universally present in all subjects, albeit to varying degrees. Both the container and contained functions happen largely unconsciously, according to Bion.

2 Affect, Biography, and Watching Reality Television

Introduction

Reality television consumption has often been discussed by scholars in terms of *Schadenfreude*, entertainment, voyeurism, and class positions on the part of the viewers who make sense of the content they see (Nabi et al. 2003; Calvert 2004; Deery 2004; Metzl 2004; Hill 2005; Nunn and Biressi 2005; Hall 2006; Papacharissi and Mendelson 2007; Lundy et al. 2008; Baruh 2009, 2010; Bagdasarov et al. 2010; Sender 2012; Skeggs and Wood 2012). Many authors have also critically discussed the ideological aspects of the genre. For instance, Angela McRobbie argues that the development of reality television goes hand in hand with the neo-liberal practice of 'eradicating welfare and social security in favour of self-help, and personal responsibility' (McRobbie 2009, 34). Consequently, a model neo-liberal individual is created by reality television programmes. Many scholars draw on the ideas of Michel Foucault in their critical analyses. When thinking about reality television, the idea of surveillance naturally comes to mind. These formats present a form of discipline and the active workings of power that is both shown on television and potentially adopted by audiences, as much research suggests (Ouellette 2004; Wood and Skeggs 2004; Bratich 2007; McCarthy 2007; Ouellette and Hay 2008a,b; Weber 2009). Related to this, makeover shows in particular have been criticised by feminist writers for their ideology (McRobbie 2004, 2009; Di Mattia 2007; Sherman 2008). Scholars argue that sexist and heteronormative stereotypes of what it means to be a woman, to be beautiful, and so on are depicted in these shows (Wilson 2005; Jackson 2007; Wegenstein and Ruck 2011). In a more positive light, Katherine Sender (2012) and Annette Hill (2007) have stressed that audiences use reality and makeover shows in a complex and nuanced way to make sense of their own lives, problems, and relationships.

While these works represent an important contribution to reality television audience research, they lack considerations of embodied-affective modes of viewing and instead rely more on cognitive accounts of viewers. This chapter discusses two case studies and supplements them with data from other interviewees. All data was collected as part of a research project on audiences of *Embarrassing Bodies* and ten individuals were interviewed in total. Following on from Chapter 1, I place an emphasis on affect by returning to Freud (1981a,b) and his affect model; Anzieu's (2016) notion of the skin ego; and Bion's 'container-contained' model (1963), which Anzieu incorporated into the concept of the skin ego. I argue in this chapter that the interviewees' engaged with *Embarrassing Bodies* in complex, contradictory, and ambivalent ways. Additional themes that summarise aspects of the viewing process are also discussed. They are containment, voyeurism, and entertainment. I explore each of them in separate sections and begin with containment below.

The Doctors as Maternal and Containing Figures

The interviewees spoke warmly of the *Embarrassing Bodies* doctors and how they interacted with the patients on the show. The doctors were described as 'caring' (I5, 235), 'genuine' (ibid.), 'brilliant' (I6, 93), 'friendly' (I2, 557), as putting people 'at ease' (I7, 177) and 'good with people' (I7, 181), 'professional' (I5, 233), 'using language that people may identify or relate to' (I9, 263), 'approachable' and 'friendly' (I10, 178–180), 'showing empathy and kindness erm and not judging' (I8, 282–283) and 'comforting' (I6, 141). There was general praise for them. As far as the interactions between the doctors and patients are concerned, the research participants regarded them as very professional and amicable: 'I think they, they're very respected. The, the doctors treat them with, with respect and courtesy. I don't think, they're not dismissed, erm, they're all taken seriously, erm, yeah I think they get good treatment hopefully' (I3, 269–271), said one woman. Another interviewee remarked,

> I think they're all very friendly and, erm, like they are the sort of people I would trust, they do come across like they love what they're doing and, erm, generally GPs don't have a good reputation in this country from what I've heard. [...] I think all of the doctors are really nice and sometimes I would get awkward in a situation that they are but they seem to be very confident and still compassionate, they are very down to earth when they are treating the patients.
>
> (I6, 95–103)

Apart from one research participant for whom the doctors were not important – she did not really remember them – all other participants said they liked the doctors and felt a connection to them. One said, 'I quite like Dr. Pixie, she seems quite nice, I'd quite like to be like her, if I was a GP' (I8, 267–268). The research participants regarded the doctors as professional, friendly, and respectful. The doctors are not only celebrities but appear as medical professionals who seem to be able to diagnose everything and have a solution in mind when presented with a medical problem. I will now discuss one interviewee's responses in more detail with regard to containment (as defined by Anzieu 2016).

Case Study #1: Ellen

> Ellen was in her 50s and worked in the media industry at the time of the interview. Illness played a part in her life in so far as she grew up with a close family member who suffered from ill health.

One of the first aspects of her life, Ellen[1] told me about, was the experience of growing up with a family member who had a chronic illness. It 'ruled our life' (I2, 77) and structured the way the family lived to some extent. For example, 'it sort of dictated what sort of food we ate as well' (ibid., 85). Recently, Ellen remarked that the family member's condition had worsened and resulted in a family visit to A&E one night:

> I mean they couldn't tell for ages what it was and were actually sending him home until they spotted, one of the, one of the doctors thought she could see some air on the, erm, in his bowel on the X-ray and thought 'Oh I think I know what's happened' so [...].
>
> (I2, 121–124)

In the interview she told me about the impact the illness had on the family life as she was growing up and suddenly remarked,

> having said that, it's just made me realise that I, one thing I did forget about my life and I suppose I tend to gloss over, is that I had a mini, sort of, I don't even know what, it wasn't a breakdown, it was like a sort of depressive period myself.
>
> (ibid., 144–146)

She had an incident during a mock school exam as a teenager and was unable to take the exam. It is helpful to include Ellen's description of the incident here because it illustrates how an affective body state was recounted and re-emerging as memory traces as she spoke:

> I remember, I remember feeling fine, feeling, it was a French exam and I remember going into the classroom, I remember that and I wasn't worried about this exam in the slightest and, erm, and I sat down and I remember, I remember looking at the piece of paper that the questions were written on and I remember it is quite a sunny day and I remember looking, I remember sitting there just keep looking

at it, looking at it and I suddenly thought 'I can't read it, I don't know what it says!' and it wasn't, it wasn't in French, it was in English and I couldn't make the words sort of sink into my head. It was really bizarre and I've never experienced it since and it was just, I was sort of reading the words but the meaning, I couldn't understand the meaning and nothing would sort of go into my head. I remember sitting, I remember, I remember sort of looking out the window thinking 'OK, calm down. Just take a minute and then look back again.', everybody was busily writing away and I thought 'Don't panic', just you know and I looked back again and I still couldn't do it and I remember just packing up my pencils in my pencil case and putting it in my bag and getting up and saying to the teacher 'I'm sorry, I can't do this.' and I just walked out of the classroom. And I didn't go back to school until, I actually did my A levels and I just remember, at the start I remember crying quite a bit when I got home.

(I2, 147–162)

From a psychoanalytic perspective, one could suggest that this incident had resided in her unconscious and was recalled by her in the interview as a result of free association. This incident is also about the body and an experience of a body not functioning or refusing to cooperate (similar to many of the bodies that are shown on *Embarrassing Bodies*). The recounting of the incident might also have been accompanied by affect. For Freud, any memory is connected to affect. It is possible that in the act of talking about the experience, which is primarily about an affective experience that showed itself in a kind of dispossession of the body, Ellen re-experienced some of the affect in the interview.

She may have also remembered it and talked about it in the interview because she (unconsciously) hoped for further clarification from me. I, as a university researcher, may have been (unconsciously) perceived as someone with knowledge and authority by her, similar to a psychoanalyst. Even though I had not acted like one or sought to reproduce a therapeutic situation. Another reason why Ellen remembered and recounted her experience may be that I had also shared troubling and possible unexplainable aspects of my body with her. She may have felt that we had something in common and as a result felt able to share an intimate episode of her life history. Naturally, I did not and could not offer any clarification or commentary on the episode. I asked her:

J: Mhm and you never sort of tried to erm understand what you know why …

I2: … No, I don't know why because I, the minute I did my A levels and I wasn't at school, I was fine and I remember, yeah I remember having a period of sort of just being in that zone where you, you can't, you know, you just, you don't know why, you just sit there and then just, just discover you're crying. You don't know why you're doing it, it just sort of happens.

(I2, 187–191)

No one explained the experience and feeling of bodily dispossession, of a body that spoke itself without her conscious control. A doctor gave a diagnosis as to why this had occurred, but she regarded it as 'complete and utter bollocks' (ibid., 167). She did not know why she had had the breakdown or what could have caused it. '[...] yeah that was a strange and I still don't know, as I say, don't know what that was about and I've not, I've never had it since' (ibid., 176–178). After hearing those narratives, I felt very touched that Ellen had shared them with me. In the days following the interview, I reflected more on them and why I had felt so touched and somehow been affected by them. I realised that I, and every one of us, have the same desire that Ellen articulated: a wish to receive an answer to or explanation for aspects of our bodies that we have or that function in a specific manner. We may not be able to explain or understand them and none of us have chosen them. I associated a feeling that my disability (see Introduction) had similarly come upon me, without much choice and agency like Ellen's momentary episode of a body that was out of control. This image of bodies that become and embody specific states (a disabled body, an ill body, etc.) is of course also very present in *Embarrassing Bodies*. The bodies are shown as bodies that show a specific medical condition and are then diagnosed and granted medical treatment. These processes can be further thought about by drawing on the psychoanalytic notion of containment and I do so in the remaining part of this section. Such a desire for containment was shared by Ellen and other interviewees. I felt touched that the atmosphere and unconscious connectedness between us had enabled such narratives to emerge. This theme of an affective experience or bodily condition that remains unexplained appeared again during the interview. Another incident relating to her close family member was discussed by her towards the end of the interview:

[T]he old, the old doctor is god sort of NHS is rapidly disappearing and that can only be a good thing cos' quite often they aren't and, erm, you know, don't get me wrong, there are plenty of them that do fantastic jobs but, erm, I'm still, still very bitter and twisted about the, the specialist that didn't happen to spot the fact that my [family member] had a large tumour growing in his bowl, even though he stuck a camera up there and said 'Oh dear, I can't seem to get the camera through, there is a bit of a blockage.' and then didn't do anything about it but, erm, my sister and I had to let that one go.

(I2, 682–689)

These quotes suggest that illness (like in many other of the interviewees) has played a part in Ellen's life. She experienced doctors who either could not tell and explain what had happened or gave incorrect diagnoses. Referring to her family member's health condition, she remarked that the doctors kept changing their minds what the right treatment was: 'I don't know whose making the decisions in this but it appears that nobody is' (ibid., 245–246). When I asked her about the *Embarrassing Bodies* doctors, she remarked,

> To actually see the doctors on the programme undergoing it themselves, you then feel confident that they obviously know what it feels like and what it entails to have certain tests and certain treatments done so I think that's, erm, you know again that sort of demystifies it a bit for you.
>
> (I2, 548–551)

The fact that the doctors on *Embarrassing Bodies* also undergo certain tests and treatments makes them appear more equal with the viewers. It is this joviality and authenticity that are key characteristics of the genre that was voiced and appreciated by her here.

A little later on in the interview, Ellen said that, to her, the encounters between the doctors and patients sometimes felt 'a bit like a, you know, long lost friend coming back' (ibid., 559). She called the show 'slightly unbelievable because they get such a continuity of care like that, whereas most of us will have to tip up at the surgery and see whichever bloody doctor we can get in to see' (ibid., 561–563). She called it 'a utopian version of a doctor-patient relationship' (ibid., 559–565) – one she nonetheless seemed to aspire to. Ellen liked the doctors, but one might also interpret her sentences as articulating a desire for the continued (and free) care that is administered in a perfect relationship in the show. This idealised and televised relationship is one of care, warmth, accessibility, extensive medical knowledge, and constant availability, like an ideal mother to the baby. Here one can apply the ideas of Anzieu (2016) in order to argue that the doctors were perceived in affect terms as maternal figures, who enwrap, contain, and hold both the patients on the programme (according to the interviewees) and the interviewees in the skin envelope. The doctors contain the research participants and their own bodily anxieties, uncertainties, and experiences related to the body. This perception of the doctors is of an idealised nature. The doctors themselves are ill sometimes, have a bad day, or come across as unpleasant (like anyone else), but those experiences take place *off* the television screen. This allows for a division to occur. The doctors can be easily constructed as caring and motherly because – to Ellen and the other interviewees – they only come across as such on television; other qualities are absent. We may refer to such idealised descriptions of the doctors by the interviewees as acts of 'self-reflective appropriation' (Sandvoss 2005, 118). Viewers reflexively related the doctors to their own biographies when they mentioned that they would like to be treated by them or meet them. It is open to debate to what extent the interviewees were aware of and reflected on their appropriations of the doctors as maternal and caring figures. Was it an appropriation to them or rather an accurate description of how they saw the doctors? Sandvoss's term is useful because I argue that viewers established and appropriated specific characteristics of the doctors in their narratives that were outlined earlier. The interviewees constructed the doctors. They discursively excluded other qualities of the doctors that did not fit the idealised image they had created. However, the theme of containment was very strong in the data and I continue to explore it in this section.

Didier Anzieu (2016) remarked that the baby forms mental images of being contained and sharing the same skin with the mother that are based on sensory experiences of touch and responses of being held and contained (see Chapter 1).[2] The sense of being held by the mother or father creates a sense of security for the baby. This is underscored further by touch and the voices of the parents that hold the baby and respond to any feelings of distress or pleasure in an adequate manner (ibid., 101). Anzieu stressed the sensuality as well as the virtuality of being held and contained, and the description of this process can be enriched by drawing on the ideas of Wilfred Bion (1963) as he himself did. In the case of *Embarrassing Bodies*, the doctors cannot actively respond to the viewers but the interviewees witness container/contained scenes (they described it in a likewise manner) in the programme between the patients and doctors and this possibly results in their desire to be contained which ultimately could offer a containing function for them. Resulting from being contained is what we broadly call psychic growth, as Thomas Ogden explains,

> [T]he contained grows as it becomes better able to encompass the full complexity of the emotional situation from which it derives.
>
> (Ogden 2004, 1358)

Barry Richards (2007) argues in relation to media news coverage that the latter is often anxiety provoking or shocking at first but is then put into context, explained, managed, and contained (see Hill 2007, 88 for the same argument):

> The unbearable images of famine or bomb victims continue to appear and to resonate, at the same time as the voice-over or other footage may have given us images of aid workers representing hope and fortitude. [...] In the era of late modernity and vanishing tradition it is the media which have taken over from traditional authorities' key powers to shape our minds.
>
> (Richards 2007, 63–64)

Be it news coverage or *Embarrassing Bodies*, something affective, the unspeakable or unbearable, is explained, diagnosed, digested, and made bearable here. Ellen spoke of *Embarrassing Bodies* as 'dehorrifying' and 'demystifying' aspects of medicine, we may now identify an underlying, psychic dimension of the programme. In feeling contained, uncanny, horrific, or mysterious aspects of the interviewees (and their bodies more specifically) are contained and made bearable. Explicitly, they are *named* as conditions and explained by the doctors. A bodily state or condition that may have been experienced in pure affect terms without an explanation or words to describe it is being named by the doctors. This act of naming does not have to be in relation to the interviewee's bodies or a condition they might have but it suggests that there is an answer and treatment for everything that is given by the *Embarrassing Bodies* doctors. This is a distinct characteristic of many reality television and makeover formats: the knowing and authoritative expert. Formats have *recognizable* features that always remain the same and this may increase audience loyalty (Hill 2007; Moran 2009; Chalaby 2015). The reoccurring and recognizable characteristics of *Embarrassing Bodies* that make it identifiable as a format (the same hosts, music, logos, studio are used in each episode) may be seen as formal characteristics that contribute to a feeling of containment in the viewers. While the show featured different patients and also introduced new segments over the years, its core scenes and sequences remained the same: doctors who diagnose and initiate treatment of patients. While each episode may present the unknown and unknown patients, viewers know that the structure of the show is going to be the same (theme music, graphics, doctors, etc.). It is not only the doctors but also the structure of the show that may contribute to a desire for containment in the interviewees. The interviewees responded, naturally, to these core scenes of the container/contained between doctors and patients by articulating how compassionate, professional, caring, and good the doctors were. Anzieu stressed that the experience of containment occurs in the relationality of mother and baby. We could argue that a similar relationality is shown in the show between patients and doctors and desired for by the viewers. They may experience *Embarrassing Bodies* as an affective interface (Kavka 2009) that binds them to the doctors. This notion of being bound or connected to the doctors was expressed in narratives about them that I have reproduced at the beginning of this section. It was articulated by the interviewees but may essentially refer to affective bodily states and a bodily desire to be held and contained.

Returning to Ellen, the desire and fantasy of being contained may have been a result of the experiences she has had with her own affective body states and real doctors that were precisely *not* of a containing nature. She spoke twice of the *Embarrassing Bodies* doctors as 'demystifying' things for her as a viewer, and this could suggest, from a psychoanalytic perspective, that she had the desire to have some of her own experiences that are related to the body to be demystified. Instead, she experienced doctors that were of little or no help.

Voyeurism and Entertainment

The desire of being contained was a crucial aspect of the interviewees' way of viewing the programme. Another aspect was voyeurism. As much research on reality television suggests, audiences engage with the former for reasons of voyeurism. Naturally, voyeurism is something that is less socially accepted than other motivations and few interviewees openly talked about their viewings of *Embarrassing Bodies* in a way that alluded to voyeurism. This is not surprising because they may have had fears of being frowned upon by the researcher. A few quotes nevertheless exemplify this notion and one has reason to believe that voyeurism played a part in watching *Embarrassing Bodies* because things are shown that – unless one is a doctor – one would never see off the television screen. Voyeurism may relate to two aspects: entertainment and affect. I will explore each in turn. When talking about why they watched *Embarrassing Bodies*, one participant said,

> Also I think that everyone is just a little bit nosy by nature, aren't they? So they want to see what everyone else is doing or what's wrong with them that might be wrong with you or not wrong with you.
>
> (I3, 48–50)

We could say that the participant also talked about her own self here when emphasising that everyone is like her. In going back to the container/contained model, we can conclude here that perhaps she (unconsciously) wished to know what or if there is anything 'wrong' with her own body. A little later on in the interview, she said that she had 'maybe a grotesque interest, a morbid interest in' (I3, 197) *Embarrassing Bodies*. She regarded it as 'extreme' (I3, 198) and 'shocking' but 'in a good sense' (I3, 206). Upon my question if she was quite drawn to *Embarrassing Bodies*, she replied,

> Yeah! But I guess, I don't know whether that's just me personally or people in general, erm, partly people are just nosy and they wanna know what is happening in other people's lives but also it's, erm, educational as well. You never know, your friends or family that's been previously undiagnosed and you've seen it on there and you think 'Oh, maybe it could be that!' and you could go and suggest that to them. I don't know. Although, erm, perhaps it's also, teaches people to be more acceptive or tolerant of other people if they have anything that could be deemed embarrassing so I think there was a

few people on there with body odour issues and things like that and they were horrifically embarrassed by it. I'm sure there were places they could have been teased and perhaps would think it's because their hygiene is poor, not because they have a particular illness so it's educating people about the reasons why, behind some people are the way they are.

(I3, 209–220)

This quote also further underscores the containing/contained motive. In feeling contained, the programme enabled the interviewee to be more accepting of her own body, of 'the reasons why' she is how she is. We may almost detect a sense of relief in seeing other, imperfect bodies on screen here. This also shows the uniqueness of the medical reality genre but particularly of *Embarrassing Bodies*, a programme that is not concerned with hegemonic ideas of beauty but about everyday – and rare – medical problems that are shown, talked about, and treated. It goes beyond the superficial but explains why people are the way they are. Additionally, the potentially unconscious viewing motives of voyeurism *were made conscious* through the interview situation here ('everyone' is nosy) and censored by the ego because from the superego's point of view, voyeurism is not socially acceptable. Judging from these quotes, voyeurism may be entertaining, even exciting for some, as the next quote shows more profoundly.

I think it's very, it is entertaining, I like the sort of production style of it, you know it flows very well and, erm, it feels wrong, I must admit, it feels wrong sometimes watching it for entertainment but you know what I mean, it's, erm, I find it very interesting, although I've always been interested in medical stuff like that so.

(I2, 357–360)

Again, we may see here how the viewing position was carefully negotiated as a response to myself and my question. The interviewee (Ellen) suddenly had to account for her reasons for watching *Embarrassing Bodies*, something she possibly had not done before in much detail. She openly said in a free associative manner that the show is entertaining (possibly because of its voyeuristic qualities) and then realised that this 'feels wrong' and quickly deployed the motive of medical education like the other participant. Both participants' utterances were produced through free associations and then corrected or somewhat moderated by consciousness. Upon my question if she watched it because it is entertaining and a sort of guilty pleasure for her, Ellen replied,

Yeah in a way. It's not really a guilty pleasure, because I don't feel guilty about it, I actually learned so much from it and I think it's you

know I think anything that can make you a bit more of an understanding person and can help you empathise with people's situation
isn't really a guilty pleasure [...]. Occasionally where you do sit and
you don't mock them as such but you're just like 'Oh for god's sake,
how did you not do anything about that for years?' so yeah it's quite
entertaining in that way I suppose you get to, you don't get to laugh
at other people's misfortune, you don't but it's just, erm, there are
some people who are fairly unbelievable.

(I2, 364–377)

The entertainment aspect was carefully spoken about here and it is not
quite clear what, for the interviewee, marked the exact entertainment
qualities of the programme. Another interviewee said, 'I suppose anyone who watches it has got a general, in a weird way to be entertained
by some of the grossness that can happen to the body' (I7, 76–78). A
third interviewee stated that the show 'is quite good entertainment, it's
usually on, I find it like light relief from all my problems' (I10, 150–151).
A female interviewee remarked in a confessional tone,

> I do also think that people watch it for entertainment value and, and
> I think that I'm probably being guilty of that as well to be honest.
> [...] I mean I probably haven't been entirely honest, like I have to
> admit there are sometimes, when I've watched it and I thought "Oh
> my god that person is so stupid".

(I8, 472–478)

Another interviewee also commented on the funny qualities of the show,

> [Y]eah about the presenters they always find quite a lot of humour
> in it as well and sometimes it is funny, or if you see somebody 'Oh
> my god!' cos' you may laugh, cos' it is part of how we are isn't it?
> Somebody may come in and say 'I've got' without showing it, erm
> 'I've got massive testicles' or something like that and you would kind
> of laugh and you want to know what it is.

(I9, 275–279)

As I argue below, entertainment may link to affective modes of viewing
in relation to voyeurism. Whatever is deemed an entertaining aspect of
the show by the interviewees symbolises an affective and pleasurable
discharge of, as I argue following Freud, experiences or thoughts about
one's own body and the uncertainties and anxieties associated with it.
Describing something as 'entertaining' may relate to defensive reactions.
Viewers see something they are not supposed to see and in not knowing
how to respond, respond with uneasy laughter. Such scenes were then
labelled as 'entertainment' in a deferred manner during the interviews.

The entertaining qualities may also relate to seeing embarrassing conditions that the viewers would laugh at or find amusing because they did not recognise themselves as having them or relating to them (*Schadenfreude*). However, it seemed difficult for the interviewees to talk about the show also being entertaining and there was relatively little mentioning of it in the data. These analyses may read rather speculative and it is not clear *what* was entertaining about the show.

As they spoke about entertaining aspects of the programme, the interviewees were coming to terms with such motivations and seemed cautious and careful not to expand on such narratives. A male interviewee, Peter, also presented some mention of entertainment:

I7: I do kinda partly watch it for educational as well as the entertainment.
J: And what is entertaining about it?
I7: I think it's just, well, for instance, is it last week's episode in the new series? Just things like that poor chap who had all those scales on his feet. I mean I've had a little bit of hard skin and thought that was horrible but just seeing to the extremes it can go to, it's incredibly interesting, I find it interesting anyway, fascinating and at the same time you know obviously it can be quite horrible at times as well so I don't know whether I've got some sort of sick part of me but obviously it is incredible to see what sort of things can happen to bodies, all our bodies really. I think as well probably the makers know that cos' they do obviously want things like that [chuckles].

(I7, 90–100)

Similarly to Ellen's quote discussed earlier, Peter had to account for his viewing motives and give reasons why the show may be entertaining for him. Rather than speculating further what the entertaining qualities may be for interviewees, I wish to focus on the discursive (de)construction of those entertainment narratives by interviewees. From the data alone, I am unable to conclude *what* the entertaining qualities of *Embarrassing Bodies* were. Peter presented a shifting position. He described the show as entertaining in a free associative manner but then corrected his narratives and used other words to describe his motivations: 'interesting' and 'fascinating'. His description of the 'poor chap' with scales on his feet (much more extreme than Peter's own hard skin) alludes to *Schadenfreude* and taking pleasure in others' misfortune. Peter then proceeded to shift to a more serious discussion and described the show as 'horrible' at times and wondered if there was a 'sick part' in him that watched the show or was entertained by seeing horrible things. The quote may exemplify a 'discursive shifting' (Hills 2005, 43) and an attempt to frame the viewing in a certain way that actually moved away from entertainment but as Peter spoke and expanded he wondered if there was a 'sick' part in him. It is Ellen and Peter's quotes in particular that are interesting for they show the shifting and process-like narratives that were less governed by rationality and more uttered in a free-flowing manner. They point to the psychoanalytic understanding of the subject as one who is never fixed but in processes which are embedded in the social world and intersubjective relations and are subject to change. Following Hills (2005), who discusses a similar narrative of an interviewee who showed discursive shifting, we could interpret such narratives as a repression through conversation (Billig 1999). Billig theorises repression as an act that occurs in conversations by, for example, changing the subject. Both Peter and Ellen changed the subject midway through their narratives. While Ellen acknowledged the entertaining qualities of the show, she then went on to explain what things were *not* entertaining for her and concluded that she merely thought of some of the patients as 'unbelievable'. She said she did not 'mock' or 'laugh at' the patients, but it is not clear what the entertaining qualities of the programme were for her. Similarly, Peter did not really answer what exactly he found the entertaining qualities to be and he possibly could not because, I argue, they were related to an affective, pleasurable discharge of affective bodily states that related to anxiety and uncertainty about his own aging body. While Billig's (1999) reworking of the Freudian concept of repression may offer us some insight into the discursive dynamics that occurred, I argue that his theory may not adequately illuminate the narratives presented earlier. It is beyond the scope of this chapter to engage in detail with Billig and other discursive psychologists (e.g., Timpanaro 2010; Parker 2015) who have criticised Freud and psychoanalysis more generally. Billlig has paid little attention (see ibid., 214) to the Freudian concept of 'negation' (Freud 1981m) that at least to some degree describes the same mechanism as his theorisation of repression-through-conversation: a conscious (and discursive) move of shifting, denying, or changing a narrative (Johanssen 2014). We may think of these narratives as being examples of conscious changes of the subject, but I would grant them less agency and consciousness than Billig has. With Billig's work alone, we may not quite analyse how or why Peter and Ellen seemed to return to what, in Billig's eyes, they had presumably repressed through changing the subject or not talking about it more: entertaining qualities of the show. Rather than simply not mentioning or denying entertainment outright and then moving on to different narratives, both interviewees returned to these aspects after they had denied or avoided them. They spoke of the show as entertaining, then did not provide more clarifications on the topic and described the show in different terms ('fascinating', 'interesting', 'unbelievable') and then implicitly *returned* to the theme and noted that it felt 'wrong' (Ellen) or 'sick' (Peter) to watch the show for those entertaining reasons. Rather than repression, or unsuccessful attempts of repression, I would characterise such contradictory narratives as free associations that were situated at the intersection of consciousness and the unconscious. For instance, Ellen's expression of 'Occasionally where you do sit and you don't mock them as such but you're just like "Oh for god's sake, how did you not do anything about that for years?"' (I2, 372–377) may be seen as free-flowing utterances that are only partly characterised by negation or repression but are also characterised by a dynamic narrative that encompasses looking for the right words and phrases to describe Ellen's responses to viewing. The show may have been entertaining for interviewees because it made them feel better about themselves and led to affective discharge. In that sense, they may not have been able to talk much about the entertaining qualities because they relate to affect and are in tension with discourse. I outline this point more by focussing on voyeurism and affect below.

Voyeurism and Affect

Voyeurism has distinctly affective dimensions (Fenichel 1995). As I have spent some time outlining the Freudian take on affect in Chapter 1, I will now enrich these theoretical discussions by drawing on some more data. Some interviewees spoke of the excitement they felt when watching *Embarrassing Bodies*.

> Excited. Erm, yeah quite that's why I like to record it cos' I hate the adverts, I need to be on it! Like, I kinda like stop because I want to see what happens next and I don't like when they talk too much, I'm just like 'no, no, show me, show me everything.' Erm, yeah (1), excited is the word, it's quite sad.
>
> (I6, 77–80)

> I'm always excited to watch it, cos I wanna see what's on next! [laughs]. Erm, I just find it really interesting.
>
> (I3, 222–223)

Another participant remarked that they would personally never go on *Embarrassing Bodies*, 'unless I had some bizarre, rare presentation that was so exciting I needed to share with everybody' (I5, 410–411). The word 'exciting' is very striking here and I will return to it in the Conclusion. I suggest that it serves as a placeholder in an attempt to describe and verbalise affect (Wetherell 2012; Ellis Tucker and Harper 2013) and the 'affective glue' (Kavka 2009, 37) that binds the viewers to *Embarrassing Bodies*. The interviewees who used the word 'exciting' did not – and possibly could not – really specify further what they regarded these exciting qualities to be. Exciting was used to mark an affective state that is experienced in the viewing process. It is linked to entertainment and positive feelings on the surface but, more specifically, I argue that the previous quotes suggest voyeuristic viewing tendencies. For psychoanalysis, voyeurism is regarded as 'voracious unfulfilment' (Metzl 2004, 429). It knows no end. Voyeurs 'have to look again and again, and to see more and more, with an ever increasing intensity' (Fenichel 1995, 319), as Fenichel stresses. Peter said in this context that he thought when watching a particular scene '"Why am I watching this for?" but it's incredibly sort of, erm, compelling to sort of see, isn't it?' (I7, 133–143).

As with the quote of the other interviewee reproduced earlier, who admitted that it 'feels wrong' at times to watch *Embarrassing Bodies*, the voyeur is compelled to gaze while knowing it is wrong to gaze at something one is not supposed to see.³ The interviewees who want to see what is on *next* exemplify this. For them, their excitement can never be completely satisfied because there is the promise of an ever more embarrassing/extreme case to be seen. One participant said that for her, *Embarrassing Bodies* had

> come to a natural end, cos' I've seen most of the things on there, so I don't watch it as religiously but again it's one of those things that if you're home and it's on in the evenings, I watch it.
>
> (I5, 100–102)

Another quote exemplifies this further:

> I quite like Malaria or something like when they pick up on pretty (1) exciting things rather than just (1) boring, like I don't mean to be harsh but like dermatitis and acne yeah it is, when it's really bad [...]. STIs are a bit boring now cos' you heard it everywhere, when they go on the beach and they talk to people like what they do over the weekend when they're drunk, you're just like 'Yeah, we all know this'.
>
> (I6, 177–184)

These quotes suggest that voyeurism is an on-going process without end. It needs to be pushed further, from one extreme case to the next. The excess of affect in reality television that I discussed in the Introduction is implicitly talked about by the interviewees here. There is always the promise of more. Arguably, this is how *Embarrassing Bodies* itself has evolved over the history of the show. It is useful at this point to recall how (Freudian) psychoanalysis understands voyeurism. Fenichel (1995) has defined the act of voyeurism in the following terms:

> Voyeurs are fixated on experiences that aroused their castration anxiety, either primal scenes or the sight of adult genitals. The patient attempts to deny the justification of his fright by repeating the frightening scenes with certain alterations, for the purpose of

achieving a belated mastery. This unconscious significance of scoptophilia is most clearly seen in those cases in which gratification is obtained only if the sexual scene the patient wishes to witness fulfils very definite conditions. These conditions then represent either a repetition of conditions present in an important childhood experience, or more often a denial of these very conditions or of their dangerous nature.

(Fenichel 1995, 319–320)

Achieving this mastery in the viewing process is key here as many of the participants in the sample had experienced deeply troubling and, in some cases, traumatic experiences in their childhood. In that sense, voyeurism is not only about affect and entertainment but also about repetitive viewing to achieve mastery over bodily states. I unpack this further below by focussing on one particular interviewee.

Case Study #2: Martha

> Martha was a postgraduate student at the time and had an interest in psychoanalysis. She came to the United Kingdom to study for her degree and had been living here ever since. Health and illnesses have played a role in her life in a number of ways.

The interview with Martha was the longest one I carried out and I felt that of all participants, she was the one who opened up the most. She talked at length about her biography and shared some intimate experiences with me. I felt honoured and touched that she shared her life with me the way she did. It may be that Martha opened up to me because I had opened up to her about my body and subjectivity before the interview had begun and in that way the psychodynamics of the interview may have been structured accordingly.

After briefly talking about where she was born and her family, she said that 'there was always a reason for me to go to the hospital, infections, things' (I1, 48). With regard to her family, she said that 'I am the one who provides the answers with emotions of how they feel so I am that stone of emotional enrichment' (I1, 63–65). She regarded the interview as 'one of the least times that someone asks me to talk about myself' (I1, 125–126) because normally 'no one ever asked me' (I1, 129). She mentioned that she often has turned to television programmes in times of emotional upheaval or crises when she 'was feeling alone and lost, I was going to programmes that really helped me or contained me' (I1, 189–190). 'Those were my friends and they gave me some answers [...]' (I1, 426).

Two experiences related to the body can be related to her consumption of *Embarrassing Bodies*. Martha gave a vivid account of the hospitalisations she had mentioned before:

> Yeah, well, I, when I was three I fell down and hit my forehead and, erm, half of my forehead skin was peeled off like an open book, so you see here I have a stitch on my forehead and, erm, for some reason growing up I always had food poisoning, for some reason and, erm, always, I was going, I have been three, four times for urine infection so they had to do some invasive procedure which I was awake and very painful to, erm, give direct medicine to kill the virus so you know that image of me being, don't know seven, on the hospital table and I have, you know, ten doctors around me, inserting a tube from the urine tract and I was awake and I could see everything was so painful. I think it's one of the most painful moments and I could actually see myself crying from pain.
>
> (I1, 235–243)

Shortly after describing those experiences to me, she remembered another experience that related to sexualised violence in the street when she was a teenager. This experience left her feeling 'a bit uncomfortable with my body' (I1, 256). She said because of the role hospitals have played in her life she has developed an awareness of her body. She regularly went to health check-ups to make sure everything was fine.

For a time in her life, she felt uncomfortable with her body and used to cover it when she would go running, for example. 'I used to go running and wear a really long coat to cover every side of my body' (I1, 495–496). She liked *Embarrassing Bodies* very much and described it in the following terms:

> I like the idea of medicine, of treating something because all the things treat, healing and I think, I think with the *Embarrassing Bodies* programme it's not only they heal the surface of the skin, okay, we do some injections and the glands stop to swell or whatever, it heals the emotional part because these problems that cause a bit of trouble when I see actually that, I don't know if all of them find treatment, like every, but I have watched many of them, erm, I even feel emotional because I feel like 'Wow, I bet it feels like such a relief of actually dealing with things'.
>
> (I1, 526–532)

She emphasised the healing aspects of *Embarrassing Bodies* many times in the interview: 'how they always have a treatment for everything, how they have an answer for everything' (I1, 577–578). I would argue that this sentiment relates to my earlier discussion of the container-contained dynamic.

In going back to Fenichel's definition of voyeurism as a substitute for troubling or traumatic childhood experiences, I would argue that engaging with *Embarrassing Bodies* may have presented a substitute for these experiences for Martha and other interviewees. This involved an addressing of conflicts in order to achieve mastery over them that is mostly unconscious. As Fenichel remarks, 'voyeurism is based on the hunger for *screen experiences*, that is, for experiences sufficiently like the original to be substituted for it [...]' (1995, 319, italics in the original).[4] The relation between voyeurism and the viewing of *Embarrassing Bodies* is important here. The screen on which it is shown provides a space for subjects to (unconsciously) project aspects of their biographies on. When I asked Martha if her watching of the show was related to how she felt about her own body, she answered, 'Don't know, I think it's, I think it's curiosity' (ibid., 956). At this point in the interview, she did not see a connection between her own body and the programme.

Both *Embarrassing Bodies*' scenes that are commonly regarded as private or taboo and the programme's narrative of healing and cures are of significance here. They made it an important object (or rather process) for the participants, one that aids them in addressing troubling experiences because it sends out signals that enable an engagement (the aspect of voyeurism that made interviewees tune in and watch the show) and signals that promise a cure (the narrative of the helping doctors, the successful surgeries, the healed patients, etc.). Voyeurism is in this case not only to be perceived as something negative or taboo – even though ontologically it might be the case – because epistemologically the voyeuristic look aids the interviewees in facilitating an encounter with experiences that occurred in their childhoods or at an earlier point in their lives. Voyeurism is here additionally not, as Freud believed, centred on sexuality or castration anxiety. Even though there are many patients on *Embarrassing Bodies* who have conditions that are related to the genitals, the interviewees tended to portray themselves as receiving no sexual gratifications from seeing them. Contrary to classical psychoanalysis then, voyeurism in this case is not to be seen as neurotic or damaging for the subject's well-being. Instead, it can be understood as a vehicle that enabled an encounter with inner experiences of subjects. Voyeurism seemed to have initially triggered the interviewees' interests in *Embarrassing Bodies*. I asked them if they could remember when they watched the programme for the first time. They seemed initially drawn to it because of the (unconscious) potential of voyeurism, of seeing something one is not supposed to see. One female interviewee remarked, 'I can remember just thinking, oh, my first thoughts were "Oh my god!" which I think a lot of people thought' (I5, 108–109). Another interviewee explicitly mentioned voyeurism when he said, 'Well, probably, as I've said, you know a sort of mixture sometimes of horror, fascination, almost voyeurism I suppose' (I7, 106–108). Similarly, Martha told me about her fascination with the human body and how she loves 'watching everything' (ibid., 963) that happens to her body during a medical procedure.

> I was actually telling the doctors: "Tell me what you do." and I want to look at all the instruments you know and I wish I could have a mirror to look, which of course was impossible but I was very quiet and calm.
>
> (ibid., 966–969)

Upon hearing this, I made an interpretation and asked her, 'And would you say this is also related to, erm, you say you have a lot of knowledge and you like to observe closely and, to sort of being in control?' (I1, 998–999). She replied,

> Yes. Oh my god yes. That it is, yeah a lot. [...] I think yeah, I think you are right, something about controlling but also I am very equally scared, probably I am equally scared deep down that's why I wanna be so in control of the body because of the fear of something happening. [...] I guess this, this is what Embarrassing Bodies does, it doesn't leave you in the dark about something that you might not know.
>
> (I1, 1000–1036)

At this point, Martha realised as a result of thinking about her relationality to *Embarrassing Bodies* that there might be a connection between aspects of her biography and her viewing of the show. This quote underscores the theme of voyeurism that I have deployed in connection with the skin ego and the container/contained model when discussing interview data in this chapter. From a psychoanalytic perspective, the control that Martha talked about and which was made conscious in the interview situation summarises the voyeuristic viewing that is concerned with mastery and control, a desire to be contained and to know about one's own body. This feeling of being in control and of learning about medicine and the body is facilitated by the programme.

Affect, the Abject, and Language

There were also parts in Martha's narrative that suggest a very affective and embodied viewing experience. When we talked more about the show, she described the first time she watched it:

> I think the first one was, erm, a woman had a problem in her genitalia area. She was observed by the doctor and I think it kind of attract

my attention because I was so surprised how the camera will zoom in so much and I think it was myself a curiosity about someone else's body but also a complete astonishment of how can a camera go that close and how does the person feel [...] I couldn't believe with my own eyes [...]. I have this kind of morbid fascination to look at people's body.

(I1, 558–571)

In support of my argument for these voyeuristic tendencies, there seemed to be a sense of surprise and disbelief. Martha asked herself how difficult it must be for the patients to live with the conditions they have. There is a sense of surprise, curiosity, and amazement on her part: 'I'm like how is it possible, how is it possible for the body to have this kind of difficulty, I mean how is her everyday life, how does she deal with it?' (I1, 758–760). Another interviewee remarked, 'Sometimes I see people with conditions that I just, number one, couldn't imagine ever existed [...]' (I2, 348). A third interviewee said,

I think it was just quite shocking that people were either willing to come on TV and show everyone they had this thing that could be deemed embarrassing, erm, but also illnesses or disease that you didn't even know exist and some of the treatments for them, where you didn't realise that things were so invasive or shocking.

(I3, 201–205)

Initially, participants portrayed themselves as being shocked or surprised by what they saw on screen. Words like 'morbid', 'horror', 'shocking' or 'invasive' are used and they evoke notions of affect and the abject (Kristeva 1982). If something is experienced as abject, one cannot help but look both in horror and fascination. It becomes clear that the bodies on *Embarrassing Bodies* are identified with and disidentified with at the same time. Research participants portrayed themselves as being shocked and taken aback by them, yet at the same time they may feel empathy and compassion for them. This marks a dichotomy. By seeing the abject bodies, the interviewees can be thought of as being in a potential 'narcissistic crisis' (ibid., 14), as Kristeva (1982) remarks. The abject relates to something that is always already lost in the ego: a coherent sense of a whole and unified self. It is as if the abject is experienced as affectively *contagious* through the television screen and it is thus not surprising perhaps that the interviewees' initial reactions were so affective. One interviewee remarked in this respect: 'yeah if it's all too real then I do, don't know, it could be me, it can still be me, I can catch anything and be affected' (I6, 203–204). Another man said, '"Eeeurgh" you are imagining the pain but that's what it is, you are imagining the pain, you don't know what it is like' (I9, 409–410). For the interviewees, there may be a latent fear of becoming like the patients and at the same time there are feelings of pity and compassion and also hope because the bodies on the show are turned from being abject into healthy and normal bodies again and the doctors represent an element which is distinctly non-abject.

This element of the affective was partly queried by me when I asked the interviewees if they were sometimes shocked by some cases on *Embarrassing Bodies*. It is of course difficult to put these affective reactions into words because they precisely relate to moments that are beyond language and signification but this question was nonetheless an attempt. As André Green put it so aptly, 'Affect may allow itself to be expressed by language, but it is essentially outside it' (Green 1999, 48–49). All participants were quick to point out that they can deal with most of the conditions on *Embarrassing Bodies*. However, there were specific moments for all of them when they had to look away from the television screen. Martha outlined her reaction to the image of the woman's vagina that I discussed earlier in more detail:

> Erm, no, just the surprise, I mean I have never seen something so magnified. I mean we all have an idea of how, especially women, we have an idea of how it is but this kind of, it was so magnified, erm, I might say, probably for a few seconds I might felt a bit like 'eurgh'.
>
> (I1, 647–650)

More narratives may be included for discussion at this point:

> Erm, not very good at watching needles go in, don't know why, I have to look away at that point. Don't like, can't watch things with eyes that freaks me out and can't watch anything that involves boobs being pulled around. Breast augmentation just makes me feel ill and liposuction because I don't know why, it's just so widespread now it appears that and nose jobs as well. Those three things really weird, nose jobs, boobs jobs and liposuction, I, I struggle to look at them being done. I don't know why.
>
> (I2, 491–496)

> I was shocked last week with the chap, the chap who had his eye removed that was that was ama-, I guess almost I wanted to look away, part of me does that and part of me always wants to look so that I think that's probably the most shocked I've ever been to be honest and the fact that he's still sort of talking so normally, I've never seen anything you know as quite extreme.
>
> (I7, 114–118)

Affective moments (that possibly may have qualities of the abject or shock) were tried to put into language by interviewees here. Ellen repeatedly said that she did not know why she has to look away from the television screen sometimes. She emphasised her affective bodily reaction ('makes me feel ill'). The other participant expressed being 'shocked' when seeing a particular scene. Martha has gone 'eurgh' while watching the show. But what about the moments of shock or the description that a participant has to look away? How can one make sense of them?

I would argue that we see here how voyeurism is tied in with affective responses that make participants look away, only to resume their screen gaze moments later. Peter said that a 'part' of him always wanted to look. There were moments in the consumption of *Embarrassing Bodies* that are marked by a turning away that could have unconscious roots. If we recall my discussion of affect in Chapter 1, the reasons that provoke an affective reaction can remain unconscious. The interviewees in my sample did not know why, or were unable to say why they have to look away sometimes. This is supported by the point that they cannot explain their affective reactions any further.

This could be understood as a disidentification. There is an irrational fear on part of the viewers I interviewed that they might catch a disease or condition they see in front of them. It could also be understood by drawing on more social reasons. Some sequences might be rendered too taboo for a particular interviewee because one is not supposed to look at certain images: for example, a breast augmentation surgery. From a Freudian perspective one could argue that in such situations, they look away or cover their eyes because the superego demands it. However, an alternative interpretation can also be put forward. I shall return to this point of affective viewing in a short while.

We can conclude that these affective moments support the theoretical conceptualisations of the television viewing experience as an *embodied* one. The ego is always a bodily ego. The sudden turning away of the face or the whole body from the television screen shows that viewing is more than just a cognitive operation. The whole body seems to be involved and this turning away is involuntarily, governed by what one might call 'affective' forces in the interviewees' bodies that they cannot describe any further.

Conclusion

It was the task of this chapter to provide an overview of common themes that emerged in the interviews of my research project on *Embarrassing Bodies* audiences. The overarching themes presented in this chapter were (1) the doctors who viewers unconsciously regarded as containing and maternal figures, (2) entertainment, and (3) voyeurism (and its affective dimensions). From the perspective of media studies audience research, these themes that converge around the experiences and narratives of an embodied and affective mode of viewing might be regarded as contradictory. How does all of this fit together? I suggest that the themes are *ambivalent*, yet they all belong together. From a psychoanalytic perspective, they are not contradictory.

From a psychoanalytic viewpoint, an apparent desire to be contained constituted a key moment that also marks the (unconscious) appeal of *Embarrassing Bodies* for the interviewees. It shows that the interviewees may be unconsciously and consciously invested in the show. It enabled them to compare themselves with the patients and to be potentially more accepting of their own biographies and experiences. I underscored this by focussing on two interviewees – Ellen and Martha – in more detail and by exploring the complexities that underlie their consumption of the programme. These are to be seen in relation to their biographies and how experiences that relate to health and illness have had an influence on them watching *Embarrassing Bodies*. As I have stressed in the Introduction, the interviews occupied a key position here. I can only argue that some aspects are originally of an unconscious nature because they were rendered conscious through thinking about and replying to my questions. Phrases like 'it's just made me realise' or 'now I remember' that were uttered by participants support this claim. It was, as I have argued, both my unconscious and conscious actions and utterances that were connected and angled, as Freud says, in the manner of a telephone towards an interviewee's unconscious, thereby establishing a connection. It was, to some degree, free association that enabled unconscious fantasies and memories to become conscious. This is absolutely crucial because, I would argue, had I not relied on psychoanalysis as a methodology and theoretical framework, these aspects would have remained absent both for the interviewees and myself alike. In that sense, what I have learned from interviewees about their consumption of the show is always incomplete because they – and myself and my own consumption of it – are only partially known to them and myself. Some aspects are conscious, some aspects were rendered conscious in the interview, and others remain unconscious. The relationality between subjects and the show is thus multilayered. This can be exemplified further by the following quote from Peter, answering my question of if *Embarrassing Bodies* had changed him in any way: 'Well (1) I don't know about any specific example, as I say I don't, it, it may have done subconsciously more you know [...]' (I7, 309–310). This unconscious connection between *Embarrassing Bodies* and the interviewees' biographies is explored further in the next chapter where I specifically look at their inhibition to tweet about the show.

Notes

1 All interviewees' names have been turned into pseudonyms in this book.
2 Anzieu (2016) lists both 'holding' and 'containing' as functions of the skin ego and we can conclude that he borrowed the concepts from Winnicott (2002) and Bion (1963).
3 This taboo is lifted by *Embarrassing Bodies* itself through framing everything as a medical show. Hence, it is okay for the viewers to see what they see. This is mirrored in the discourse of medical education that was frequently deployed by interviewees in this context.
4 Fenichel (1995) refers here to Freud's concept of 'screen experiences' (Freud 1981c) [1899] by which Freud understands a memory that has significance in relation to a repressed experience that it is substituted for.

3   Unable to Tweet
Inhibition and the Compulsion to Share

Introduction

This chapter features more data analysis from the research project on *Embarrassing Bodies* audiences. It presents data on users' Twitter behaviour and introduces the Freudian concept of inhibition in that context. Following from the previous chapter, I argue that the programme resulted in such affective responses to the show in the interviewees that they may have been unable to engage with it on social media. *Embarrassing Bodies* has had a strong Twitter presence (through an official profile and the doctors/hosts' individual Twitter profiles), but the interviewees in my research project all expressed how inactive they were on Twitter about the show. Yet they were using the platform for other purposes and actively tweeted about other things. It seemed that there was a discrepancy between the interviewee's active Twitter use and their conscious (and unconscious) exclusion of tweets on *Embarrassing Bodies*. I explore this further through Freud's notion of 'inhibition', which refers to a self-selected restriction of a situation to avert the affective experience of anxiety. Inhibition may be regarded as a subjective state that protects against unintended or undesired encounters, ideas, or actions. On the surface, it may appear that interviewees chose not to tweet about the show because such Tweets may be considered embarrassing because of the show's trashiness or vulgarity. However, as discussed in Chapter 2, *Embarrassing Bodies* affected the interviewees in such powerful manners that they had difficulty in explaining discursively. The interviewees were also not really able to say why they did not tweet about the programme. As I argued in the previous chapter, I therefore suggest that the programme facilitates an unconscious connection between aspects of their biographies that relate to their bodies (anxiety, trauma, uncertainties), but this connection was not made by the interviewees. Many interviewees talked to me about aspects of their bodies and how they felt about them (this often related to anxieties, uncertainties, or traumatic bodily experiences), but this was in no relation to their consumption of the programme. I therefore suggest that such experiences were facilitated through the viewing of the programme but that the interviewees were not aware of such a connection. This is amplified through their inhibition to share anything about the programme on Twitter. As a result, we could argue that the falling silent on Twitter is an unconscious act of resisting the very idea behind social media: that we should share everything about us and others. Not tweeting about the programme is thus an act of protection on the part of the users in order not to publicly engage with aspects of their bodies.

Social Media and the Demand to Share

The Internet, in general, and social media, in particular, have been described as spaces that are made up of and enable *sharing* (John 2013; Meikle 2016). Sharing may be an ambiguous term that is difficult to define as Wittel (2011) and Kennedy, J. (2016) have noted. Sharing, the creation, distribution, and engagement with user-generated content online has been extensively linked to labour, exploitation, and alienation on social media. A point that is more fully discussed in the next chapter. Some thinkers have also linked it to creativity, participation, and political agency online (e.g., Jenkins 2006; Dahlgren 2013). In this chapter, I am interested in exploring how social media platforms are fundamentally designed to enable, facilitate, and to a degree *force* users to share content and reveal aspects about their own subjectivities online. This is often discussed in relation to gift economies and how sharing online may constitute acts of gift giving and reciprocal exchange (Cammaerts 2011; Jarrett 2015; Kennedy, J. 2016). Josie van Dijck (2013) has shown that users on social media negotiate sharing in relation to changing privacy norms and policies. While the term 'sharing' has a long history in computer culture and of course elsewhere, it has reached a new prominence in relation to social media (Kennedy, J. 2016, 464). Jenny Kennedy has produced a useful framework of different definitions and usages of the term sharing in relation to the contemporary. One aspect of the framework is particularly relevant one for this chapter: 'Sharing is defined in relation to disclosure and affect, meaning to make oneself available to others through some form of sentiment articulation' (Kennedy, J. 2016, 468). On social media, in particular, sharing becomes 'affective' (ibid., 469) and a form that aims to 'provoke social intensification' (ibid., 469). This does not mean that users automatically share and reveal everything about themselves, they are careful and cautious in light of who could see what they create and post online (Stutzman et al. 2012). I return to this aspect in more detail in due course in this chapter. 'Sharing is never employed neutrally', as Kennedy has remarked elsewhere (2013, 129). The characteristics of social media interfaces are not just that Facebook, Twitter, Weibo, Instagram, and so on provide the opportunity for communication, but the interfaces (and the companies behind them) depend on, what they term, the 'sharing' of content. Without content created by users, they would most likely cease to exist. In that sense, sharing is a rhetorical device used by many social media services:

> Social media platforms use the rhetoric of sharing to establish their function as facilitators of social engagement. Here are some typical assertions: 'Facebook helps you connect and share with the people in your life'. 'Find out what's happening, right now, with the people and organizations you care about' says Twitter. 'Share your life in photos' invites Flickr, 'Keep up with your friends and share your stories with comments & notes'. YouTube, likewise, is situated as a facilitator of social relationships, offering through their iPhone app 'more ways to share with the people you love'.
>
> (Kennedy 2013, 130)

I am interested in exploring the incentive to share from a psychosocial perspective a little more, before contrasting it with the inabilities and inhibitions by the interviewees to share content in relation to *Embarrassing Bodies* on social media. Rather than living only in an age where there is a demand to enjoy, as most famously Slavoj Žižek has argued (e.g., Žižek 2007), there is also a demand to share. Sharing becomes a euphemism in this case for producing, disclosing, and revealing information as content online. Whether such practices can really be defined as 'sharing' remains disputed (Kennedy, J. 2016) and I would argue that the term is not quite suited. As Kennedy has argued, sharing is framed by social media companies and commentators in the media as the norm, showing that one is sociable, open, reflexive, and creative. 'Good subjects post, update, like, tweet, retweet, and most importantly, *share*' (Kennedy 2013, 131, italics in original). Sharing is constructed as a social good that is beneficial for all. It is no coincidence that the very usage of the term 'sharing' evokes notions of parental and authoritative teaching (in nursery or primary school settings, for example): 'sharing is caring'[1], young children are told and one of the fundamental skills they learn in their early years is to share toys with others and not to be too possessive of them. Sharing here becomes simultaneously a command that is exercised so that the child may experience the joy in sharing, most often through playing with others. For children, sharing is constructed as an ethical and human practice that they must follow and obey to become responsible and good subjects. Sharing becomes a demand to the *individual* child to be *relational*. The injunction to share results in strong traces in the superego, which, ideally, shall be present for a subject's entire lifetime. As such, sharing symbolises the ability to momentarily part with and let go of objects while the infant is able to retain an introjected imago of them and take pleasure in using them with others. Throughout life, sharing is an act of social and cooperative qualities which enables feelings of love, friendship, and relationality both individually and collectively. It also means individuals are able to engage with others, take part in group activities and find their position within a group (Anzieu 2016).

Sharing 'is by definition a positive social value and bestows a warm glow upon that which it touches' (John 2013, 199), as John puts it beautifully. Russell Belk (2009) has argued that the quintessential and one of the primary acts of sharing is mothering. 'In giving birth the mother shares her body with the fetus and subsequently shares her mother's milk, nurturing, care, and love with the infant' (ibid., 717). We may return to Anzieu's notion of the skin ego (2016) at this point, for it underscores the nature of sharing between mother and baby. 'This care is given freely, with no strings attached and no expectation of reciprocity or exchange' (Belk 2009, 717). Belk writes about the origins of sharing. However, psychoanalysis holds that there is indeed a strong reciprocal nature between mother and baby (and other primary caregivers), which is highly charged through fantasies, desires, and expectations on both parts. The baby (is [un]consciously expected to) respond/s to the given milk, care, and love, and it is often the (in the m/other's eyes) insufficient or excessive manners of responding that are cause for psychic distress. As noted in Chapter 1, for Anzieu, the experience of sharing in the relational environment between mother and baby is both actual and illusionary-virtual. The baby has the fantasy of sharing a common skin with mother.

> The paradox of signifying contacts lies in the fact that a mother who is attentive not only to her baby's bodily needs but also to its psychical ones does more than simply satisfy these needs: by the sensory echoes she sends back, as much as by the concrete actions she performs, she shows that she has correctly interpreted them. The baby's needs are satisfied and at the same time so is its need to have those needs understood. This creates both a wrapping of well-being, which it cathects narcissistically, and the illusion, essential for the formation of the Skin-ego, that the person on the other side of that wrapping will respond immediately, and in exact complementarity, to its signals; this is the reassuring illusion of an omniscient narcissistic double always at its beck and call.
>
> (Anzieu 2016, 47–48)

This illusion that the other will respond immediately lends itself to characteristics of informational capitalism today (Dean 2009) which are marked by an intensification of communication across time-space that results in accelerated speed and a desire (and often expectation) for almost instantaneous replies to emails, messages, or posts. The allure of an immediate response is both present on social media interfaces and suggested and implied. I type a Tweet and hit the 'tweet' button, and immediately the Tweet appears for me to acknowledge that it has been circulated into existence; the very architecture of Twitter suggests that others will immediately like it, retweet, or comment on it. How disappointing if a Tweet fails to gain any traction and remains presumably unnoticed! When I first joined Twitter, I used the platform to merely read other Tweets and remained inactive. I was largely dissatisfied with Twitter and experienced a feeling of lack. Something was missing. This changed drastically when I started using the platform properly and how Twitter wanted me to use it: by actively producing content and engaging with others. All of a sudden, I gained more visibility, others were retweeting my Tweets and commenting. I was rewarded with feelings of recognition and acknowledgement. I had become a 'good' social media subject.

Whereas the skin ego is overcome as the baby matures and develops her own 'thinking-ego' (Anzieu 2016), Anzieu notes that there are sociocultural spaces and phenomena that resemble the skin ego (as discussed in the previous chapter about the *Embarrassing Bodies* doctors and the viewers' relationship to them). The psychoanalytic session resembles the skin ego in so far as that it opens up 'a safe space for the patient against overwhelming sensations (of sight, sound, smell, etc.)' (Anzieu 2016, 261). I have argued that the *Embarrassing Bodies* viewers I interviewed articulated a desire for containment which ultimately remained unfulfilled. Social media may similarly relate to our desires for containing and safe spaces that enable healthy forms of expression and communication (Johanssen 2018). This illusion is also propagated by social media platforms through the very use of the word 'sharing' and the various official narratives that are about care, safety, privacy being valued, and so on. Social media platforms present themselves in similar notions as a therapist that happily receive endless data streams in a stream of consciousness manner. Nicholas A. John has related the use of the term 'file sharing' to a general use of the word 'sharing' that is situated within therapeutic culture:

> However, I would like to argue that the force of the term file sharing also and importantly lies in the sense of sharing as a type of interpersonal communication, one that implies proximity, openness, and honesty. This sense of sharing is clearly central to what is termed the therapeutic culture or discourse.
>
> (John 2014, 205)

Social media thus appeal to and resemble a wider cultural trend that suggests that it is important, healthy, and liberating to disclose and engage with our inner feelings, anxieties, and desires (Johanssen 2012). However, as has been widely discussed, such spaces do not make for safe and healthy spaces but are instead characterised by ambivalence, fragility, and hatred as well as love, cooperation, and support. Many scholars have shown that individuals are careful in how and what they share on social media about themselves (Solove 2007; Stutzman et al. 2012; Baym 2015). Sharing and distributing content online are done, while users are mindful of privacy, ethical, and legal issues. However, such studies implicitly presuppose that sharing is a conscious process largely guided by rationality and reason. In this chapter, I discuss exemplary data that points to an inhibition and unwillingness to share certain aspects of individuals' subjectivities (their loyal consumption of *Embarrassing Bodies*) which were shaped by conscious as well as unconscious dimensions. Sharing may be restricted and strategic, but its underlying reasons are often located more deeply in our life histories. While subjects may be specifically interpellated through social media and wider cultural narratives' injunctions to share, which are themselves partly rooted in super-egoistical demands, such practices are not without limits.

A Silent Audience?

Some interviewees specifically mentioned that they do not talk about *Embarrassing Bodies* with others. One participant, who watched it with her partner, only talked about the show while they were watching it and not afterwards:

> Yeah I think we react to things as they happen on the show but mostly it's to say how shocking that thing is or how awful it must be for that person, or you know, squeaming a little bit at some of the surgery scenes erm but it's not really something that we talk about after the show's finished unless it is something that someone else brings up in conversation 'Oh did you see that episode the other day?' but I don't really hear many people talking about it, erm, in social circles or anything. You see people tweet about all the time throughout the programme, erm, but I think outside of its air time it's not talked about that much.
>
> (I3, 373–381)

She added that she thought that the programme was generally not 'considered polite conversation' (I3, 384). Another interviewee liked to talk about *Embarrassing Bodies* but was regularly told to 'shut up' (I2, 604) by colleagues who 'think I am weird that I sit and watch these things' (I2, 606). While six interviewees expressed that they had watched the programme with friends or partners at times, many also said they never talked about the programme with anyone. A related quote can be included at this point:

> I guess Embarrassing Bodies falls into like trashy a bit, some people would call it slightly trashy, like expositional sort of telly and I think

that's true but what I like about it is like that it does provide some kind of support network for people and that you might watch it and go 'Oh' and so I think that's kind of interesting, I think it's doing a job in some way, it's not just like a disgusting show, it's like informing and educating people.

(I10, 43–48)

This might be interpreted as the banality of reality television, that it is not worthy of conversation, but I argue that more complex reasons for not talking about it may be at stake here. Some people did express that they talked about the show with friends or partners:

I was at university and we used to watch it in our flat, I lived with five guys at uni and we found it like hilarious cos' you know people getting their bums out and stuff, it's just like and it was the sort of thing where you talk, you talk about it with people and you were like 'Did you see that guy's bum?' yeah so probably about I don't know six years ago?

(I6, 168–172)

Here, the social context of viewing it amongst a group of male university friends could lead to the perception of the show in lighter terms that relate to entertainment and *Schadenfreude*, and that may also relate to internalised, unconscious norms of masculinity that advocate 'laddish-ness' and not opening up to more insecure and fragile embodied ways of living and relating to others (Yates 2007). While these insecurities may still have been present within such a group of males, they may be unconsciously defended against by laughing at the patients and shouting 'Did you see that guy's bum?' The same interviewee had also expressed in the interview that he found the show 'like light relief from all my problems' (I10, 157–158). He said, 'I think shows like this do make you appreciate, you know, everyone is like critical of themselves but shows like this they put a perspective in people, people go through a lot worse, like scary stuff' (I10, 331–333). There are different narratives within the same interview that point to entertaining aspects of the programme but also more reflective dimensions that describe the programme as fulfilling more serious functions for the interviewee. Such ambivalent[2] accounts were present in many interview transcripts. A female interviewee also talked about watching the show with others:

[T]wo friends of mine, we used to watch it all together on television and you know sometimes we laugh, not at them, but for example that guy with the smile we found him so adorable, so cute that he tried to smile so much and we felt actually, our hearts like sunk for him so at some point I think we had dinner and we actually put

Embarrassing Bodies because it creates a sense of discussion among us so, we were eating and watching it, so yeah that might not be nice to eat and watch all these things but no it wasn't, you see, I don't find it repulsive and it didn't do nothing for my food, actually it creates discussion among a group.

(I1, 920–928)

This quote also describes a more communal and social viewing experience. The group of friends watched the show while having dinner. The interviewee described it as if it facilitated discussion and compassion but also moments of laughter that point to entertaining dimensions. Both of the quotes may allude to voyeuristic moments as part of the viewing process. While some interviewees watched the programme with others, only four explicitly stated that they engaged in conversations about it.

Internet and Twitter Use

In total, nine of the ten interviewees made use of the Internet when it comes to medical information and had visited the *Embarrassing Bodies* website as part of their online activities. They all seemed to maintain a critical distance towards information they were presented with online, yet attributed special trust to the *Embarrassing Bodies* website. One participant said she had occasionally visited the website, while she regarded the Internet in general as potentially dangerous when searching for medical information:

I suppose the advent of the Internet as well has meant that there is so much you can look up and read about and if there are specific conditions, you can look and it helps you to formulate questions that you want to ask doctors and things like that. They must hate it, they must hate the internet, doctors. Must be the worst thing that's happened to them [chuckles] but, erm, my parents aren't of the generation that do that and of course sometimes the internet is quite dangerous when you look up these things but at least it gives you things that you can ask but, erm.

(I2, 261–267)

Another participant regarded *Embarrassing Bodies* as the prime source for their medical information. Rather than looking at 'dodgy websites' (I7, 316–317), he turned to the programme as a trusted and accurate resource. Another participant made use of the website to compare parts of her body to the pictures uploaded to the galleries to see if she 'was in the nation average and stuff like that' (I6, 247–248).

One may interpret from these quotes that *Embarrassing Bodies* is a highly trusted brand for the participants. One of its key benefits is access to medical information. The trust extends from one medium (television) across to another (the Internet). It is carried over by the *Embarrassing Bodies* programme brand as it is recognised through the logo, official accounts, and the doctors' accounts on social media. This may be a general marketing move in order to enhance visibility (Johnson 2012). Maintaining such a brand that is itself part of a wider channel brand is crucial for channels (Johnson 2007, 2012). The *Embarrassing Bodies* brand and its attributes may signify information and trust to the viewers, and while they did not talk about it with many people, they articulated having a very close connection to the programme that is increased or at least maintained by using the website or following the doctors on Twitter. One participant specifically called *Embarrassing Bodies* a brand and stated that the doctors were 'very professional, very nice, they're very good, like, faces for the brand' (I10, 186). I return to the aspect of branding in a moment. As I had recruited all research participants on Twitter, they were all using the platform, albeit to varying degrees as far as their interaction was concerned. Highfield et al. (2013) have stressed that Twitter may act as a 'virtual loungeroom' (Highfield et al. 2013, 405) that may connect audiences, particularly when viewers tweet during the broadcast of an episode. This may contribute to a 'shared sense of watching' (ibid., 406) among atomised individuals or groups. Murthy (2013) has similarly stressed Twitter's abilities for social communication. For users, tweeting may serve the purpose of 'self-affirmation' (Murthy 2013, 28) of their subjectivities. It is a way of showing the world and themselves that they exist. In the case of the research participants, some preferred to remain inactive on Twitter and they only used it to read other people's Tweets, while others actively tweeted. Those five who were active in terms of sending out Tweets only very occasionally tweeted about *Embarrassing Bodies* and did not engage in extended discussions about it. One said,

I3: I don't really like talking about that much on Twitter, just, I like reading what other people tweet about but I think that it's so open and people's opinion vary so much and there's always clashes and people who are just out for an argument. It's not something that I want to get involved in.

J: So would you say you are not that active on Twitter?

I3: Yeah, I follow more than I tweet. I mostly tweet things that are a bit funny or erm something to do with Yoga or sewing or an offer that my friends might like so I retweet that. I don't take part in debates on Twitter because I think that can just lead to huge arguments. Dr. Christian is a prime example of that, everyone's, he is very getting into Twitter arguments with people and they're sending him sort of horrible things, so it's not something that I wanna be part of.

(I3, 402–412)

Another interviewee remarked that when he tweeted about the programme, he did so in a light-hearted manner:

> Yeah erm on Twitter but maybe not to anybody in particular but sometimes if I think if something may be I know something comes on and they do close ups of that and I would make a joke of it and go you know put something there and I always put the hashtag so that people watching that programme will see that and people know what I'm talking about erm because obviously there are a lot of other people I follow, who follow me who are watching it as well so they know what I'm talking about but it always light hearted not anything erm there's no derogatory or there's nothing bad about it, I just make humour of it really, just for that purpose of that because I am you know when you are on Twitter and you don't know anybody, they might have hundreds and hundreds of followers but you know they are all strangers really if you know.
>
> (I9, 382–391)

There is very little serious discussion of *Embarrassing Bodies* on Twitter in general. Many Tweets make fun of the programme and its patients. One can conclude that *Embarrassing Bodies* does not make an easy conversation topic. 'At the very least, Twitter provides a new channel for the conversations that have always occurred around television' (2013, 407), Harrington, Highfield, and Bruns suggest. But what about conversations that have hardly ever occurred, before or since Twitter's existence? Twitter may have led to more discussion around the live broadcasting of television content (such as sports matches, for example), but my discussion complicates the aforementioned quote and scholarship that stresses social media's potential for sharing, dialogue and interaction (e.g., boyd 2007; Marwick 2013; Murthy 2013) because my data suggests that there are times when users choose not to share certain information. Of course, there are no set rules on what Twitter, or social media generally, is for and how it should be used (Couldry 2012; Hills 2014), but the (corporate) intention behind the social networking site is that people generate and share content (Murthy 2013; Fuchs 2014). As Murthy has highlighted, health issues are actually being discussed on Twitter, and many users reveal cancer diagnoses on the social networking site, for example (ibid., 128). In that way, Twitter, along with online forums and other social media platforms, may create virtual 'patient communities' (ibid., 116) that contribute to a 'dialogic' rather than 'monologic' (ibid., 124) health discourse. This is to some degree the case on Twitter as the *Embarrassing Bodies* doctors' often receive medical-related Tweets. However, the interviewees did not express such dialogic forms of communication. It seemed that there was a discrepancy between the interviewee's active Twitter use and their conscious (and unconscious) exclusion of Tweets on *Embarrassing Bodies*. It appeared that many people did not want to talk about *Embarrassing Bodies* with others, let alone on Twitter where everyone could see such a Tweet. One interviewee, who worked in medicine, remarked that she mostly followed others (including the presenters) on Twitter: 'I follow them but I don't really, I don't put much on Twitter because obviously the job I do and that's a public forum, so I am cautious of what I put on Twitter, so I don't put much on there but I do kind of follow people on there' (I5, 400–402). Marwick and boyd have remarked (2010) that particularly on Twitter audiences are more difficult to know and manage for users. They are invisible because anyone may see someone's Tweets and they can be re-tweeted beyond immediate followers. Whereas in the offline world, one can manage different and multiple audiences and separate them from one another more easily, on Twitter they have collapsed into one amorphous mass. This makes impression management (Goffman 1959) difficult. As a result, users may imagine rather than fully know who their audiences are and how their Tweets are perceived by others. They are cautious as to what information they might reveal through a Tweet and may try to target Tweets to different audiences, through hashtags, for example, but this attempt may be difficult at times. Users may be in a tension between what is perceived as a performed and an authentic self. While Marwick and boyd (2010), for example, describe the act of audience management on Twitter as a conscious one, it is helpful to refer to Aron Balick in this context, who theorises social networking activities by drawing on D. W. Winnicott's (2002) notion of 'the false self'[3]:

> it tends to be the false self/persona that becomes the vehicle for our self-expression on status updates and tweets, to the exclusion of other aspects of our wide ranging and multiple subjectivities. In expressing ourselves in this fashion, we are protecting aspects of our subjectivities that we feel less happy about projecting into the world.
> (Balick 2014, 19)

This protecting may occur both consciously and unconsciously. There seems to be a sense of silence and invisibility around *Embarrassing Bodies*. Such silence and invisibility may be further explored through the notion of inhibition.

Inhibition and Freud

The term 'inhibition' refers to a psychoanalytic notion first developed by Sigmund Freud. 'It is difficult to find a systematic theory of inhibition in either the works of Lacan or of Freud' (Vanheule 2001, 110), but the term appears in a number of Freud's works in particular. Essentially, he postulated that his time was a time of repression of sexual instincts that led to specific symptom formation with regard to inhibition. In one of his earliest texts on hysteria, Freud and his colleague Joseph Breuer regarded repression as a mechanism by which things are 'intentionally repressed from [...] conscious thought and inhibited and suppressed' (Breuer and Freud 2001, 10). In his early writings, Freud defines repression as an act of fending off or averting ideas or states that arouse unpleasure in the subject. Repressed ideas cannot be consciously thought but may slip through the unconscious in fragmentary form. There is thus always a struggle between unconscious ideas being kept at bay and them forcefully being released into consciousness. One impulse inhibits another impulse in that sense.

> An impulse or urge is present which seeks to release pleasure from a particular source and, if it were allowed free play, would release it.
>
> Besides this, another urge is present which works against the generation of pleasure — inhibits it, that is, or suppresses it.
>
> (Freud 1981i, 135)

More generally and not in relation to repression, Freud also regarded inhibition as a conscious effort of precaution or a restriction in order not to experience a particular symptom (e.g., anxiety or phobia). Inhibition may be regarded as a subjective state that protects against unintended or undesired encounters, ideas, or actions. This may also express itself discursively in changing the subject in a conversation, for example, or in feeling unable to adequately converse with others at all (Billig 1999). When the ego is occupied with a specific task that may be overwhelming (mourning, for example), it inhibits its use of psychic energy for other tasks. This notion refers to Freud's economic model of the mind that seeks to make the optimum use of its energy and is arguably less important for us here. However, while inhibition may refer to a conscious act, its underlying reasons and specific motivation that led to inhibition can be *unconscious* to the individual. In that sense, inhibition itself can be a symptom (which masks the underlying problem) as well. It is the task of the psychoanalyst to explore together with the patient what the reasons for a particular kind of inhibition may be if that inhibition fundamentally limits a person's healthy psychic functioning. In other words, what does the symptom through which inhibition is expressed mean in relation to its underlying, unconscious cause? This kind of inhibition may have occurred in relation to the interviewees' inability to tweet about *Embarrassing Bodies*.

Inhibition may also occur unconsciously as a protective mechanism by which the superego restricts the id's impulses that would threaten the ego if consciously expressed or enacted.

Inhibition is in close proximity to repression, and we may therefore explore it in more detail at this point. Psychoanalysis understands repression as an act whereby an idea is rendered unconscious by the ego but is continuously, dynamically pushing for release into consciousness. Repression occurs in response to an undesirable, unpleasurable impulse that is aroused either internally (through thoughts or affective states) or through external perception. 'Through repression the discharge of an excitation that provokes displeasure is inhibited' (Vanheule 2001, 111), as Vanheule puts it in referring to Freud's early, neurological model of the mind that seeks to limit internal and external stimuli. In that sense, inhibition is used here in the biological-neurological sense by Freud. 'Freud states that repression ultimately aims either at inhibiting an instinctual impulse from being turned into a manifestation of affect or at inhibiting and deflecting the excitatory process in the id' (ibid., 111). However, as noted, the repressed content is pushing for release. This danger of the 'return of the repressed' produces anxiety as a primarily affective state in the subject.

> Although the act of repression demonstrates the strength of the ego, in one particular it reveals the ego's powerlessness and how impervious to influence are the separate instinctual impulses of the id. For the mental process which has been turned into a symptom owing to repression now maintains its existence outside the organization of the ego and independently of it.
>
> (Freud 1949, 32)

What follows from repression is thus a 'struggle against the symptom' (Freud 1949, 33) which inhibits healthy psychic life. The symptom essentially refers to a substitute of the repressed content that 'carries on the role of the latter' (ibid., 37) through continually renewing the demands of the repressed to activate itself in some shape or form to conscious awareness. The symptom is nonetheless a compromise formation between what has been repressed and the demands of the superego. Any symptom is thus a kind of distorted, psychic outlet for the repressed elements while the ego tries to organise them into a functioning mode of existence. It 'adapts' (ibid., 35) the symptom to the external world. When Freud attributes the symptom with 'a certain impairment of the capacities of the individual' (ibid., 35), it is clear that he understands it as an inhibiting force for the subject. As a result, the symptom is closely merged with the ego and may, in some cases, be actually very valuable. Obsessive-compulsive symptoms (such as excessive cleaning or self-cleansing) make the subject feel 'better than others' (ibid., 36) precisely because of her symptom. What may be regarded as inhibiting from the outside may therefore not be experienced as such by the subject. Any symptom is created to avoid anxiety, or rather, as Freud specifies, a symptom is generated in order to avoid a particular, dangerous situation that has been anticipated or envisioned through the generation of anxiety (Freud 1978, 53). A symptom may be defined as something that inhibits the subject in a twofold manner. It inhibits against the generation of anxiety through avoiding a particular situation or thought and, second, it inhibits the subject's psychic health more fundamentally.

Additionally, inhibition may also occur in the subject without symptom formation. As inhibition is a consciously experienced process, it involves restricting the ego. Consequently, Freud defines inhibition as 'the expression of a restriction of an ego-function' (ibid., 16). Inhibition thus means that the ego has given up on parts of itself in order not to experience a psychic conflict that would need to be repressed. As we have seen, the symptom is the consequence of repression and is related to inhibition, but inhibition can also be used to circumvent repression as such. In this way, whatever would elicit the psychic conflict is cathected and maintained in an energised, charged-up state but never released.

> In the case of repression, cathexis is displaced from the conflict-related idea to an associated element that becomes the symptom. In this case the function implied in the conflict is maintained. The associated amount of excitation is displaced onto an element outside the scope of the direct conflict-situation.
>
> (Vanheule 2001, 124)

Vanheule (2001) provides a useful synthesis of the different forms of inhibitions that Freud (implicitly) discusses:

> a decrease in the pleasure of exercising a function,
>   a decrease in the ability to carry out a function,
>   an interruption of the carrying out of a function by the appearance of anxiety,
>   negative reactions (for example, anxiety) when a person is obliged to carry out a function, a hampered functioning because of conditions attached to the function, and a prevention of the exercise of a function by security measures.
>
> (Vanheule 2001, 112)

However, Freud (1949) also discusses a type of inhibition that may paralyse the subject in relation to a particular state precisely *because* she wants to enact that state but cannot due to the inhibition. Inhibition, then, may not always function in order to fend off repressed fragments and anxiety but may also be related to more benign feelings of shame or a fear of embarrassment that refer to a specific situation which an individual wishes to overcome but cannot. In relation to that, inhibition may be enacted as a self-punishment in order to avoid a psychic conflict. The superego restricts the ego from pursuing a particular activity, for example. This may have been the case for the interviewees.

Inhibition on Social Media

It seems that all the social media aspects of *Embarrassing Bodies* (apps, a website, Twitter presence, Facebook page, etc.) did not contribute to dialogue or exchange of opinions but made for an asocial media that worked almost exclusively in one direction. Even those participants who occasionally tweeted about *Embarrassing Bodies* did not talk about it with others on Twitter but merely sent off Tweets about it. One interviewee, who was very active on Twitter, remarked in this context,

> [I]t is a little bit less sensitive on something like Twitter but I think everyone on Twitter is trying to be funny and I think everyone is trying to be recognised as being sharp and I think that kind of leads people to be actually a lot meaner than they would be in real life.
>
> (I10, 191–194)

For example, the interviewees who did tweet about the show merely sent off tweets but did not respond to other Tweets that mentioned *Embarrassing Bodies*. Such practices may be explained with a growing awareness of privacy in relation to personal data as subjects continue using social media, as Stutzman et al. (2012) suggest in their longitudinal study of Facebook users' public disclosure of personal data. For their sample, they identify 'a robust trend of declining public disclosure' (Stutzman et al. 2012, 31), while users simultaneously shared more information privately with their friends on Facebook. Marwick and boyd, as well as Stutzman, Gross, and Acquisti, note that there may be an increased awareness of 'silent listeners' (ibid., 29) who users do not know very well on social media. As a result, they are cautious about revealing personal information. While such sentiments may have played a role, I argue that the interviewees in my sample were unwilling and partly inhibited to tweet about *Embarrassing Bodies*, due to affective and unconscious constraints.

Yet, whereas all other interviewees remained silent on Twitter about *Embarrassing Bodies*, nine interviewees followed the doctors/presenters of the show and had tweeted them at times. There seems to be a contradiction, then, between their relative silence about *Embarrassing Bodies* on Twitter and the action of following Dr Pixie, Dr Christian, or Dr Dawn. Matt Hills (2014) notes that for users, 'SNS themselves take on an intensely subjective significance combined with intersubjective meaning' (Hills 2014, 195). This tension between a subjective significance of *Embarrassing Bodies* and social norms and audience expectations that may have prohibited users from revealing such a subjective significance may be resolved through following the doctors. The act of following someone on Twitter may be considered as a more passive move in this case. It establishes a connection that remains relatively invisible to others and may not be shown unless an interviewee would retweet Dr Pixie's

Tweet, for example. Even though the interviewees were not keen to talk about *Embarrassing Bodies* on Twitter, the 'follow'-function still allowed them to remain connected to the brand. This may contribute to the notion of containment that I discussed in the previous chapter. I wish to suggest that the act of following but not directly engaging with the doctors on Twitter constituted an act of brand identification and brand loyalty (Marwick 2013) that is made possible by Twitter's structure of the possibility to follow other users. In that way, users did not have to reveal that they liked *Embarrassing Bodies* through Tweets or offline conversation in the wake of fears of being frowned upon but could still remain faithful to the show and the doctors (and ultimately to the brand) in following them and in also using the official website or apps. Whereas I have suggested that the decision not to talk about the programme online and offline may be a very conscious decision in the light of social norms and superego dynamics (that are of course infused with unconscious dynamics), the act of following may have unconscious motivations that may testify of a deep brand loyalty and desire to be close and connected to the brand. Celia Lury (2004) has argued that 'the affective relations between brands and consumers, [...] typically include some degree of trust, respect and loyalty but may also include playfulness, scepticism and dislike' (Lury 2004, 10). Such an ambivalent relationship between the brand and its consumers may also be present here (see also Banet-Weiser 2012). In following the doctors, a sense of loyalty is enacted that goes beyond the television set and a mere viewing of the show. It may show the effectivity of the branding strategy of Channel 4. This dialectic of a silent following may thus point to an engagement with the doctors that is ambivalent at times. It is a more inward following that does not feature Tweets that would communicate such a following to Twitter audiences. Adam Arvidsson (2005) defined brands as being about social relations: 'Brands work as platforms for action that enable the production of particular immaterial use-values: an experience, a shared emotion, a sense of community' (Arvidsson 2005, 248). While it is useful to regard *Embarrassing Bodies* as a brand, Arvidsson's definition reaches some limits here. Banet-Weiser (2012) has defined brands similarly and makes implicit use of a psychoanalytic term:

> Brand cultures exceed the products they represent and, through this excess, offer community to individuals that assures affective connection with others as well as with themselves. Individuals often feel 'held' by the intimacy of a brand culture: participating in brand cultures feels like participating in an ethical or moral frame.
>
> (Banet-Weiser 2012, 119, emphasis in original)

While the *Embarrassing Bodies* brand may be defined through notions such as community, relationality, and shared emotions, and primarily affects that unite both viewers and patients (see also Misha Kavka's argument that was discussed in the Introduction about the relational affectivity of reality television), this 'platform for action' and 'community', as Arvidsson and Banet-Weiser call it, was not enacted anywhere, apart from perhaps through the viewing of the programme and the act of following the doctors on Twitter. Whereas other brands are (in)voluntarily publicly displayed and showcased (e.g., the Nike shoes are worn, the Coca Cola bottle is carried around, the Apple MacBook is used) by subjects who consume them and may even feel as part of a community as a result, *Embarrassing Bodies* is instead mostly consumed in isolation in front of the television screen in the living room. It is of course not a physical product that is branded and shown in public. Yet, while the programme may not be displayed by viewers in the manner of, for example, an iPhone, as I have just discussed, there may also be underlying inhibitions that do not point to the brand's immateriality alone. Catherine Johnson (2012) has argued that expanding the Channel 4 brand beyond the television channel into the Internet (with services such as 4OD) has not been without risks for the broadcaster:

> As Channel 4 continues to expand into new media platforms, its brand has become an asset to be both exploited and protected. This is particularly important because Channel 4's key demographic groups (ABC1s and 16–34-year-olds) tend to be early adopters of new technology. Extending the Channel 4 brand into new areas protects the brand's equity by helping it to stay relevant for and connected to its core audiences.
>
> (Johnson 2012, 95)

These early adopters were also present in my sample, partly due to the fact that I had recruited them through Twitter, but to what extend has Channel 4 succeeded in extending its brand and the *Embarrassing Bodies* programme brand? Has Channel 4's brand strategy failed as a result? Does the main slogan of the show 'There's no shame, we're all the same' remain valid?

> However, brands only gain value through the uses and meanings attributed to them by the public. Therefore, programme branding is an attempt not just to organize the relationships between programme extensions, but also to manage the uses to which these products are put by the public. As our engagement with media products is made increasingly visible through the internet, this becomes more pressing.
>
> (Johnson 2012, 157)

There may be a tension between Channel 4's attempt to manage the relationship between the programme brand and its online discourse by the public. I argue that the public discourse about bodies, illnesses, health-care, shame, and embarrassment that Channel 4 perhaps hoped to achieve through the *Embarrassing Bodies* brand and its presence on social media may have failed, but that does not mean that *Embarrassing Bodies* is not a popular brand. The majority of the Tweets that mention the show are of a negative tone in my experience but they still uphold publicity and discourse about the brand. The majority of the Twitter users in the sample did not tweet much about the show, be it positively or negatively.

As I have noted in the previous chapter, the programme as a facilitator of an ability to talk about embarrassing aspects of the body is not without limits. It may have also been present on an unconscious level for many interviewees in so far as it facilitated unconscious and affective memories related to their own bodies. The programme resulted in such affective responses to the show in the interviewees that they may have been unable to engage with it on a communicative level. Many expressed a deep trust of the doctors and the programme, and used the website and followed the doctors on Twitter but fell more or less silent on Twitter and in offline conversations. This may be because they and the programme unconsciously touch and activate something in themselves that they are profoundly affected by. This 'something' related to affect and problematic bodily experiences that are too private to share online and are also difficult to put into words. As a result, we could argue that the falling silent on Twitter was an unconscious act of resisting the message of the brand that users should participate and help lift the taboo of ill bodies through visible engagements with the brand. It was also an act of resistance to the sharing mantra propagated by social media platforms that users should share anything that is on their minds. Viewers in the sample displayed a loyalty to the brand in their narratives about it and their use of extra-televisual texts, like smart-phone apps and the website, and in following the doctors on Twitter. Such a loyalty is maintained in a nuanced way without public expression of it. There may be inhibitions on part of the viewers to publicly express their liking of the programme because it is not perceived as a topic for small talk. They were also so affected by the programme in regards to visceral reactions that relate to past bodily experiences that they wished to protect themselves by not disclosing such reactions on social media (Balick 2014). Such a desire for protection was the result of inhibition. There was thus a conscious dimension to inhibition which refers to not wanting to disclose that viewers thought very positively of *Embarrassing Bodies* as well as an unconscious dimension. The unconscious dimension presented a defensive turning away from the embodied experiences that I have discussed in the previous chapter by referring to Martha and Ellen in particular. A tweeting about *Embarrassing Bodies* may have established a connection between particular affective-embodied experiences and *Embarrassing Bodies*, which for reasons I do not know they (unconsciously) may have not wanted to establish.

A key argument emerges at this point. Viewers in the sample engaged with *Embarrassing Bodies* in a one directed manner. This one directionality characterised not by dialogue but by specific and instrumental requests (e.g., submitting a Tweet, looking up something on the *Embarrassing Bodies* website, watching the programme) actually led to a *more inward directed viewing* for many of the subjects I interviewed. Such a viewing is not completely disengaged with the social and interpersonal relations as the subject is always constituted by and part of the social. Instead, it may be characterised by a subject who turns towards herself. This is both triggered by *social* circumstances (*Embarrassing Bodies* is not a topic for small talk) as well as *psychic* circumstances (such as affective responses, bodily experiences, and their relationship to inhibition) that are entangled, the latter being shaped and influenced by social norms as well. I will return to this aspect later. While such practices may constitute an act of unconscious resistance to brands and ideologies, it may possibly not be regarded as a complete resistance but rather an ambivalent and dilemmatic one. The interviewees who were on Twitter were at once loyal to the brand message behind *Embarrassing Bodies* and followed the doctors, and resistant in their silence on social media and in conversations with friends or colleagues. It needs to be noted that the interviewees were actively tweeting about other topics on Twitter. My discussion bears some similarity to recent studies of both non-resistant and resistant media use, whereby subjects only use media for specific practices and consciously disregard them for others, for example only using phones to send text messages (Ribak and Rosenthal 2015), or not using media or social networking sites altogether (Portwood-Stacer 2013; Woodstock 2014). Rather than defining such practices and use patterns, the ones of this project's interviewees included, as patterns of resistance, Ribak and Rosenthal (2015) term them 'media ambivalence[s]'. Such a term includes at once practices related to use and non-use of (features of) certain media and makes space for subjectivity and motivations behind such practices. However, such studies have placed an emphasis on conscious opting out of media features and make no reference to unconscious and affective dynamics.

Twitter's Skin Ego

The sense of inhibition that I have outlined may have been particularly difficult for interviewees to negotiate in light of the dominant social media imperative of sharing, disclosing, opening up, and communicating. In addition to the use of the word 'sharing', another term can be found in abundance on social networking sites: community. The term is listed 156 times in the *Zuckerberg Files*, an online repository of all public statements by Mark Zuckerberg from 2004 onwards. On its official website, Facebook states that its 'mission is to give people the power to build community and bring the world closer together' (Facebook 2017). Facebook and other social media platforms frame themselves as bringing communities together as one, global community. As has been noted by many thinkers, communities are imagined (Anderson 1983; Pahl 2005; Studdert 2006; Walkerdine 2010). Valerie Walkerdine has described communities, for instance, the community of a former steel-producing town in Wales, as being characterised by 'embodied affective relations' (2010, 95). She looks at community in relation to the psychoanalytic notion of containment and relies on Anzieu in conceptualising community as a skin ego. While there are ample differences between the community of a former steel producing town, which finds itself confronted with social change, and the so-called communities of social media platforms, it is useful to conceptualise social media as community through the skin ego nonetheless. In his work on group analysis, Anzieu (1984) has argued that the group imagines itself as having a body in order to have an organisational structure and a feeling of togetherness amongst its members. This is similarly the case for social media platforms which, consisting of millions of members across the world, define community standards and codes that aim to govern behaviour. Through using the same platform, users feel part of the same community. There are also more implicit, unwritten rules in a community, and this was discussed by the interviewees. They needed to be adhered to in order to belong. Three quotes which I discussed earlier exemplify such rules of belonging:

> [I]t is a little bit less sensitive on something like Twitter but I think everyone on Twitter is trying to be funny and I think everyone is trying to be recognised as being sharp and I think that kind of leads people to be actually a lot meaner than they would be in real life.
>
> (I10, 191–194)

> I would make a joke of it and go you know put something there and I always put the hashtag so that people watching that programme will see that and people know what I'm talking about.
>
> (I9, 384–386)

> I mostly tweet things that are a bit funny or erm something to do with Yoga or sewing or an offer that my friends might like so I retweet that.
>
> (I2, 408–409)

These narratives characterise one particular dimension of Twitter as being a light-hearted, witty, and funny community. In addition to the unconscious dimension of inhibition that may have influenced not to tweet about *Embarrassing Bodies*, there may have also been a conscious dimension of not doing so. Tweeting about the programme in a similarly serious manner to how the interviewees spoke to me about it may have been perceived as out of place or as a violation of the skin ego that enwraps Twitter users in an (imagined) shared sense of what the platform is about. This may have added to the inability to tweet about the programme.

Conclusion

This chapter laid out aspects that concerned the engagement with the different *Embarrassing Bodies* presences on television and online. I was particularly interested in the notion of a silent audience and why many interviewees did not talk about the programme with anyone and also remained silent about it on Twitter. Yet many followed the *Embarrassing Bodies* doctors on the social networking site. I interpreted such a silent following as an identification with the *Embarrassing Bodies* brand that is slightly ambivalent. Viewers in the sample may not have been able and willing to share their thoughts on *Embarrassing Bodies* online. An aspect of the branding strategy behind the show may have failed in this particular case. The programme resulted in such affective responses to the show in the interviewees that they may have been unable to engage with it on a communicative level. As discussed in the previous chapter, the interviewees – apart from Martha – did not mention seeing a connection between their biographies and their viewing of *Embarrassing Bodies*. To me, how they talked about their biographies and *Embarrassing Bodies* occurred very much in a divided manner. No participant themselves (except for Martha) spoke of a connection between their biographies and the viewing (and choice) of the programme. It is striking, however, that all participants mentioned deeply personal, troubling and – for some – traumatic experiences related to illnesses or medicine almost immediately after I had asked them to tell me about their life history. I would not argue that these narratives merely came about as a result of the method of free association. One could conclude that the interviewees made some unconscious connections between *Embarrassing Bodies* and their subjectivities in the interview, but they were not aware of it nor had they thought about it prior to the interview. This unconscious connection may likewise show itself during the viewing process in the form of affective responses. One participant answered my question of a relation between their biography and the show in the following way:

> Erm, not directly. I think because of the situations that I've been through with friends and family, it makes me more aware and I'm more, erm, intrigued I guess by things like that but it's not what

triggered it. I have always just been interested in those kinds of things [...]. I don't think there is a direct correlation between [the biography] and why I watch *Embarrassing Bodies*.

(I3, 494–501)

Watching *Embarrassing Bodies* may represent – at least partially – an *unconsciously* made choice to facilitate mastery and affective discharge.

To return to the skin ego and the container/contained model discussed earlier, one can argue that consequently this desire to be contained is not fulfilled because no full or complete containment takes place. As I discussed earlier in this chapter, *Embarrassing Bodies* was viewed largely in a very inwardly directed manner and was not talked about with friends or family in social settings by the interviewees (except in the interview). The voyeuristic modes of viewing that form part of the whole experience of watching the show support this further. It is precisely the defining moment of voyeurism that the voyeur is *not* seen by anyone but has uninterrupted access to what they are looking at.

Week after week, the viewers saw patients being contained and healed and they also felt a sense of containment but *something* is still missing. The containment is incomplete and a residue of affect remained. This quota of affect is, what psychoanalysis would call, 'acted out' and discharged in the viewing process through moments of laughter, shock, turning away from the screen, screaming, disgust, and above all in the state of diffuse 'excitation' that three of the participants described themselves to be in. The viewing of the show may be seen as a way of discharging affects that are uncoupled from ideas: ideas that refer to bodily states, bodily experiences, or experiences related to the body that were spoken of by many interviewees but not in relation to *Embarrassing Bodies*. These ideas refer to experiences of, or thoughts about, undesired bodily states (like illnesses, embarrassing conditions, disabilities, etc.) that we all share as humans, independent of *Embarrassing Bodies*. They may refer to unconscious fears we all have of our bodies or parts of them being ill, strange, embarrassing, unknown, mysterious, or other in some ways. It is, like affect, not restricted to the interviewees.

For a moment, I wish to present more quotes that testify to affective reactions to the show before thinking about what they might entail.

Yeah, yeah, yeah definitely there's something like, you know when there's like really gross infections when you kind of think that is quite disgusting, like when things are like septic or whatever or just general like people go on there with all manner of things don't they? Erm, and like, erm, you never really know what you're gonna get but there's a few times I've kind of gone 'eurgh'.

(I10, 200–204)

I mean yeah you do get those sort of 'eeeh' squirmy moments where you know you can't even look at the screen.

(I2, 367–368)

I can watch most other things, she says gruesomely. I don't know, I don't like seeing pain, is the other one that gets me. I'm quite happy to watch operations but if it's a sort of emergency medical thing that we're watching and the person is obviously in a lot of pain and screaming and that really 'eeeuuh' gets to me. Watching pain is horrible! I can't watch that.

(I2, 514–517)

These quotes may support my theoretical framework that emphasises affect because we could, once more, interpret the interviewees as trying to verbalise an affective experience that occurs while they watch it. In the process of watching an episode, they reacted in a certain way that, as most have discussed because their viewing was so inwardly directed, it was not talked about by them. Upon hearing my question(s) they thought back to their viewing experience and relived the moment in their memory that they then talk about. I argue that these quotes suggest an attempt to render something that is not outside of language but in tension with it, putting a not-yet-expressed state into language: affect. If affect 'hesitates at the edge of the unsayable' (Anderson 2009, 78), then these quotes show how something nearly unsayable can sound in an interview situation. What is being described here is precisely unsayable but turned into a sort of sound that is, on top of that, attempted to be put into words by myself in the transcript as 'eurgh', 'eeeh', and 'eeeuuh'. What do 'eurgh', 'eeeh', and 'eeeuuh' mean here? What are they meant to describe? What lies behind them?

As André Green (1999) argued (see Chapter 1) in an affective reaction, childhood memories or experiences represent and rearticulate themselves consciously or unconsciously. If, as I have discussed, the interviewees' affective reactions relate to memories that are in relation to their bodies, I would argue that it is precisely the moment that is pinpointed in a number of different ways by the interviewees here that marks the affective discharge. The speaking of excitement; of shock; or of 'eurgh', 'eeeh', and 'eeeuuh' marks these affective reactions and their final step of discharge. They mark the discharge of a remaining affective quantity that was not responded to or contained for the participants but lurking in their bodies. In looking at the sequence and order of how these reactions might look like, something is first registered (e.g., a gaping wound) and a few milliseconds later, a viewer responds by screaming 'eurgh' or covering their eyes. If we recall that Freud described affects as two-sided – they contain the discharge and feelings of unpleasure or pleasure and can also contain fantasies. Some of the affective reactions that the interviewees have talked about are both distinctly unpleasurable and pleasurable (the voyeuristic excitement or a sense of relief for participants who have had successful treatment) but it is not clear *why*. I am not interested in speculating why these affective experiences occurred, but it is fundamental *that* they occurred. If we follow Freudian psychoanalysis here, they were related to past childhood experiences. As I have argued at length in this chapter, psychoanalysis suggests that there may have been a connection between (medical or health related) aspects of interviewees' biographies and their viewing of *Embarrassing Bodies*. This connection is heightened by examining affective experiences. From a Freudian perspective, there may indeed be a connection between affective reactions and how they are experienced in front of the television screen, together with the subject's biography and bodily experiences. What this connection exactly is or why, for instance, Ellen reacted so affectively when seeing pain or nose jobs, I cannot and do not wish to say. It can be explored psychoanalytically, yet can never be fully known.

Notes

1 Facebook itself made use of the expression in a blog post when the 'sharing' feature was first introduced (Kennedy 2013, 129).
2 The term 'ambivalence' is used here to describe some aspects of the interviewees' relations to *Embarrassing Bodies*. The term is often used in psychoanalysis and Bleuler (1952) originally defined it as an experience or thought that is simultaneously cathected with unpleasant and pleasant feelings.
3 Winnicott defines the 'false self' as a defence mechanism that is used to protect the subject against a threat by creating an altered or different character they present to the outside world (Winnicott 2002).

4 Affective Labour and the Body
Theoretical Developments

The second half of this book moves away from a focus on audiences of television and social media alone. In this and the next chapter, I discuss the increasing focus on data in the realm of the digital and how psychoanalysis may help to make sense of it. I situate the increased scholarly and industry attention on data as developments that are to do with a monetisation of data; user data being commodified on social media; and large data sets being created, compiled, and extracted for various purposes today. These developments have, on the one hand, something to do with notions and debates on digital labour, affective labour, and commercial social media, while they, on the other hand, revolve around terms such as big data, datafication, data-driven lifeworlds, dataveillance, algorithmic power, and so on. In that sense, this second part of the book seeks to make sense of the wider structural dynamics that shape media systems, and the Internet in particular, across the globe today by relating them psychosocially to psychoanalysis both on micro as well as macro levels.

Labour

As I have argued in the previous chapters, media use is partly shaped by unconscious and affective dimensions. Whereas I have characterised specific Twitter use with regard to inhibition and the compulsion to share in the previous chapter, the demands and various incitements to share offered by social media platforms primarily exist because the production of user data is what contributes to profit maximisation on those sites.

One emerging strand of research in political economy over the last decade or so has been concerned with what is referred to as 'digital labour'. In this chapter, I will outline some of the central arguments in the digital labour debate and supplement them with a psychoanalytic dimension. I will also return to some of the discussions on affect from Chapter 1 and develop Freud's and Anzieu's works on affect further to make them more applicable to the notion of affective labour online.

Critical theorists have argued that user activity on social media constitutes a form of unpaid labour that is exploited on platforms such as Facebook, Twitter, YouTube, Instagram, and other services. Drawing on Karl Marx's labour theory of value and how it has been developed by Dallas Smythe with regard to the notion of the audience commodity (Smythe 1981), user activity is conceptualised as labour. Smythe used the context of television viewing to argue that audiences are turned into commodities when they watch programmes. They and information about them (ratings, socio-demographic data) are sold to advertisers. Advertising time is bought by companies in order to access viewers' time and attention. This marks a form of unpaid labour on the part of the viewers because it leads to value-creation (Jhally and Livant 1986). Christian Fuchs (2014) has applied this argument to social media. User activity creates value for social media platforms (and other commercial services on the Internet) through the creation of content, such as location data, browsing data, or data that is uploaded in the form of text. The data thus created is turned into a commodity and sold to advertisers on Facebook, for example, who, in turn, offer targeted advertising to individual users based on extracted data about them. In this context, it is useful to offer a brief description of how Karl Marx defined labour in capitalism because many voices in the digital labour debate have drawn on him.

Marx (1976) has discussed the nature of labour in capitalist societies. Labour, as Marx has argued in the first volume of *Capital*, creates use value that is coupled with exchange value. Use value refers to specific qualities that a commodity has (e.g., a thick coat protects against cold weather in winter), and exchange value refers to the price of the commodity that the buyer has to buy in order to own it. In this process, an object, an idea, or a resource is transformed through the instruments of labour (e.g., a machine) into a new product by the worker. For Marx then, not surprisingly, labour is material, a material process by which materials from the external world are appropriated by the worker. Marx defines the labour process as follows: 'The simple elements of the labour process are (1) purposeful activity, (2) the object on which that work is performed, and (3) the instruments of that work' (Marx 1976, 284). For Marx, then, labour at the level of production is a concrete process by which materials are appropriated by the worker. In capitalism, they are given an object of labour to work on and as a result are paid for that labour which enables their survival. The subject who performs the labour has essentially sold her labour power to the capitalist; her use value is the property of the capitalist. This condition has taken over the worker's whole life, and she is only a subject in so far as she is a worker. This has been termed *alienated labour* by Marx. The worker has no control over the commodities they produce, the machinery they use, or the raw materials that are needed as part of the production process. As a result, the worker is also alienated from herself and fellow workers (Marx 1973, 1976). I return to this point later on in the chapter when discussing the digital labour debate in more detail.

Value is put together out of the value of the form of labour and the constant value: for example, that of the machinery. In the production process, extra value is produced: surplus value. This means that a quantum of extra labour power has been invested in the production process that is unpaid. Upon entering the circulation sphere, the commodity is exchanged and thus transformed into money (which will again be turned into capital), which, in order for the labour to be productive, has now become more money than that which had been invested at the beginning of the whole process. At this point, surplus value has been realised. This value is owned by the capitalist, not the workers; they receive wages which are kept lower than the all-in-all labour value invested. The capitalist's profit is equivalent to the quantity of the exploitation of the worker which equates to the unpaid, extra labour time. What one finds at the heart of capitalism is the imperative to accumulate ever more capital. This can happen in two ways: One can prolong the working day, or one can increase productivity. What is crucial for Marx here is that the capitalist manages to increase profits by increasing the work time and making the worker work longer than necessary to produce all the needed commodities and to generate surplus value (Marx 1976). As the value of a commodity is always measured in time in the Marxist labour theory of value, the increase of productivity is seen as 'relative surplus value production', as more commodities and more surplus value can be produced in the same time period.

Immaterial and Affective Labour

Marx's labour theory has been significantly developed by so-called Autonomist Marxism as well as other thinkers. For this chapter, debates on immaterial and affective labour are particularly relevant. In the age of informational capitalism, labour has increasingly become, while still a material process, immaterial and about knowledge, information, communication, affect (Fuchs 2008).

Michael Hardt and Antonio Negri (2000, 2004) and Mauricio Lazzarato (1996) have advanced conceptualisations of immaterial labour (see also Virno 1996, 2004; Berardi 2009). Broadly speaking, the term designates new forms of labour that go beyond traditional factories and workplaces and stretch into all spheres of life and are not easily recognised as 'work'. Immaterial labour

> produces the cultural content of the commodity (and) involves a series of activities that are not normally recognized as "work" – in other words the kinds of activities involved in defining and fixing cultural and artistic standards, fashions, tastes, consumer norms, and [...] public opinion.
>
> (Lazzarato 1996, 133–134)

It is the product of the labour process, which is itself material and physical, that is intangible, such as a feeling of well-being, health, or satisfaction (Hardt and Negri 2004, 108). Hearn counts, for instance, software designers, waiters/waitresses, sex workers, academics, information, computer and knowledge workers, performers, artists, technicians, and service workers (Hearn 2010, 63) as immaterial labourers. They generate less tangible commodities: relationships, code, data, ideas, knowledge, or services. According to Hardt and Negri, there is an ever-increasing need and desire for the labour process to become immaterial: 'today labour and society have to informationalize, become intelligent, become communicative, become affective' (2004, 109). This real need and at the same time *desire of becoming* is key and I will examine it in the next two chapters in more detail in relation to social media labour and fantasies of big data. Hardt and Negri argue that there is more and more reliance on communication, soft skills, and social relationships within all workplaces today. 'This labor is immaterial, even if it is corporeal and affective, in the sense that its products are intangible: a feeling of ease, well-being, satisfaction, excitement, passion-even a sense of connectedness or community' (Hardt 1999, 96).

There have been some debates within Marxism and scholarship that draws on the immaterial labour concept about its measurability and value-creation. According to Hardt and Negri (2004), immaterial labour cannot be measured, and the concept therefore seeks to move beyond Marx's labour theory of value (Marx 1976) which I briefly outlined in the previous section. As Hearn notes, 'value has moved both outside of, and beyond, measure' (Hearn 2010, 65). Some thinkers have also critiqued the argument by Autonomist Marxism that immaterial forms of labour now take precedence over more physical, material labour processes that Marx analysed in *Capital*. It is beyond this book's scope to enter into these debates in more detail, instead I am interested in the theoretical underpinnings with regard to affect when it comes to affective labour.

In an early text on affective labour, Michael Hardt has argued that '[t]heoretical frameworks that have brought together Marx and Freud have conceived of affective labor using terms such as desiring production [...]' (Hardt 1999, 89). However, apart from Deleuze and Guattari (1983, 1987) who Hardt alludes to here, there have been very few works that successfully brought together Freud and Marx specifically when it comes to affective labour. This is one of the key tasks of this chapter with regard to digital labour. For Hardt and Negri, affective labour is a component, or sub-aspect, of immaterial labour. It involves

> the production and manipulation of affect and requires (virtual or actual) human contact, labour in the bodily mode [...] the labour is immaterial, even if it is corporeal and affective, in the sense that its

products are intangible, a feeling of ease, well-being, satisfaction, excitement or passion.

(Hardt and Negri 2000, 292)

To some extent, immaterial/affective labour is also about self-care, self-improvement, and reinvention, and its heightened coming into being in neo-liberalism is obvious in that respect. I wish to go beyond Hardt and Negri here and mention other important thinkers on affect and labour that are often excluded in the affective and immaterial labour discussion. In her seminal book *The Managed Heart* (1983), Arlie Hochschild researched and conceptualised emotional labour as an act in which, for example, flight attendants had to learn how they should feel and display particular emotions in their working lives. They were trained to close the gap between how they felt and how they should feel in front of a customer to guarantee the successful selling of a commodity. Affective and emotional displays, Hochschild demonstrates, are key factors in not only generating use but also exchange value.

One particular strand that is important to discuss here is the feminist and radical feminist thinkers on reproductive, domestic, and care labour, who, as Leopoldina Fortunati (2007) has argued, in many ways are the real creators of the immaterial labour thesis discussed earlier. Angela McRobbie (2011) and Kylie Jarrett (2015) have also stressed that the 'discovery' of immaterial and affective labour by many academics as something distinctly new and rooted in informational capitalism is wrong. Jarrett (2015) has produced a detailed critique of Autonomist Marxist conceptualisations of labour because they have ignored earlier discussions on feminised labour as well as domestic, care, and service work. Discussions on immaterial labour have not fully considered the mutual relationalities between production and reproduction, between the economic and social spheres which have always existed in capitalism. To postulate the novelty of the social factory, where work time and free time are blurred, even indistinct, is untenable. Instead, there are specific spheres which are vital to capitalism that depend on women's work (unpaid domestic work, for example). Federici (2004) has argued that throughout the history of capitalism as it emerged from feudalism, social relations are fundamentally reshaped. A distinction is made between what is economically and what is socially viable. Work, as Marx also documented, is no longer organised around smaller circles such as the family. Instead, those relations are separated. Men work for wages in factories and women stay at home, or work for less than men. The housewife is constructed and propagated in the nineteenth century amidst a proletarisation of work in factories. Women were linked to reproductive, domestic labour that made them invisible. 'Importantly, it also placed the woman's labour and her body as a reward for the working man, using them to reduce the effects of alienation and exploitation found in his labour, thereby pacifying the workforce' (Jarrett 2015, 60). Additionally, as has been pointed out (Mies et al. 1988), such labour has in traditional Marxist labour theories of value been regarded as unproductive because it does not generate exchange value but merely use value. However, critiques of this approach articulate that the very act of domestic and reproductive labour serves to raise and discipline subjects into future workers but also satisfy the husband so that he may continue to work.[1] So-called 'women's work' is essentially in that respect because it constitutes and re-creates (ideological) subjectivities. These accounts allow for a more inclusive category of immaterial, or rather affective (for a better term), labour, to emerge. They include embodied, messy, and non-masculine forms of (un)paid labour, and introduce another angle on subjectivities that is helpful for this book. While Hardt and Negri have ignored much of feminist work on affect, emotion, and the mind-body dualism (Ahmed 2014, 206), another problematic concerns their use of affect itself.

What Is Affect for Hardt and Negri?

In the previous chapters, I have put forward a distinct model of what affect means from a psychoanalytic perspective. However, in many affect theories 'affect' is not fully defined and is used as a term to designate a number of processes and relationalities. Take for instance, Clough et al.'s definition of what they term 'affect-itself' in relation to affective labour:

> Affect-itself is admittedly an underspecified concept because it is meant to address the becoming abstract, and therefore becoming subject to measure that which is seemingly disparate – that is, pre-individual capacities ranging from preconscious human bodily capacities, to human genetic materials functioning outside the human body, to the capacities of computer programs to elaborate levels of complexity beyond the specifications of the program, to the capacities of bacteria to cross species now lending to a reconceptualization of evolution as well as becoming a model of bioterrorism.
>
> (Clough et al. 2007, 62)

I do not regard this definition (or non-definition) of affect as particularly useful. Affect is often in danger of being used as an umbrella term with which anything, as long as it is somewhat relational, emergent, becoming, and so on and so forth, can be labelled. While affect, based on Spinoza and Deleuze, can perhaps be broadly defined as an ability of objects and subjects to affect and be affected, there is scope to think about this further in relation to affective labour and to separate it from other forms of labour. In her auto-ethnography of working as a restaurant waitress, Emma Dowling, for example, equates affective with emotional labour (in the sense of Hochschild): 'Affect played a significant role in the management strategy, both in terms of enhancing the affective quality of the service work performed, but also in structuring relations amongst co-workers [...]' (Dowling 2007, 119). This quote could also be read as describing emotional, rather than affective, labour. I want to hold on to the notion of affective labour (rather than emotional labour) because it opens up avenues of exploring labour in different ways than theorisations of emotional labour alone can do. Treating the two as distinctive may help to further theorise and analyse the specificities of affective labour in contrast to emotional labour. Unlike Hesmondhalgh and Baker (2008), I do not think that the two should be equated or conflated. Too much work has gone into the field of affect studies that painstakingly differentiates affect from emotion (e.g., Ngai 2005; Wetherell 2012), while of course there are also thinkers who argue *against* a separation of affect and emotion (e.g., Ahmed 2014). One of the key strengths about the concept of affect, which is perhaps one of its weaknesses at the same time, is its resistance to definition, its intangibility, its refusal to be closed down through specific attributes, paradigms, and ideas. Affect studies thus open up new ways into the study of relationalities, bodies and matter, and so on. However, as I have argued in the Introduction, this also risks to make the concept an empty signifier that has been filled with various meanings by so many different scholars that it is in danger of becoming unusable because shared meanings can no longer be identified. In an effort to reach certainty and more clarity, I have put forward my definition of affect as being situated in tension with consciousness, discourse, and the non-discursive. I am fully aware that such a definition goes against the grain of much of affect studies, but it may perhaps offer some value nonetheless.

Emma Dowling notes that Hardt and Negri (2000, 2004, 2009) use the term 'affect' without fully defining its elements (Dowling 2007, 118). While I fully subscribe to Hardt and Negri's diagnosis that affective labour has increased in post-Fordism (this is particularly relevant to information and communication technologies-based work but also goes beyond it), the question poses itself as follows: What is the 'affective' in 'affective labour'? Hardt and Negri stress that the produced commodities or products are affective and immaterial: 'social networks, forms of community, biopower' (Hardt and Negri 2000, 293), for example – but what is distinctly *affective* about them as products or how they are produced? Hardt and Negri base their use of affect on the conceptualisation by Spinoza (Hardt 1999; Negri 1999; Hardt and Negri 2004, 374).[2] In the text *Value and Affect*, Negri defines affect as the 'power to act' (Negri 1999, 79). Affects 'construct a commonality among subjects' (ibid., 87) which is marked by power and desire. Affect becomes a power of transformation through and towards the commons.

If in fact affect constructs value from below, if it transforms it according to the rhythm of what is common, and if it appropriates the conditions of its own realization, then it is more than evident that in all of this there resides an expansive power.

(ibid., 86)

This has been echoed in the later writings of Hardt and Negri on the revolutionary potential of the multitude (2000, 2004, 2009). Affect, then, is not about individual bodies but about the effect of entities being affected and affecting, whereby 'events are charged with affectivity' (ibid., 88, see Dean 2016 for a recent discussion on this in relation to the crowd). The term somehow marks a relationality between and connection to other categories and is framed as such in the last sentence of the text by Negri: 'affect (production, value, subjectivity)' (ibid., 88). This makes for a useful starting point, to consider some of the formulations on affect in the later works by Hardt and Negri. In *Empire* (2000), affect is frequently evoked. Affective labour is partially about 'the creation and manipulation of affect' (Hardt and Negri 2000, 292). Care labour, for instance, produces immaterial affects (ibid., 293). 'What affective labor produces are social networks, forms of community, biopower' (ibid., 293). '[T]he media must create affects and forms of life' (2004, 108). In relation to care work, affective labour is defined as 'biopolitical production in that it directly produces social relationships and forms of life' (2004, 110). While I admit that these quotations are taken out of context, they nonetheless do not fully define what is meant by 'affect/s' and how affects are experienced, created, and produced.

The most definitive definition of affect and affective labour by Hardt and Negri is perhaps the following one:

We call the other principle form of immaterial labor 'affective labor.' Unlike emotions, which are mental phenomena, affects refer equally to body and mind. In fact, affects, such as joy and sadness, reveal the present state of life in the entire organism, expressing a certain state of the body along with a certain mode of thinking. Affective labor, then, is labor that produces or manipulates affects such as a feeling of ease, well-being, satisfaction, excitement, or passion.

One can recognize affective labor, for example, in the work of legal assistants, flight attendants, and fast food workers (service with a smile).

(Hardt and Negri 2004, 108)

However, I feel there is scope to develop the notion of affective labour through empirical examples which may perhaps shed more light on the distinctly affective dimensions of it. I wish to do so through discussing affective labour on social media. Before doing so, some more discussion of the qualities of immaterial and affective labour are helpful.

Immaterial Labour and the Problem of Embodiment

In her critique of the immaterial labour concept, Sharon C. Bolton has claimed that

> the focus on *care labour* and *kin work* is firmly tying affective la-
> bour into a form of embodied effortless labour. In other words, it is
> tying affective labour into the domestic/natural/feminine realm and
> completely loses sight of the fact that it is a form of labour and, very
> often, particularly hard work'
>
> (Bolton 2009, 4, italics in original)

While I think this criticism is a little unfair, because Hardt, Negri, and Lazzarato do not necessarily define immaterial labour as effortless, it speaks to another problem of the concept: a lack of a consideration of the specifically embodied aspect of immaterial and affective labour. I want to use this section to tease out the implicit Cartesian dualism of the mind/body that is evident in some scholarship on immaterial labour. The concepts of affective and immaterial labour, and Marx's very no-tion of the labour process more generally, are also too rationalistic and lack adequate theorisations of unconscious, and affective for that mat-ter, dimensions of the labour process. Both Freud and Anzieu can be of help here. Both the discussions on immaterial labour and the discussions on digital labour in particular are neat, clean, and rigorous but also somewhat lacking and strangely disembodied (Dyer-Witheford 2001, 72; Bolton 2009; Lanoix 2013). In psychoanalytic terms, they present a very *anal* form of theorising that lacks the messy, uncontrollable, and affective forces at stake in bodily labour. Of course, all labour is *always* embodied as well as creative (Fuchs 2012) and to an extent the differ-entiations between different kinds of labour as distinctive are a little arbitrary, as Hardt and Negri themselves have acknowledged. A focus on the immanent, rather than structural, aspects of affective labour may add a level of complexity to the concept. This has been done to an extent by feminist and feminist Marxist scholars who have reintroduced wom-en's work, feminised work, and emotional labour into the debate (Jarrett 2015), but there is scope to continue this task. Admittedly, my aim goes slightly against the grain of political economy here. Political economy *per se* is more interested in structural than in subjective analyses and theorisations of labour and capitalism (Wittel 2004), but I maintain that a combination of both is needed in order to understand relation-ships of exploitation and subjectification in today's digital age. I am not interested in advancing the (structural) discussions on how work may be changing on a wider scale or how and if particular forms of work are productive or unproductive, feminised or masculinised, emotional or affective, material or immaterial. Those debates have been and are held elsewhere (see Fuchs 2014; Jarrett 2015 for overviews). Instead, I want to take the category of affective labour as a starting point for theorising user activity on particular spaces on the Internet as being a significant creator of value, thus labour, that is specifically situated as (un)conscious-affective, embodied activity (see Krüger and Johanssen, 2014; Johanssen 2016a for steps in this direction). Angela McRobbie points out that

> [f]eminist contributions to this kind of debate [on immaterial labour] have been characterised by an emphasis on actual working practices, which is in sharp contrast with Hardt, Negri et al, who are explicit in their desire to bring post-Marxist philosophy together with a futuristic agenda for new radical labour movements, leaving little space for anything like a case study or even references to career pathways or to the actual experiences of working life in these sectors.
>
> (McRobbie 2011, 75)

The next chapter will feature a case study on the affective labour of disfigurement on social media that may add a particular perspective on what digital labour is and feels like today. Before doing so, some wider engagement with the immaterial labour literature may be beneficial.

Monique Lanoix has argued that Hardt and Negri's and also Lazzarato's conceptualisation of immaterial labour frame the labour process (as well as the produced commodities to a lesser extent) as disembodied. Seen in this vein, immaterial labour is knowledge-based and rests on mental skills as individuals and groups exchange ideas, communication, knowledge, services, and so on. 'In this sense, the corporeality of immaterial labor is thin' (Lanoix 2013, 91). Reading Hochschild (1983) with Hardt and Negri would result in regarding 'the purpose of the flight attendants' emotional labor [as] the production of comfort. That is the extent of the embodied exchange; it is thinly embodied' (Lanoix 2013, 92). Lanoix goes on to describe care work as 'thickly embodied' (ibid., 95). It is both based on speech acts as well as corporeal, affective encounters between a worker and the subject who is cared for. Naturally, this is care conducted for and though the body/bodies. It involves the touching, washing, lifting, and cleaning of other bodies through the worker's own body, primarily their hands. While Lanoix is right to argue that the conceptualisation of 'immaterial labor as primarily commodity-producing and, second, in the manner in which they [Hardt and Negri] maintain the hegemony of intellectual labor within their concept of immateriality' (ibid., 97) is problematic, I feel that her dichotomisation of thin and thick affective labour does not advance the debate. Lanoix only focusses on care labour, whereas Hardt and Negri (as well as feminist Marxists) have conceived of affective labour as encompassing a range of processes. The kind of thickly embodied labour Lanoix writes of privileges a particular kind of labour over any other labour. But any labour is always embodied. The ego is always a bodily ego, as discussed in Chapter 1. Labelling some labour practices as thinly and others as thickly embodied and thereby creating a hierarchy of which labour is really worthy of being called 'affective' is unhelpful.

It is not that Hardt and Negri's concept of affective labour is disembodied. Instead, they and related thinkers operate at times with an (implicit) Cartesian model of the subject that splits the subject-as-worker into a body and soul. For instance, Berardi has stated that in 'the history of capitalism the body was disciplined and put to work while the soul was left on hold, unoccupied and neglected' (Berardi 2009, 115). Often, Hardt and Negri write of 'brains and bodies' (2000, 295) 'the brain coextensive with the body' (2000, 365), that 'life is nothing other than the production and reproduction of the set of bodies and brains' (2000, 365). 'The creation of communication, for instance, is certainly a linguistic and intellectual operation but also inevitably has an affective component in the relationship between the communicating parties' (2004, 108). Bodies and brains, linguistic/intellectual and affective, are treated as distinct and separate categories here, while I would argue they are much more intertwined. Hardt and Negri note that 'health care workers, for example, perform affective, cognitive, and linguistic tasks together with material ones, such as cleaning bedpans and changing bandages' (2004, 109). Elsewhere, Hardt (2007) has referred to 'the body and emotions', and the idea that affects 'refer equally to the body and mind' (Hardt 2007, ix). There is an implicit dualism between the affective and the discursive, between the mind and the body, and between reason and affect in those formulations. As Sara Ahmed (2014) notes,

> When the affective turn becomes a turn to affect, feminist and queer work are no longer positioned as part of that turn. Even if they are acknowledged as precursors, a shift *to* affect signals a shift *from* this body of work. Affect is given a privileged status in commentaries such as Hardt's, becoming almost like a missionary term that ushers in a new world, as a way of moving beyond an implied impasse, in which body and mind, and reason and passion, were treated as separate.
>
> (Ahmed 2014, 206)

However, there is an exception in *Multitude* where a more fragmented concept of the body, similar to Deleuze's work, is put forward:

> For years neurobiologists have argued against the traditional Cartesian model of the mind autonomous from and capable of ruling

over the body. Their research shows instead that mind and body are attributes of the same substance and that they interact equally and constantly in the production of reason, imagination, desire, emotions, feelings, and affects. [...] If the analogy holds, in other words, it is because the human body is itself a multitude organized on the plane of immanence.

(Hardt and Negri 2004, 337)

In conclusion, the use of affective labour by Hardt and Negri may be convincing in relation to changing labour practices but it is often unclear and dualistic.

Digital Labour, the Audience Commodity, and Affect

Now that important foundations for the digital labour debate have been introduced, the debate itself can be outlined in this section. One of the earliest voices here was that of Tiziana Terranova (2000) who argued that what users on the Internet did was very often 'free labour' (2000): writing code, translating websites, providing content. Central to this is the argument that the creating of content by users on for-profit social media (such as Facebook, Twitter, or Instagram) creates exchange and use value for the social networking sites and for that reason should be understood as labour (Fuchs 2014). User-generated content forms the backbone of social media and without it those platforms would cease to exist. They depend on users uploading and sharing content. An important aspect of this debate is the audience commodity notion by Dallas Smythe (Smythe 1981). Smythe argued that watching television is an act of working because their activity of watching has been bought by advertisers who watch content as well as advertisements (see also Jhally and Livant 1986). Christian Fuchs (2010, 2012, 2014) has argued that user data are sold as a commodity to advertising clients who may then offer targeted advertising to individual users. It is for that reason that they have produced commodities through labour which remains uncompensated through wages or other means. As Jarrett (2015) elaborates, the user data which is collected and extracted is manifold: search data, status updates, customised interfaces, liking, following, sharing data, click-stream data, and so on (2015, 83). As Fuchs has argued, user data is exploited because users receive nothing in return, apart from a free platform.

The online work they perform on social media is informational work, affective work, cognitive work, communicative work and collaborative work. This work creates profiles, content, transaction data and social relations.

(Fuchs 2014, 265)

Fuchs has maintained that such activity also makes for alienated labour, because users do not own their created content, or the platforms they use to circulate it.

Kylie Jarrett has advanced this debate through her figure of the *Digital Housewife* (2015). Drawing on feminist and Marxist feminist work on care labour and domestic and reproductive labour, she argues that the creation of user-generated content on commercial social media is akin to those types of work which are often conducted by women or migrants. Such work is similarly exploited, for it remains often entirely uncompensated or under-compensated.

Some authors disagree with the digital labour theory and have argued that user-generated content is not fully owned by social media companies and can therefore not be exploited technically; that there is no wage relation and there is no work relationship; that these activities are more akin to rent than to productive labour (Comor 2010; Caraway 2011; Lee 2014). Jarrett has argued that it is precisely the history of scholarship on domestic labour that refutes those critiques. Unpaid labour is still an act of labour and does not require a wage relation to be defined as such (Jarrett 2015, 89). It is beyond the scope of this book to enter into such debates which largely concern political economic technicalities and definitions of what constitutes labour. What remains unrefuted is that users are not compensated for their content and that such content adds to the profit maximisation (albeit in complex and intransparent terms) of social media companies. User data is also, and this will be picked up on in Chapter 6 in more detail, monitored, mined, extracted, packaged, and used for various purposes. One purpose meaning user data are sold to advertisers. 'As domestic work demonstrates, there may not always be a direct or obvious line between a particular activity and monetisation, but this does not mean that it is not part of the productive machinery of capital' (Jarrett 2015, 90).

Jarrett (2015) and others (Coté and Pybus 2011; Pybus 2013, 2015) have argued that it is user activity on social media as distinctly *affective* that is exploited. This happens through relational exchanges (such as liking other users' posts on Facebook) that contribute to user data. Recently, there have been a growing number of publications on affect, specifically in relation to digital media (Gibbs 2011; Karatzogianni and Kuntsman 2012; Sampson 2012; Clough 2013; Garde-Hansen and Gorton 2013; Paasonen et al. 2015; Johanssen 2016a; Elerding and Risam 2018; Jarrett 2018). These accounts all emphasise the affectivity at stake in networked forms of communication. In their introduction to the edited volume *Networked Affect*, Paasonen et al. (2015) note that online user practices in the broadest sense (e.g., surfing the Internet, searching for something on Google, posting an update on Facebook) make for intense 'affective investments' (2015, 7) that may be 'repetitive, frustrating, and potentially rewarding' (2015, 7) for subjects. At times networked communication may be not 'merely instrumental' (Paasonen et al. 2015, 10) and about goal-directed actions but also beyond rationality and conscious control on the part of users. It is this idea of an intense form of embodied engagement with the Internet that makes affect a useful concept to work with when it comes to critically analysing social media use. As Jarrett puts it aptly, 'Rather than merely a site of disembodied rationality, the Internet is a site for physical arousal, heightened emotion and the cultivation and maintenance of rich social relationships' (2015, 121). Drawing on Massumi's (2002) and Ahmed's (2004) definitions of affect as well as Fortunati's (1995) work on domestic labour, Jarrett argues that using social media constitutes a distinctively affective mode of engagement with digital platforms and other subjects. Her model of the digital housewife rejects a neat dichotomy between treating social media activity as alienated and exploited, or inalienable and fulfilling. It is both and may produce exchange as well as use values.

However, while there is a growing interest in affect in Internet studies more generally, the term is often used illusively and in various ways by different scholars. This is partly due to the conceptual openness of 'affect' as a notion, but it risks being used as an umbrella term. For instance, Paasonen, Hillis, and Petit speak of 'affective attachments' on the Internet that are about 'articulations of desire, seduction, trust, and memory; sharp jolts of anger and interest; political passions; investments of time, labor, and financial capital; and the frictions and pleasures of archival practices' (Paasonen et al. 2015, 1). Yes, all of those may denote particular affective attachments or experiences, but what is *specifically affective* about them? In his work on *Tumblr* and its queer community, Alexander Cho (2015) has defined affect as 'a moment of suspense, a shift, an attunement between entities' (Cho 2015, 44). Veronika Tzankova (2015) has named networked affect, that is affective relationalities and communication online, as 'a complex set of intensities associated with rational and nonrational modalities' (Tzankova 2015, 62). Affect may 'produce meanings that are only implicitly articulated in online discourse and representations' (ibid., 62). While such expressions are taken out of context by me here, they make for rich and rewarding starting points to think about what affect online, or affective online communication, may be and how we can make sense of it. These citations are neither exhaustive nor representative of scholarship on affect and social media, for example. Instead, I would like to argue that there is scope to specify how one particular angle – a psychoanalytic one – on the topic may add definitions and perhaps provocations to it.

Conclusion

In this chapter, I have outlined the developments from Marx's labour theory of value to the Autonomist Marxist concepts of immaterial and affective labour. I focussed on Michael Hardt and Antonio Negri's (2000, 2004, 2009) work in particular and argued that their use of the term affective labour is dualistic and lacks conceptual clarity. Given that many thinkers draw on these categories when it comes to critical discussions of social media use and digital labour, more inherent and concrete conceptualisations of affective and digital labour can be useful. Kylie Jarrett (2015, 2018) has made important contributions in this respect.

In the next chapter, I will be turning to empirical data to explore the particular messy, ideological, economic, and subjective dynamics of embodied affective labour on social media. I do so by drawing on and further developing the psychoanalytic model of affect.

Notes

1 How such forms of disciplining are done has been extensively theorised by the German psychoanalyst Alfred Lorenzer (1986) in his works on the interaction forms between mothers and children (Krüger 2013; Krüger and Johanssen 2014).

2 Hardt and Negri define their use of affect, drawing on Spinoza, as follows: 'In Spinoza's thought, in fact, there is a correspondence between our power to affect (our mind's power to think and our body's power to act) and our power to be affected. The greater our mind's ability to think, the greater its capacity to be affected by the ideas of others; the greater our body's ability to act, the greater its capacity to be affected by other bodies.

And we have greater power to think and to act, Spinoza explains, the more we interact and create common relations with others. Joy, in other words, is really the result of joyful encounters with others, encounters that increase our powers, and the institution of these encounters such that they last and repeat' (Hardt and Negri 2009, 379).

5 Affective Labour on Social Media

In order to illustrate the theoretical debates which have taken place so far, I will discuss some exemplary data from a research project on individuals with facial disfigurements.[1] The project focussed on their use of social media in particular. While they of course constitute a particular group of people with visible bodily differences, their narratives may still point to wider dimensions of digital labour on social media today and how it can be theorised as embodied and affective. All social media users who were interviewed in the project used Facebook, Twitter, Instagram, and YouTube to varying degrees to display their own subjectivities, primarily through disfigurement or bodily difference. This act of negotiation of their subjectivities was fundamentally about a particular embodied characteristic (a disfigurement) that was itself turned into affective labour for social media companies. I regard it useful to explicitly frame their engagements with social media as *labour*, rather than mere use, self-representation, affordance, or online activity, not only because of the exchange value-generating aspect which has been discussed at length in the previous chapter but also because the interviewees implicitly spoke about their self-representation in a vocabulary that was about labour and alluded to notions of entrepreneurialism, affect, self-surveillance, and self-branding. Second, the notion of labour is useful to theorise a particular set of user practices which, perhaps unlike more banal and mundane uses of social media more commonly referred to in the digital labour literature, constitute acts of labour around a lack. Those acts of labour thus not only constitute affective labour, as Hardt and Negri define it, but also labour as an intense, psychic process that is about coming to terms with trauma, the body, and what it means to be different in a media saturated age today. Subjects do not only have full control over their own bodies but have little control over the user data they circulate online. This can be linked to Marx's notion of alienated labour whereby workers produce commodities that make them alienated from themselves and their produced goods. The interviewees experienced a similar kind of alienation in relation to their bodies (as well as their data). I theorise this form of affective, alienated labour as labour-as-lack by drawing on Jacques Lacan (2002) and André Green

(1999). Labour that revolves around and also directly addresses a dimension that is lacking: the not-disfigured subject, notions of beauty, of being a useful citizen, and others. By continuously engaging in acts of self-representation that are about their disfigurement, users unconsciously and consciously spoke of it in relation to what they lacked, a 'normal' appearance. The lack also comes to symbolise a desire to gloss over it by assuming subject positions that are characterised as beautiful, successful, and agentic. Additionally, the lack also articulated itself in interview narratives more generally that suggest that users were not fully able to put into words how they felt when using social media, to fully express who they are online. This affective dilemma was responded to by referring to what they were *not* or had not: a 'normal' face, smooth skin, fully functional hands, and so on. We can see how affect operates on multiple levels and layers that will be untangled more over the course of this chapter. This form of self-representation could be read as a form of labour that is encouraged by the very structures of social media which enforce acts of representation based on users' subjectivities. This lack is itself attempted to be filled by producing ever more data about the self. Rather than labelling such practices as forms of 'playbour' (Kücklich 2005), or necessarily fun and fulfilling activities, they constituted intense forms of engagement that are fulfilling and important to the users, but equally intense, difficult and at times emotionally draining.

Social Media and Different Bodies

I will begin this chapter by discussing one interviewee's narrated biographical details in more detail. They can help to show how media usage is shaped by life histories. Jayne, in her twenties, survived a house fire when she was a baby. She sustained burns on 70 per cent of her body. She lost her hair and parts of her fingers and toes in the fire. Speaking about her experiences in primary and secondary school, she remarked,

> Yeah, so a lot of people would say turning a blind eye or like, I don't know, I was always, I was always in a dream-like fantasy world, I was always like, I don't know like, I always go to my own little bubble and it sounds really stupid and a lot people, say, I can't ignore it, but I always just went in my little dream world and so that's what I always kind of done, so when stuff like that did happen, I noticed a change in behaviour but I just thought oh they're having like a troubling time at the moment, it's not, I leave you to it, you know, it didn't really click, I guess it was a bit, I don't know, you could say it was a bit of ignorance.
>
> (I3, 120–127)

This narrative echoes the skin ego, discussed earlier in the book. Here it became a kind of cocoon made of fantasy, which Jayne called her 'bubble'. It protected her against outer, unwelcome experiences by peers at school. Being in a bubble suggests an orientation towards the inner, an inwardness, a subject who is floating blissfully, perpetuated by and through fantasy. However, this bubble was also the result of a strong support network of friends and family who supported her whilst growing up. Jayne was part of a children's burns club and described it as 'amazing, cos' we all connected, like I always say, we're not connected in blood, we are connected in skin' (148–149). Being with other burns survivors, allowed her to 'have a break and just be yourself' (151). Growing up, she was confronted with a changing body, like everybody, but because of many hospital treatments, her burns and scars change throughout her life:

> Like with burns where it doesn't grow, it just pulls and like normal skin grows and stretches, where burns doesn't, so and reconstructive surgery and it is altering an image that you already see in the mirror, so you may get used to a scar, you may get used to a burn but then you're having surgery and it may get altered and then you develop that kind of attachment to your original burns which is weird, so kinda like it's, I don't know how to explain it, it's kinda like, it just kinda knocks you for six, so it and it just makes you feel like a bit alien having this new burn, or this new scar, or this new skin graft, you're like 'Oh what is this?', will that bother ya, that little skin graft, but not having burns since you are eighteen months that is really weird erm but like where it doesn't grow or stretch it may like leave, it might make, so for example, I can't explain it, can you see here? [Points to her arm].
>
> (I3, 189–200)

This quote exemplifies how one aspect of Jayne's subjectivity, having burns, affected her. Her body was so fundamentally altered through changing skin and hospital treatments that it bothered her. This narrative rendered a particular affective experience of growing up with a changing body into words, but the experience could not be fully captured. 'I can't explain it', she said to me. Growing up with burns made her mature sooner than other children: 'I had to mature way sooner than people my age, like when I was a thirteen year old, I wasn't really a thirteen year old, I was more like a thirty-one year old in a thirteen year olds body' (307–309). Living with burns was framed through affective terms that emphasised bodily functions and an embodied relatedness to being in the world. This being in the world was often described in bodily terms but was not necessarily named through the use of a particular signifier:

> You know, I remember actually, you know, I didn't even really consider myself, or I had, the word disfigured, I didn't even attribute

that word to myself until, like, until, I think it was on my last operation, so I would have been about 20-ish. I met my surgeon, and he
said, 'Oh yes, this...' He said a comment like, 'Oh yes, this type of
disfigurement blah, bah, blah. I was like, 'Ah! I'm disfigured?' I was
like, 'Oh yes, of course I am.' But I just always saw myself as wonky,
or you know, I don't know, I just never.

(I5, 355–361)

The word 'disfigured' comes to bear particular attributes and the interviewee was affected by a surgeon calling her disfigured. She had not
really thought of herself in such terms. It can often be the social world
and other people that make us and reinforce us as the bearer of a particular kind of subjectivity. In this case a disfigurement. While we may not
have thought of ourselves in that way, it is clear that we will *always* be
as such, because bodily differences are recognisable and (un)consciously
enforced by others. In this example, difference and its explicit naming
was needed in order for the surgeon to fill his professional role and act
upon the interviewee through surgery or medical advice. This notion of
difference and being made aware of it was also discussed by another interviewee. Speaking about her media consumption, Jayne favoured reality television and documentaries. 'I've always been fascinated in like real
life stuff, I felt like I was different and watching documentaries about
people being different was like "Oh my god, look, they're different like
me too!"' (278–280). This focus on difference was also present in her
use of social media, which had evolved from more secluded, bubble-like,
towards an open display of her body:

I was never that open on social media, apart from my personal Facebook but doing the catwalk and photoshoots and getting more involved in fashion erm and it's allowed me to be more open about
myself, so on Instagram, I do more shots of, less shots of, selfies,
more shots of my full body and I never used to do that.

(I3, 433–436)

Another female interviewee spoke about whom she followed on Twitter:
'I try and follow as many charities, as many charities, but also ones
that are appropriate to me erm to support' (I2, 232–233). Those quotes
suggest that much of the social media use revolved around a particular
aspect of the interviewees' subjectivities and life histories. Rather than
emphasising a variety of use patterns, interviewees spoke of how their
bodies were also reflected in who they followed and engaged with on
social media. Such expressions suggest a form of affective labour which
revolved around specific elements that had to do with the interviewees'
bodies. As they started using social media, many had to learn to come
to terms with very different responses to their alleged bodily differences.

Responses which were often aimed at their bodies. One female, who had created her own Facebook page, said in this context,

> I made a mistake when I first erm started my page [...], I remember just taking a picture of my back and that was it, so all you see was burns and it got quite a lot of negative, yeah and a lot of negativity come from, cos' I think I had like an open page and I had loads of followers and literally built three and a half thousand friends and fifteen hundred followers but a lot of the followers were literally like from India, from different parts of Asia and they were mainly the ones that they would say, they'd say 'pretty' and 'slut' so there was kind of, yeah they were putting me down and saying 'Eew that's disgusting, that's ugly, put it away, cover up', they were not happy with it, another thing that I've learned is that when I've gone abroad to other countries erm if I show off my scars, they tend to laugh at me, almost like it's a joke and I get that quite a lot, I was in Bulgaria last year and I had people filming me.
>
> (I2, 565–574)

Another interviewee explicitly disagreed that her cleft lip and palate was a major part of her subjectivity.

> The cleft lip and palate is part of my identity, but it's a small part. It's not the first, like, if you were to ask me to write down ten things about myself, it might not even feature on that list.
>
> (I5, 537–540)

However, later on in the interview she commented on her Instagram use:

> I think the biggest thing, so on Instagram, like, occasionally I will see a photo of myself, and I'm like, 'Oh, that really highlights my cleft.' And I'll be like, 'Oh, please use the one where it's less visible.' Like, or less apparent. So yes, so that's something that Instagram has, kind of, like, the way that I see, the way that I take photos of myself, or that other people take of me, you know, there are angles and there is, but then, again, that's kind of problem that everybody has, I think. Everybody has, like, unflattering photos and angles, and more. So I, yes, like everybody else I'll be, like, 'Can you use that one of me please because it looks a bit better than this one?' [...] So if a photo is taken of me from a, sort of, side angle on this side, my face looks very dented. I'm like, 'No!' So yes, so, photos, yes, photo editing and things like that. But, yes, but there are, I think it depends on how you use Instagram as well. Mine is to, kind of, document my life.
>
> (I5, 575–594)

Those quotes suggest that affective labour played a major part in the subjects' social media activities. Many articulated an openness and pro-activeness in their sharing of their disfigurements. Bodily difference not only made for a major part of their everyday lives but it also led to heightened forms of awareness as well as self-surveillance when it comes to social media use. Interestingly, both quotes emphasised the *individual* and their function in maintaining their social media profiles. Rather than attributing the negative reactions to her photo to the other users, the interviewee spoke of her 'mistake' she made in uploading a photo that was perhaps too explicit in showing her burns. The other user similarly voiced the need to upload photos which showed who she really was but in a moderate, 'less visible' manner. Such narratives illustrate the affective labour conducted by the interviewees which was about creating feelings of ease for themselves as well as for other users. I return to this point in a moment when discussing the entrepreneurial self on social media. As the previous quotes suggest, this use of social media is often conducted in relation to imagined and real others, who may judge through comments, likes, shares, or (re-)tweets. This was also done in view of the danger of trolling. Many expressed fears of being trolled or abused online but this did not stop them from using social media. Instead, it strengthened their desire to show the world who they were, even if this also included potential trolls. 'It [trolling] is at the back of your mind but I try not to think about it too much' (I1, 273). 'What's the worst that can happen? Get memed, trolled? They are just a random person on a computer at the end of the day' (I3, 457–458).

> There's the kind of tweet where you just want to just reach through the screen and just slap. Anyway, so, conversations like that where you just engage more than you should do and try and explain and it's just, it can. [...] So, I do find that with social media sometimes that it can be this cycle where you feel like you have to have the last word and that's not very healthy, but for the most part it's great.
>
> (I4, 512–513, 529–531)

Having a physical difference was both embraced and also exceeded, the quotes suggest. Another interviewee responded to my question about her Twitter bio:

> J: You have written in your little description or bio that you have [a particular condition] and you've written, you are not defined by it?
> I1: Yeah. I try to stick by that quote as much as I can really, erm yeah. I don't wanna be defined by how I look or what my disabilities are. I am just as capable as everyone else.
>
> (I1, 258–263)

This double dimension of living with a disfigurement but of not letting their subjectivities be dominated by it was at the heart of the social media labour of all interviewed. Sally, who had missing fingers, also spoke about how her embodied subjectivity was taken up and used by others, and travelled from physical to online spaces:

I4: I do get that on tubes, of people, like, taking photos of my hands.
J: Really?
I4: Yes.
J: What do you do when that happens?
I4: Well, it's really awkward. I always think that I'm going to do something amazing, you know? I'm going to be, you know, I'm going to say something and I'm going, and I just don't because normally they're ...
J: Well, it's hard to do that.
I4: Well, also because they could be like, I'm not doing that, you know?
J: They could deny it.
I4: Unless they were right in front of me, like, zooming in, they could pretend they're not doing it. You know, I can see that they're doing it and they're laughing and they're sharing it with their friends or whatever.

(I4, 619–632)

The narratives situate social media use as an embodied practice that is oriented towards and in tension with affective intensities, other social media users, and social media interfaces. I wish to theorise them further through the skin ego (Anzieu 2016) at this point. Users spoke of their relationship towards social media platforms as if they were embraced by them in a skin ego-like manner. Social media provided a space for them that enabled engagement with their own subjectivities and other users. Such enabling spaces may have contributed to a sense of security and feelings of containment for users in the first place. However, such spaces were periodically ruptured and disrupted through abuse or hateful comments. Rather than feeling secure and held at all times, their social media use was described in ambivalent terms and was always in danger of being threatened by others. This anxious state resulted in a heightened self-surveillance of how they looked and what they posted online. This state is primarily characterised by an affective, objectless experience that hovers over practices of self-representation. It produces a constant gaze upon one's self in order to anticipate how something may be perceived or responded to by others. It is an act of affective *labour* because it ultimately seeks to create the perfect product that both the users as well as others on social networking sites are pleased with. The subject turns towards and upon herself in relation to how others may respond. This required a heightened sense of the affective atmospheres on social media and how, for example, a particular photo may enhance or disrupt them. Such anxieties were also responded to with a focus on agency and autonomy in the face of uncontrollable responses. Users were determined to show themselves who they really were, while at the same time anticipating and negotiating undesired responses (Nakamura 2015). In her work on calling out racism and misogyny on social media, Lisa Nakamura has shown that it is often through unpaid, digital labour of individuals, not the platforms themselves, that toxic content is challenged. This form of labour is itself often challenged and accused of censorship by others. There is thus a tension on social media when specific positions (sexist, racist, ableist, etc.) are challenged. For the interviewees, social media activity as labour was similarly constituted in the aforementioned narratives as an affective fragility which was both feared and embraced. It is akin to the definition of the labour process given by Marx earlier, because it involves a goal-directed crafting of elements of subjectivity towards a product (of which many users are not aware that it is turned into a data commodity). This is partly driven by social media's excessive ideological demand to be authentic, real, and relatable. Rather than creating a particular version of themselves, or adopting a false self online which Turkle (1984, 1985) and also Balick have discussed (2014), the interviewees were keen to demonstrate authenticity.

The Neo-Liberal Subject on Social Media

In an earlier quote, Jayne had spoken about her social media use becoming more open and public in recent years. This embracing of the emphasis of sharing content on social media also came about because she was starting her own charity.

> It came about cos' when I have surgery it's not like a week recovery, it's more like month, or two months out, sometimes like a bit longer, like burns take long time to heal and it was something to keep me busy and like take my mind off the pain and stuff, erm at the moment it's like a hobby but you never know somewhere down the line it could turn into a freaking, multi-million pound organisation where it needs my constant attention 24/7 erm but that's in the long run but I've got loads of ideas and I'd love to meet with erm Sir Alan Sugar or Richard Branson but erm that is just a dream right now but erm I think it's amazing, it's got so much potential, I've just gotta remember to start small and not to run before I can walk cos' I get so excited about it, I just do everything at once yeah.
>
> (I3, 565–574)

Apart from the more general dimension of digital labour as affective labour outlined previously, there were many narratives in the interviews which referred to neo-liberal ideology of the entrepreneurial self. Many scholars have argued that social media is increasingly used by individuals to promote themselves, brand themselves, and manage their digital reputation through conscious self-performance (e.g., Hearn 2010; Abidin 2014, 2015, 2016). Subjects not only bring themselves to the labour market online, but they also generate their own advertising campaigns that can be seen on social media and personal websites in order to be noticed and acknowledged by other users (friends, colleagues, recruiters, etc.) as unique individuals. This, as Matthew Flisfeder (2015), has argued always constitutes a production of a particular form of subjectivity, rather than acting as a holistic, or complete representation of the individual (see also Singh 2016). 'The ideology of social media works by objectivizing the subject rather than by producing subjectivity' (ibid., 555). As Flisfeder emphasises,

> we invest time in deciding what to say in our status updates; we invest time in building (and maintaining) a network that makes us appear desirable to others; all of which requires us to be rather self-reflexive if we are interested in producing a Self that is to be desired by others, and which will help us develop a desired reputation. Suffice it to say that a lot of work goes into the construction of the Self and one's digital reputation in social media.
>
> (Flisfeder 2015, 559)

Crystal Abidin's work on social media influencers has highlighted the strategies used by this relatively new kind of user group which often depend on a close relationship with a loyal user base. In the case of branded content, users are actively encouraged to perform (unpaid) 'visibility labour' (Abidin 2016, 86) for influencers by talking about advertised products, promoting, showing, and buying them. Affective labour on social media is thus often, echoing Hardt and Negri's conceptualisation, about relationships, communication, passion, and individuality. Such tropes were present in Jayne's narrative about starting her own charity, which she heavily promoted on social media to gain attention and, ultimately, financial backing. '[W]ith social media, you gotta master it, you gotta learn it' (I3, 472), she said. Her route towards the creation of the charity was similarly framed in the entrepreneurial terms one finds uttered on reality television shows like *The Apprentice*: starting small, having long-term goals and working hard in order to achieve success. The charity was not solely described as a charity in the previous quote, but rather like a global corporation which is a 'multi-million pound organisation' that demands the constant attention of Jayne as the CEO. This organisation was made possible through financial investment by Sir Alan Sugar and Sir Richard Branson, two of the most notable public figures of entrepreneurs in the world today. These narratives arguably constituted a fantasy and positioned Jayne as an entrepreneurial subject with agency and ability. Two qualities she may often lack as she is recovering in hospital. She spoke of those periods of having to take time out multiple times in the interview:

> Having burns it's not like normal skin that grows and stretches, it tears and it just doesn't grow, so you gotta constantly have that reconstructive surgery and skin grafts and it's like a life sentence, never having a day off, so for a lot of people having a stable career is not an option so you gonna be in that all your life and that was a fear for me and that's why I wanted to do something like this and so it makes me feel like I'm doing something valuable with my time rather than just wasting it, sitting around, waiting for my recovery to finish and it'll be something that I want other burns survivors to get involved in as well, give them something to do and keep them busy and it could be something that they could put on their CV and it's helping them get back into society as well.
>
> (I3, 576–585)

The fantasy of the agentic entrepreneurial subject who makes her own luck may be an important (unconscious) driving force in Jayne's life. She unconsciously reproduced a neo-liberal ideology in the previous quote which emphasises the importance of work, of being productive, of work as valuable, of only the working subject being part of society. This is not meant to critique or discredit Jayne's account but rather to point to how ideology is (unconsciously) adopted rather than questioned. Wouldn't it be companies' responsibility to provide flexible modes of employment for burns survivors and others who have to take time off work for various reasons? Instead, the responsibility was put on the subjects themselves and importantly on herself by Jayne. In Jayne's words, this narrative may symbolise a further retreat into her fantasy bubble. One that was very important for her because it helped her to manage the long, idle periods in hospital. It also helped her to gloss over aspects of her subjectivity which are often framed as lacking and inadequate in ableist discourses in the media, for example. She emphasised at multiple times during the interview that she was creating the charity individually and then sought support from others:

> Initially, there was a group of us but I guess I am the driving force behind it, I am like, I could say I'm like the brains and stuff, like, I am like the main man and so I've got like people in the burns world that I wanna input and help me out.
>
> (I3, 528–530)

This desire of becoming an entrepreneur and successful charity owner also manifested itself in Jayne's affective labour by promoting herself and her charity on social media.

> I posted a picture of me doing like an over the shoulder shot and erm and I got a lot of interest from all over the world actually, it kinda went viral in America erm and it was mainly supportive comments but then I noticed a few negative ones like 'Oh why would anyone wanna see that, it's horrible' and then like 'If I was in your class, you'd definitely be bullied' and stuff like that, it's like whoa, it was a bit of a shock to my system cos' I know it's out there and I was aware of it but it never happened to me, or if it happened to me, no one ever told me and I've never been like aware of it yeah, directly and so that was interesting, got like, I weighed the pro's and the con's and I realised out of the thousands of likes and views and comments, there was only what five negatives ones and so the ratio is like ridiculous and it's irrelevant so I kinda just feel that you do have your idiots out there and if I come across them and it's up to me how I deal with it, at the end of the day a lot of people would crumble or it would be a shock to the system and dampen their spirit and their personality but I thought 'Wait, let me do another one'.
>
> (I3, 439–453)

Another interviewee, Rose, who was also creating her own charity coincidentally, expressed a similar narrative:

> I am doing this all on my own, I mean I had, I've got like the little website which erm I had help with but I am gonna start doing that myself and so a lot of it is done on social media like Instagram, Twitter and Facebook, I've got over 2000 people on my Facebook group and that's still building [...]. I think if it did become a little bit negative I'd definitely look at myself and think what is it I am doing wrong? And I think what I tend to do is just keep it erm not too happy happy cos' otherwise people go 'Oh that's crap, it can't be like that all the time' but I just always thank people, I always reply to people as well which they seem to like and then they come back with another reply saying 'You're great' and yeah I don't know what I am doing but it seems to be working, oh sorry another one was when I started out I actually put my swims onto erm the Vitiligo, a Vitiligo support group and erm straightaway a lady jumped in and said 'We're not disfigured, how dare you.' And then another lady said 'If she knew anything about Vitiligo, she'd knew that we can't erm access the water, Chlorine' but which I don't think it's totally true cos' I've checked it out and they can and the Vitiligo Support UK on Twitter, they continually re-tweet my stuff yeah erm so what I did was I removed

myself from that group and just thought I leave that for now and just reach out to the charities, the bigger organisations, learn about them, learn about them and the skin conditions and the health conditions cos' you've also got cancer scars and you got all types, it's so many to learn about erm and it's just not to upset anybody and make sure that any words that I use, they use, sort of little and not too much.

(I2, 519–567)

Both narratives tell of the management of entrepreneurial subjectivity online. Jayne was keen to emphasise to me that her picture had gone viral and the second interviewee emphasised that she had over 2000 members in her Facebook group in an enthusiastic tone. The implicit allusion to big data and an accumulation of contacts and the links, shares, and retweets that go with them seemed important to both. Such statistics suggest success and visibility online, where more rather than less connections matter. They are made possible through the affective labour of sharing photos and content about their embodied subjectivities. Both interviewees spoke of the affective relationalities that they were situated in on Instagram and Facebook, respectively. They weighed the pros and cons of having to deal with negative responses. The second interviewee's ways of using her Facebook page signifies affective labour in so far as she attempted to create a warm atmosphere, always thanking other users and replying to their posts. This attempt to always be 'good enough' (Winnicott 2002), of providing the right measure of comments and engagement, seems akin to the skin ego. Affect became the binding glue here in connecting users with the entrepreneurial subjects. It makes for, what Sara Ahmed (2014) has called the 'stickiness' of binding people together. It is something that needs to be continuously reproduced through acknowledging the other users, through holding them in an affective cocoon without alienating them. Not too much, not too little. Sally, who had her own YouTube channel, spoke about this in a similar way:

I4: The way to grow your channel and obviously to engage with your audience is to reply to a lot of people, so I do try and read what everybody writes. Yes. I think some people think that I don't do that. I do find it quite funny when people leave comments, talking about me as if I'm not there, like, she does this, or, she does that, and I'm here.

J: How does that make you feel?

I4: I just find it quite funny because they're not doing it in a, thinking that I will ignore them. They just assume that I'm not reading it. I find that quite funny. I normally reply, saying, hey.

J: I'm here.

I4: I'm here. How are you today? Yes.

(I4, 430–440)

Affective labour is thus utilised to manage relationships and 'a feeling of ease, well-being, satisfaction, excitement, passion-even a sense of connectedness or community' (Hardt 1999, 96). The creation of welcoming, good-enough affective atmospheres may also constitute an unconscious, defensive attempt on the part of the users who had their subjectivities undermined on many occasions in their everyday lives through comments on their bodies by strangers. In order not to be vulnerable to such responses on social media, the creation of particular atmospheres may serve such purposes.

Self-Value and Exchange Value

Sally similarly used social media to promote her own subjectivity which focussed less on her bodily difference but was still based upon it to some extent. In contrast to the other two interviewees who had only begun to found their own charities, she was, one could say, a successful online entrepreneur. She was a writer with her own YouTube channel that she used to promote her own work and also to review books and vlog about bodily difference.

Sally had worked in the creative industries for a number of years since graduating from university. She had recently quit her day job to focus on being a full-time author. She also said that she earned some money through her YouTube channel. 'I've got enough followers that that's also part of my job now' (I4, 197). She seemed more established in terms of being a successful creative worker than Jayne and Rose and was more conscious of her working conditions and how they related to the production of exchange value online. She was

> born with a rare condition called ectrodactyly-external dysplasia-clefting syndrome, which is EEC syndrome. It's a form of external dysplasia which meant that I was born with no, well, with lumps of skin and bone for hands and I had no tear ducts. So, my eyes were very dry and I couldn't cry, so I had operations on, my first operation when I was three months old and I've had dozens of operations on my hands and on my eyes. It's a clefting syndrome, which means I have more or less of certain things.
>
> (I4, 34–40)

Similarly to earlier quotes from Jayne and Rose, Sally spoke of how her bodily difference was commented on by other people, but she also used this difference to raise awareness through her affective labour:

> definitely a way to raise awareness of certain topics because I think when you have a disfigurement or any kind of, like, impairment – or maybe this is just me – you assume other people also notice the

things that you notice like the villain trope, but I realise people don't notice them. They don't have the privilege of having it rammed, you know, down their throat. Like, you know, they have the privilege of not seeing that. So, yes, I do want to talk about that and that wasn't a reason for me to start the channel at all, but it has become a reason why I continue doing the channel and doing certain aspects because I think it's... yes. It's important. I've got this platform. I want to use it for ... it sounds so pious – I want to use it for good things – but I do, you know, so, yes. That's definitely one reason.

(I4, 468–477)

The labour that is done through the social media activities of all the interviewees is undoubtedly very important. It helps to disrupt hegemonic ideas of beauty, normalcy, and ultimately what it means to be human online. This raising of awareness of bodily difference was an important aspect of Sally's affective labour on YouTube. Engaging with her own subjectivity through social media was presented as an act of empowerment for her.

I was on Twitter, I think I've been on that for about eight years – I think so – and that's, obviously that's just text, so it's not you. Well, you know what I mean. People can't see the person behind the words, so that's my safe social media. Then Instagram came in and then YouTube started and I didn't want to start a YouTube channel because I thought that, well, you know what the Internet's like. There's a lot of haters out there and if you look a certain way, sometimes, like, people just don't like it. So, I wasn't going to start my own channel, but then I was persuaded to by my friend and I'm glad that I did and I think that in doing that I've become much more confident and will now talk about these subjects where I just wouldn't talk about them before because they're, I would be made to feel as if they were taboo subjects and I suppose the Internet also connects you with people who you would never meet but you have similarities with. I didn't know anyone else with a disfigurement at all, so, like, it was like my own echo chamber inside my own body. Like, I couldn't talk to anyone about it because, who understood at least. So, realising that it's a conversation and that a lot of people feel like that makes me feel more passionate about wanting to actually talk about these things. So, I do think it's helped not just other people who have disfigurements who I know have found my videos and have messaged me and said, you know, they now can start conversations with other people, but has helped me.

(I4, 394–413)

The mostly text-based nature of Twitter was described here as not being able to fully capture subjectivity, and perhaps affectivity more than anything else. YouTube and vlogging was described by Sally as being more able to show her subjectivity, or a particular version of it, online. YouTube may have allowed her to turn affective experiences and states outwards, rather than keeping them inwards. The expression of being in her own 'echo chamber' inside her body is interesting in this context. Similarly, to the inhibited Twitter use of the *Embarrassing Bodies* viewers which I discussed in Chapter 3, Sally felt inhibited in sharing aspects of her subjectivity online until she joined YouTube. YouTube allowed her to connect with others and contributed to a feeling of passion, a heightened affective intensity associated with having an audience and being recognised by like-minded individuals. Rather than text-based social media platforms, YouTube perhaps allowed for a more containing association between affect and idea of her embodied subjectivity (see Chapter 1) through video, rather than just text or images. It may be subject to debate if YouTube can really be classified as an online community, but there are users who have created a sense of community through relational communication (Burgess and Green 2009). For Sally, the acts of being seen by others and of being able to present herself may have played a key role in this context.

Sally was the only one I spoke to who displayed an awareness of YouTube's business model and the economic structures behind it. The tension between a kind of self-value; use value; and exchange value, exploitation, and a sense of satisfaction was discussed by her in more detail:

> So, on YouTube every, the algorithms are a bit wonky because they don't want you to know exactly how it works, but I think it roughly works out that you get about a dollar per thousand views. So, it doesn't make you rich unless you've got millions of followers or anything like that, but it does make me, like, a few hundred pounds a month and then I can work with companies. [...] Yes; a couple of hundred pounds a month and then work with companies to do sponsored content occasionally.
>
> (I4, 200–209)

> The thing is, because it's all so secretive, you don't know what percentage that is for YouTube that's earning from, you know, I don't know what YouTube gets for those, but I think it's, I'm okay. Obviously it's always nice to earn a little bit more money, so if that was the case, I'd be fine, too, but I don't stress about it so much. [...] I'm sure that probably YouTube is making a shit-ton off of, you know, like, Zoella and Tammy Burr and everybody who's, like, got millions of followers, but I wouldn't have a platform otherwise, so it's not my job as in, you know, it's the only thing I do, so maybe if it was my actual job, a fulltime job, I would feel differently about it, but

really it's just a part-time thing that brings in a bit more money and I'm thankful for it. Yes. Like I said, I don't know the ins and outs of how much YouTube makes, though I'm sure it's a lot.

(I4, 558–575)

Her affective labour was described as tied in to a broader value system, but she did not complain about inequality on the platform. To her, the remuneration of YouTube labour was equated with business models in the creative industries such as the production of books. Many people were part of the production process, and authors could only receive a relatively small amount of money per book. Sally seemed to be fine with YouTube's underlying inequality and was more focussed on using the platform to her advantages.

'Intensifying affective states and building affective connections is the essence of the work we do when using social media, which in turn places affect at the core of the digital economy' (Jarrett 2015, 117), as Kylie Jarrett puts it (see also Coté and Pybus 2011). This intensified affective state arguably allowed Sally to vlog about her bodily difference but also constituted the unique selling point (USP), if you will, for all the interviewees and their social media activities. They used themselves and their own bodily states to produce heightened affective relationalities on social media. Jarrett argues that such affective intensities are key to corporate social media business models, for they allow monetisation and extraction of data and user engagement that includes but also exceeds mere discourse (as in text generated through comments), this is particularly the case through the emoji-buttons on Facebook, the retweet function on Twitter, the like and dislike buttons on YouTube, and the ability to accumulate friends and followers on all those sites. They symbolise and produce affective relationalities between users that are immensely valuable to the platforms. User-generated content, such as YouTube videos, Facebook posts, profile data, and so on, may constitute the important backbone of any data commodity. However, they also constitute use value, as Jarrett (2015) has stressed. While such practices may be exploited, they are meaningful to users at the same time. 'User affect is not user data' (2015, 155), but it is already implicated in user data and transformed into data. User-generated data may itself be regarded as affectively created content which is often discourse-based but at the same time is in tension with discourse. Elsewhere (Johanssen 2016a), I have argued that, for example, user discourses on Facebook are often of such a passionate-affective nature that rationality and neat, logical discourse become entangled, disrupted, and broken by affective experiences. Such experiences are attempted to be rendered discursive in a deferred manner through writing about them. Something similar may occur through the affective labour of the interviewees discussed in this chapter. Their creation of content and, importantly, how it was responded to through comments, liking, sharing, and retweeting always constituted affective-bodily states that were reflected on and turned into online content. Rather than characterising social media or user-generated content and interactions *per se* as affective, I would argue that there is a particular temporality at stake when it comes to affect and its transformation into online content. Online publics are not affective *as such* (Papacharissi and de Fatima Oliveira 2012; Papacharissi 2015) – but are rather made up of various strands of affective relationalities which themselves are the outcome of particular temporal-spatial processes. Affect is a process, as I have argued in previous chapters, and to speak of social media or online publics as affective or affect-laden may be only the beginning of exploring them. Sally's earlier quote details a process, a journey from moving from a more inhibited use of social media towards a more affective expression on social media. Particular affective-bodily states are not simply transferred online but are felt, reflected on, and then turned into affective-discursive data on social media. They were then reflected back upon in the interviews. Affect moves. It moves the subject and also moves other subjects and objects. Jayne's and Rose's descriptions of their affective experiences with both positivity and negativity on social media similarly described affect as a kind of wave that flooded them and to which they responded through particular actions online. Jarrett's term of a 'multiphasic model' (Jarrett 2015, 137) of digital-affective labour is useful for thinking about the complexities of social media activity (see also Qui et al. 2014). While Jarrett uses the term to discuss different phases in the production process of digital labour, I use it slightly differently to denote different phases and life cycles before, within, and after acts of digital labour (see, e.g., Baym 2002; Boellstorff 2008; Harrington and Bielby 2013 on life cycles and audiences). Rose's narrative may exemplify how such a multiphasic model of affect may look like. She had created a video of herself which showed close-ups of her face and body, along with dramatic music, whilst she spoke about her burns and how they had affected her life. She recounted the responses after having posted the video on social media:

> I released so much and I didn't realise that I would and everything that I spoke about, it was just like erm I've taken this coat off and I am now free like that's exactly how I felt and I went home and I realised that I was a changed person, just from the video and what made it even better was the fact that people started to see it, they started to comment, put it on YouTube and put it on my Facebook page so all my cousins, family, friends they all see it and everybody was telling me what an amazing woman I was and to hear such good feedback and hear such lovely messages it just made me feel so good, so now I've gone from that negative person into this all positive me.
> (I2, 440–447)

Yeah, yeah, yeah and erm actually I touched quite a lot of people cos' there were people that were suffering with depression, bipolar, erm a guy contacted me via Messenger and he said to me that he had lost his mum a year earlier and he was very close to his mother and he said he was on his way to work and he watched the video and he cried all the way to work and it was the first time since he lost his mum and he wanted to thank me, that's amazing, really that you can reach out to so many different people on so many different levels and so and then suddenly I started to draw in this audience that wanted to know more about me so I thought if I'm gonna do this, I'm gonna do this right and make sure it's for all the real reasons that I want and not what anyone else wants, no one's gonna tell me anymore, I'm gonna take the lead and do what I think should be done, you know, like I've said, I'm not in, I never created [her charity] for many or fame, I've created it because I want people to not go through what I went through, it's as simple as that, you know, everyone can change their lives, it's just knowing how, knowing how to deal with it.

(I2, 455–468)

Those quotes may exemplify the important aspects of affective labour that resulted in meaningful and empowering consequences. Rose's expression 'I released so much' is reminiscent of the Freudian discharge model. The video allowed an affective discharge for Rose to occur, of both diffuse affects that had possibly been repressed or negated by her. She mentioned during the interview that she had often tried to hide her burns and had seldom spoken about them with friends. It was important that the video was seen and acknowledged by people online. It made her 'feel so good' and contributed to a pleasurable affective state within her and within her social media circle. The second quote speaks of the empowerment she felt and that the video enabled her to 'take the lead' and do things right. She felt proud that she touched so many people with the video which arguably means it was a success in raising awareness of her story as she began to create her own charitable organisation.

A Multiphasic Model of Affective Labour Based on Freud

The Freudian affect model that I have presented so far in this book and supplemented with Anzieu's notion of the skin ego can be further developed at this point. His discharge model may be critiqued for an implicit stimulus-response mechanism that lies at the heart of it and one would associate it with old media effects models. While the affective responses to *Embarrassing Bodies* undoubtedly occurred in response to specific scenes, because viewers spoke about them in the interviews, Freud's model is still rooted in a specific relationality between media content and media users that relates to *particular* moments only. To theorise affective labour through Freud requires one to go a step further and to partly un-couple his affect model from particular stimuli. Affective labour is still subjective and yet relational, but, as discussed through selected interview narratives, it is not tied to specific moments or responses alone. Instead, a multiphasic model of affective labour refers to already embodied, af-fective bodily states that influence affective labour, which are turned into user-generated content based on specific bodily conditions, and so on. What I think is particularly useful about Freud's model is his distinction between 'affect' and 'idea', for it allows to hold on to both discursive as well as extra-discursive states and how they are entangled.

The basic, underlying principle of Freud's affect model shall be re-tained: affect is situated at an axis of pleasure-unpleasure that tones par-ticular, subjective experiences. Affect is an energy within the subject that may be mobilised at particular intervals, as highlighted in relation to the *Embarrassing Bodies* viewers, but it is always in an idle state within the body. Ruth Stein pointed out that it may not be completely beneficial to only regard affects as discharge processes:

> if affects are discharge processes that are centrifugally directed, that is, tending away from the psychic apparatus, then they would necessarily be evanescent and self-exhaustive, tending to run their course until they ceased to exist. This is in marked contrast to the important, persistent role affects have in dream theory. There is an inherent contradiction between seeing affects as fluid discharge pro-cesses and seeing them as relatively stable indicators of meaning or of missing thoughts.
>
> (Stein 1999, 17)

Affects as stable indicators of meaning for a particular subject are a use-ful starting point for thinking about the affective labour that is *always already* shaped by a person's subjectivity and biography, as discussed in this chapter. In her discussion of Green's (1999) development of Freud, Ruth Stein has argued that the former 'seems to conceive of affects as our relationships, our energized relationships, to an experience and ul-timately to ourselves. Affect is seen by Green as a kind of perception of "otherness" in oneself' (Stein 1999, 134). This formulation is very useful because it moves away from an overall emphasis of affect-as-discharge which I have put forward earlier and towards a model that sees affect as lingering inside and around the subject. I do not wish to do away com-pletely with the notion of affective discharge, as some psychoanalysts have done (see Stein 1999, 46 for a discussion). Affect as 'the relation-ship to an experience' (Green) is also a useful description for thinking about the particular examples of affective labour that I have discussed in this chapter. The individuals I spoke to had, like all of us, specific relationships to embodied experiences of living with bodily differences which fed into their social media use. The other notion stressed by Freud and Green which I have discussed at length in earlier chapters refers to affect as an experience of self-dispossession. This may occur to anybody during an affective experience, but for subjects who are made to feel 'other' (because they belong to a specific ethnic group, or have a disability), such dispossessions are particularly amplified and reinforced vis-à-vis the social world. Such bodily states of otherness are particularly affective because of how others respond to them and ultimately create them through speech acts and actions. I wish to think through this idea of bodily dispossession a little more through Jacques Lacan's notion of 'lack' (2002) and André Green's (1999) concept of 'negative hallucination'.

Affective Labour as Lack

While it is open to debate if Lacan gave any consideration to affect in his work and I would argue that *jouissance* is not similar or the same as affect in the Freudian sense (Green 1999; Stein 1999; Johanssen 2016b), his idea of the *lack* touched on numerous times in his seminars and in his famous mirror stage text (2002) is useful for this project. Lacan, and perhaps psychoanalysis more generally, makes clear that there is an 'alienation that occurs when we become our selves in relation to others' (Goodley 2011, 123), as disabilities studies scholar Dan Goodley has put it. Lacan famously argued that in the mirror stage, the young infant misrecognises herself in the mirror as a unitary, holistic being rather than a fragmented, dependent one. This image conceals the lack of agency, autonomy, and coherence (Lacan 2002). There may be some common ground between Anzieu (2016) and Lacan here in terms of the illusionary fantasy of agency that the baby and young infant develops. For Anzieu, the baby has the fantasy of sharing a common skin with mother and of being a complete subject. However, Anzieu's model places an emphasis on phenomenology and affect, whereas Lacan prioritises language, vision, and the gaze (Anzieu 2016). For Lacan, this lack is constitutive of the subject, the subject is the gap in the structure of the symbolic order that she enters into. Subjects spend their lives trying to catch up with a lost and idealised sense of self through finding themselves in others. Although universal, the notion of the lack may be particularly felt by people with disabilities:

> Disabled people's experience can only be understood in relation to alterity.
>   The creation of the devalued 'Other' is a necessary precondition for the creation of the able-bodied rational subject who is the all-pervasive agency that sets the term of the dialogue.
>   (Ghai 2006, 79, cited in Goodley 2011, 129)

Goodley has similarly argued that cultural discourses around disabilities are often manifestations of (unconscious) projections whereby it is others – disabled, queer, racialised people – who are lacking, incomplete, or 'other' in some shape or form (Garrisi and Johanssen forthcoming). Such ableist cultures are responsible for often creating disabilities in the first place because they metaphorically and practically disable subjects in their everyday lives (Campbell 2009). However, what was striking about some of the narratives collected in this project was that the individuals constructed *themselves* as lacking and somehow incomplete, rather than (only) being made to lack by others.

> Lacan is clear: all bodies refuse to match up to the original *imago*, never re-find the original desiring (m)other and, crucially, are castrated and rejected by the symbolic. *The tragedy is that non/disabled people do not recognise that we all share the experience of alienation and that different bodies, whether fe/male, queer/normative, black/white, all, to varying extents, are destined to fail to meet the demands of the symbolic.*
>
> (Goodley 2011, 134, italics in original)

Another person I interviewed spoke about the difficulties of having to face definitions and judgements, but her narratives also indicated her own difficulties at times of coming to terms with her cleft lip. She spoke in much detail about an experience of working in a shop as a teenager:

> Then he said something like, to my boss above me, like so she was behind me so he kind of spoke over me, and said, 'It's great what you're doing here.' She was like, 'Oh, yes, to have young Saturday people in.' Like thinking that maybe he was referring to the fact that I was a young person. Then he said, 'Oh no, yes, I used to work with disabled people, and I think it's great.' I can't remember what his exact words were. But he basically thought that I was disabled. I kind of like, it went over my head, and then it kind of sunk in and I looked up, and my boss looked a bit horrified, and I was like, like, I didn't know if it was because I was being a little bit slow or because of the way I looked. Then his face kind of, dropped and realised what he'd done, and I kind of backed up, my heart just sunk. I'd had conversations … so my dad went nuts when I got home, because obviously he was like, 'No, I have a cleft and you're not disabled.' And I've spoken to disabled, or, an individual with a learning disability about this before, a friend, and they were like, 'Whoa, what are you saying about learning disabilities, is that a bad thing?' I was like, 'No, it's nothing against you, but if you don't have one, and then for a that to be inferred on the way that

you look, when you're fourteen and an impressionable, hormonal young woman, that sucks.' They were like, 'Oh yes, okay, fair enough,' that's because actually, her learning disability, nobody can see it, so nobody, if that had been in her in that situation probably wouldn't, she wouldn't have had any comments, like that's something that she kind of has to offer up. But yes, I was like the only way he could have come to that conclusion, like, well I think then, yes, it was evident that he just said because of the way I looked, and kind of assumed that I was disabled. I was, like, 'No, this doesn't stop me from doing anything, I just look a bit wonky, go away'. So that's like something that kind of stuck with me.

(I5, 157–183)

This narrative may not be immediately relevant to her affective labour online, but it may point to a specific embodied form of identity and biography which influenced the interviewees' usage of social media. I would argue that the specific forms of social media usage that I have discussed in this chapter point to a usage around a lack which is both cognitively reflected on and affectively felt. This lack has, in Freud's terms, an ideational and affective dimension. Much of the narratives that I have quoted in this chapter may point to a dilemma which is both empowering but also difficult to come to terms with for the interviewees: a self-performance online which very often revolved around and responded to who they were (not). The affective labour on social media may be empowering because it gives the individuals with bodily differences a voice and it challenges ideological and hegemonic appearance standards and stereotypes online. Much of the affective labour was about the individual subjectivity and conducted in an entrepreneurial manner that actively embraced difference on social media and used it as a kind of unique selling point for the individual and her labour. However, many of the quotes suggest that this active self-marketisation often had to be negotiated in relation to others who challenged it, or made for a 'normal' majority who was not different. Such labour practices were thus always in relation to what they were not. They played with difference and use it to gain attention, but they could also be draining, exhausting, and traumatic when confronted with trolling, for example. The affective labour of the individuals I spoke to thus made for intense practices that were not only about the subject's (un)conscious relationships with themselves but also made for intense practices that aimed to keep up affective relationalities that maintained followers and friends who comment, share, and engage with the individuals. This desire and need to create a good enough affective atmosphere online is a crucial aspect of the affective labour and alludes to Hardt and Negri's definition of the term. This notion of affective labour-as-lack can be further supplemented with André Green's concept of 'negative hallucination' (1999). Developing Lacan's mirror stage where the child gazes into the mirror, Green creates the particular scenario of facing a void. 'Where the image of the subject ought to appear in the mirror, nothing appears' (ibid., 202). 'What is lacking in the subject is not a sense of his existence, but ocular proof of it' (ibid., 202), Green continues. Such formulations are not meant to pathologise the interviewees, but they may help in further theorising their social media use and how it was influenced by the social world, their biographies, and their affective dimensions in particular. Green argues that the subject may feel a sense of absence of her representation which is accompanied by rising anxiety. Anxiety is a highly affective state which lies uncoupled from specific ideas or objects (Freud 1981h). 'What is lacking [for the subject] is not the sense of existence, but the power of representation' (Green 1999, 202). There may be a tension between who the subject feels she is (her existence) and who she thinks she is (a representational idea). Instead of being mirrored as an idealised Other in the mirror and by others throughout life, the subject is confronted with a void of the Other. 'The subject is referred back only to his corporally experienced presence' (ibid., 202).

> The anxiety affect expresses the effort on the part of the ego to reach a representation of itself at all costs. He seeks himself elsewhere, everywhere, around himself, outside himself and finds no palliative to this excess of presence. He tries to rejoin that lost image that is missing, and it is that impossibility of finding himself again that is responsible for the anxiety. He is lacking to himself, for this empty reflection is experienced not as pure absence, but as a *hallucination of absence*. It is because the image is covered over with a hallucination of lack that the subject tries, beyond that hallucination, to find his representation again.
>
> (Green 1999, 202, italics in original)

This lack is enforced by the social world, norms, belief systems, and others who respond to the subjects who have bodily differences. They can never quite fully acquire the status of a subject and may negotiate a sense of subjectivity in relation to themselves and others. Sally spoke about an experience which can be used to exemplify this.

I4: When I worked as a bookseller, people would refuse to take change off me. They would ask to be served by somebody else, but I was the only person there. You know, people in the shop asked me, like, you know, could I dress myself. Someone asked me if my parents had considered abortion. Had I done something bad in a previous life? All this is stuff, just imagine what they say to people who have, like, major disfigurements, you know? Like, I can pass a lot of the time, so, I don't know. A woman once told me that she thought I was just the right amount of disabled because she could still ...

J: The right amount?

I4: The right amount because she could still identify with me as a human being.

(I4, 640–650)

Those shocking statements reveal how subjectivity may be questioned and undone by others. A similar experience was reproduced earlier when one interviewee spoke of being referred to as 'disabled'. She did not want to be labelled as such because she feared it may have stopped her from achieving things in life. The subject is more than a disability or a bodily difference. This being made to lack by others can be a traumatic experience that sticks with people and is felt affectively as an anxious state. It may partly explain the need but also difficulty of presenting the self on social media. Social media may serve to acknowledge and value the subjects but at the same time it may not negate the subjects' real existing differences. This acknowledgement of the lack by others on social media as a form of solidarity and support was, for instance, talked about by Rose in recounting the reactions to her uploaded video. What made the types of affective labour described here perhaps more challenging than other kinds of affective labour was the fact that the interviewees actively used their own lack as a kind of branding strategy to raise awareness and acceptance of it. This made them subject to positive as well as negative responses and was spoken about in terms of creating good enough affective atmospheres.

Another, but related, aspect which renders the concepts of lack and negative hallucination useful for theorising affective labour was the relationship between subject and other. The interviewees often spoke about their subjectivities in relation to ideological categories such as 'success' and being a productive and useful citizen (as detailed earlier). Those categories may have served as placeholders to cover over the negative hallucination and lack in order to find a representation again that could be communicated to me not only in the interviews but also online: the agentic, successful subject. This (unconscious) desire for representation was also spoken about in relation to the body. It was particularly framed in relation to one category: beauty. Green has argued that

Negative hallucination is not the absence of representation, but *representation of the absence of representation*—though the sense of the term representation here is not that of 'second best', since it entails a distancing of the subject, who is, by definition, absent. It is much more a condition of possibility of representation than representation itself.

(Green 1999, 223, italics in original)

Such a condition of possibility of representation was negotiated on social media in particular but it was also discussed more widely in relation to the individuals' lifeworlds. The move from negative hallucination to the ability of representation would be, in Green's terms, referred to as positive hallucination (Green 1999, 203). The subject is able to cover over the lack with a representation that she recognises. This has been similarly discussed with regard to selfies and bodily agency, for example (Tiidenberg and Gómez Cruz 2015). Such struggles for recognition were handled on social media as well as beyond. Many interviewees spoke about their bodies in relation to 'beauty' and what it meant to be beautiful.

> Well it's got to the point where erm you know it's almost like saying 'Okay that's beautiful' and then everyone believes that's beautiful erm you know like I think because what I've learned, because I was a beautiful young girl and I never knew it until now, I can now see everyone as a beautiful person and I can see everything as beautiful, so I always find something that's beautiful so erm when, I think when the media are saying 'That's beautiful, that's how you should look', people automatically, think that's true and to me it's ridiculous, it's almost a bit like a brainwash in in a way erm and obviously there's so much with body confidence and body image at the moment and there's a lot of young girls out there, wanna be, have big booties and little skin, skinny waists and it's all over the Internet, you know it's absolutely ridiculous that everyone wants to look this certain way and and I noticed that over the years how things have changed cos' I remember, say like 10, 15 years ago, if you had a big bottom, then you had a fat bottom but you got a big bottom now it's the way to look, you know and so I do find a lot of what they say and put into people's minds, you know that we tend to believe that's the right way to be and that's what beauty is and it is so sad and what's sad about is is that for example, me walking into a poolside in a Bikini and I got a bunch of girls in the pool staring at me and actually laughing and that is sad you know because they, they, that's, to, to them, I look disgusting and I shouldn't be in a Bikini and to me I'm beautiful and I don't care, you know and to me they're beautiful as well but regardless of how they look, if they're big, small.
>
> (I2, 294–317)

> My and some friends recently went to go and see Wonder Woman and came out, all of us felt rather inadequate after that, because she's beautiful, and I don't know how much they kind of photoshop, but then afterwards we were googling Wonder Woman's, I can't remember what her real name is, the actress, but then we found out that she's had a kid. She's had a kid and she looks like that. So yes, we all felt, like, very inadequate.
>
> (I5, 485–491)

Both narratives may exemplify the struggle, which we all face to some extent, of keeping up with ideological beauty standards defined by the fashion industry. The fashion industry, through social media, magazines, and so on, will always tell the individual that they are lacking and can improve their body. While beauty standards may change, as discussed by Rose earlier, the idea of being beautiful is strongly linked to ideology in contemporary capitalism and as Judith Butler has shown in her work on gender is closely linked to notions of performance and self-labour (Butler 1990). Becoming and being beautiful is a process, so we are told, which requires affective labour on the self through the use of cosmetics, hair removal, and so on. While the interviewee's account of feeling inadequate in comparison to the artificially created on-screen beauty of *Wonder Woman* is perhaps constitutive of the Lacanian lack, Rose challenged hegemonic ideas of beauty and exclaimed that everyone is beautiful, no matter what they look like. However, the term 'beauty' always implies that something is beautiful and something else is not. Beauty can only exist in relation to non-beauty, or ugliness. Psychoanalysts argue that referring to something or someone as 'beautiful' is always an act of idealisation of that object or subject. 'Beauty is human subjectivity expressed in ideal form' (Hagman 2002, 662). 'The yearning that we experience before beauty is for an experience that is ultimately unattainable, which is already lost, perhaps forever' (ibid., 668).

The recourse to beauty as a reference point always implies normative judgements, and such judgements are amplified through expressions that someone is beautiful or that everybody is beautiful. Beauty remains a realm where social acceptance and values are negotiated. Disfigurement and bodily differences were reinscribed into beauty discourses and practices of representation online by the interviewees in order to be accepted by others. Such forms of embodiment are thus aestheticised so that they can be shown. It is through the mentioning of 'beauty' that the interviewees were able to include themselves in the realm of the beautiful. In both being critical of hegemonic ideas of beauty but at the same time appropriating the notion of beauty to claim it for themselves and critique hegemonic beauty ideals, the interviewees reproduced the ideological impetus behind the beautiful which dictates what counts as beautiful and what does not.

Being referred to as beautiful or comparing oneself to others perceived as beautiful was also difficult at times. As one interviewee discussed,

> Sometimes that will happen when I'm sat next to a friend who is, you know, I have some friends who are beautiful, like really stunning, and I'm like, and they'll be saying this to me, and I'm like, "Okay, of all the times I've been out with you, no adult has ever told you, come up to you and randomly declared how beautiful you look, and you definitely are, you know, like, society's, kind of standardised

measure, so why do I get it?" The only reason I can get it, like, conclusion I've kind of drawn is that they're, like, doing this over compensating thing for the cleft, and they're being nice and they're trying to make me okay, but I really don't need rescuing. I'm fine, like, you know, so that's another thing that adults do.

(I5, 202–211)

I don't like it when people over compensate, and I don't like it when people are mean either. I want everyone to be in the middle so I get irritated when people say, "Oh, that's the most, like, you're the most beautiful person I've ever seen." I'm like, "Okay, that could just be your opinion, or you could just be saying that, you know, because you're like, oh I need to say this to rescue you." I don't need rescuing, you know.

(I5, 792–798)

Being referred to as beautiful may have felt excessive and patronising to her at times. While it may be easier for an individual to gloss over their own lack through particular self-definitions (which may include being beautiful), the act of being made beautiful by an other may instead reinforce the experience of lack and associated anxieties of not being a coherent subject. Being made to lack because of bodily differences may lead to a mistrust of aesthetic judgements by others that one is beautiful. Having a disability myself, I can empathise with such narratives and relate to a sense of paranoia and questioning if flattering statements by others are really genuine or meant as mere acts of comfort.

I feel like people worry and focus about little things in life and if you go through a trauma, or you've got a difference, you see the world in a different light, there is more to life than appearance and I know appearance is a big thing in the world we live in, I guess sex sells, you gotta be attractive and that's what's gonna make you money at the end of the day, and if you look different you might feel you've not got a chance to compete like erm they shut you down before you even got into the race erm but I feel like now that I am old enough, I can, [...], maybe not in the same way as these Page 3 girls, not that I wanna be a Page 3 girl but erm I can be appealing and I can be good looking and I can have the hair colour and rock it and just as good as this other girl.

(I3, 211–220)

Jayne's negotiation of beauty and its mediated forms suggests a contradictory account. One the one hand, there is more to life than mere appearances and at the same time sexuality and sexist representations of it through the Sun's 'Page 3 girl' were evoked by her. Female sexuality, appearance, and having a successful career were framed in a neo-liberal vocabulary of success, competition, and winning. While such characteristics were dismissed by Jayne, she simultaneously compared herself to the Page 3 girl – an idealised set of appearances that can never be obtained in real life – and embraced them at the same time through stating that she could be 'as good as this other girl'. This other (girl) was constructed as an idealised, yet dismissed figure who perhaps exemplifies the struggle with ideological representations of beauty we all face today. It served as a (rivalry) fantasy representation that may have helped Jayne to situate herself in relation to it. A state of being that could always be desired and yet never fully reached. Her lack was covered over through fantasies of becoming a CEO, running a successful organisation and being as beautiful as a Page 3 girl. I do not mean to critique such fantasies. They may have given her a sense of agency and desire for the future, but they equally tell of ableist ideologies that implicitly and explicitly tell individuals like Jayne that they are always lacking and will remain incomplete. Yet she may have internalised such fantasies. 'The sense of beauty can also function to reconcile and integrate self-states of fragmentation and depletion' (Hagman 2002, 671), as Hagman notes. Jayne spoke about such feelings of lack and incompleteness too:

> For someone a big achievement might be, I don't know, getting the next job, or getting a promotion or going on holiday to their tenth favourite destination in the world, mine is like getting up and not smashing a glass, it's walking to the other side of the road without chucking over and it is I feel like those small things to me are really big deals and like other people with burns have similar, like opening the front door, facing the world that is a huge achievement, yeah.
>
> (I3, 101–106)

Rather than being the agentic and successful subject she had presented herself as in other times during the interview, the aforementioned description shows the lack and feelings of inadequacy in relation to mastering every day skills and activities. Such feelings have not only come about because of anxiety or a particular embodied subjectivity – which may make life harder to navigate at times – but also because of ableist cultures that respond with ignorance or disrespect to bodily differences. While the earlier narratives symbolised unconscious and defensive responses to experiences of lack through presenting particular subjectivities online, the previous one may exemplify a conscious negotiation of lack that takes account of insecurities. Such conscious negotiations were conducted on social media in particular. Rose spoke about a friend and her sharing of content on social media:

[S]he had breast cancer, had both her breasts removed and then just one night, I don't know, I think she must have had a few too many as we do and erm she started to take loads of really, not very nice pics of her chest, now to me, there is, something I've learned, there's two ways to that, you can either do it, just like, it is forgotten or you can do it in a nice way, you know, there's different ways of taking pictures, you know it's her chest but at the end of the day there are different ways of doing it and there are a lot of role models out there at the moment, there is a young girl with psoriasis, she takes lovely pics and she is a young girl and she has such a big following and people love that and she is embracing her body.

(I2, 595–603)

What is striking about the forms of self-representation discussed so far is their visual nature and affective labour. Many of the interviewees referred to notions of beauty and were keen to emphasise their representability online and offline. To some degree, they were using mechanisms which they themselves also implicitly critiqued, the notion of the beautiful, self-branding, ableism, sexism, and so on, to campaign for bodily diversity. In framing themselves as lacking, they turned themselves into (data) objects which are then commodified on social media. The lack as a kind of fundamental alienation from ourselves which we all face, albeit to different degrees, is amplified because of data alienation. Some voices in the digital labour debate have argued that because users do not own their data on social media, the social media platforms, or the data that is sold on to advertisers, they are alienated from all three (Andrejevic 2011; Fuchs and Sevignani 2013; Fuchs 2014; Krüger and Johanssen 2014; Johanssen 2016a). This does not mean that their experiences of using social media may not be useful and fulfilling for them (Jarrett 2015). The discussion of Rose's friend and her pictures by her may exemplify the negotiation of lack and of negative hallucination through affective labour. It was important to Rose to share photos of bodily differences online 'in a nice way' so as possibly not to offend anyone. In that sense, beauty was specifically linked to an aestheticisation of the self online through specific practices (such as engaging with others, uploading the right photos). A lack only becomes tolerable – to others and to the individual – if it is presented in an aestheticised form. Such affective labour which has to be good enough, somewhat aesthetic and engaging follows the demands by social media platforms, which were also discussed in the previous chapter. Users must share, engage, and communicate with each other in order to be visible and acknowledged. '[D]oing YouTube in particular, that control you have over your own content is really empowering and I think once you break out of that and you can see people being themselves and sharing things and talking about things openly' (I4, 253–255), as Sally remarked. This demand to be authentic is part of the ideology of sharing. Authenticity in this case means a carefully constructed subjectivity around a lack which always needs to remain good enough.

Conclusion

This chapter discussed interview data from a research project on bodily differences and social media representation. I theorised the interview narratives about self-representation as forms of affective labour. I discussed their narratives about self-representation in more general terms in relation to feared trolling and responses by others on social media. I then went on to pay some attention to narratives about self-branding that signified an entrepreneurial sense which was brought to the fore through their affective labour. The affective labour was by many presented as engaging and good enough (Winnicott 2002) in order to reach a maximum of followers, comments, and shares. I ended this chapter by relating the affective labour to Lacan's lack and Green's negative hallucination.

While I have characterised the practices of self-representation as forms of digital labour which are exploited and alienated from the outset, I wish to stress that they are immensely valuable to the individuals nonetheless. They spoke about getting a sense of use value, empowerment, agency, and politics out of them. Such practices were done with a cause to disrupt often implicit but also explicit sexist and ableist content on social media that portrays bodies as white, slim, and able. While negotiating and to a degree appropriating such qualities was not without difficulties for the interviewees, I would argue that such acts of self-representation are very important because they disrupt social media hegemonies. While the narratives discussed in this chapter are also pointing to internalised neo-liberal ideologies which are reproduced, they are at the same time resistant of them and carve out spaces both online and beyond for people with bodily differences. Only classifying them as exploited, affective labour would not do them justice.

In the previous chapter, I argued that Hardt and Negri's concept of affective labour and how it has subsequently been taken up by digital media scholars is dualistic and lacks concrete dimensions as to what is specifically affective and embodied about such labour. Scholars of digital labour have tended not to focus on inherent characteristics of the term. In this chapter, I have enriched the field by showing how digital labour, and affective labour in particular, looks like for individuals on social media. Digital labour on social media is specifically affective. It is messy, contradictory, (un)conscious, and psychosocial. Only treating it as a flat category for structural discussions in political economy is insufficient. My discussions have added more dimensions to this very useful and important concept.

In an important study on affective labour about the responses to the 22 July terrorist attacks in Norway on a platform by a Norwegian newspaper, Steffen Krüger (2016) has argued that the forum encouraged and demanded of its users to present themselves in particular ways: 'Present yourself as affected in an affective way, i.e. in a way that is moving and engaging to others' (Krüger 2016, 204). While the particular community Krüger writes about may have little in common with the affective labour on Twitter, Facebook, YouTube, and Instagram that I discussed in this chapter, there is a common element which regards the compulsion to share specific content. Krüger has maintained that the newspaper online community only allowed for specific accounts of being affected to be published online: the ones that were in tune with a socially acceptable narrative of mourning, shock, a sense of loss, and so on. 'Affectedness thus turned into compulsion, and this compulsion, driven by commoditisation, fed into a more general structure of feeling that rendered suspicious any attempt at taking issue with problematic emotions' (ibid., 204). A similar policing strategy may have been evident in the interview data that I discussed. However, it was the users themselves, rather than social media platforms, who policed their own actions and the type of content they shared online. To reach the maximum and most engaging level of affecting other users through their content required a form of self-surveillance and aestheticisation of their created content. The affective labour thus comes to stand as the ultimate bearer of authenticity and a real, embodied self which is able to engage with and affect others on social media – to some degree, as I have similarly discussed in Chapter 3. There is a limit to the affective labour because it required careful selection and orchestration of content to be shared. In the article *Affective Economies*, Sara Ahmed has argued that 'emotions work as a form of capital: affect does not reside positively in the sign or commodity, but is produced as an effect of its circulation' (Ahmed 2004, 118). Drawing on Freud's ideas on affect and Marx's labour theory of value, Ahmed argues that affect acquires value over time through being circulated. Affect is the effect of relational circulations between bodies, signs, and objects. The more they are circulated, the more affective value they can (potentially) accumulate. Affects may thus appear 'as objects with a life of their own, only by the concealment of how they are shaped by histories, including histories of production (labor and labor time), as well as circulation or exchange' (2004, 121). Bodily differences, as exemplified by the interviewees, and their representations online may show how these differences have acquired a life of their own that may be controlled by the interviewees but is equally owned by social media companies and responded to and appropriated by other users. They gain affective value through being situated and circulated on social media. They stick to different elements throughout the process of online circulation. The more the stories of bodily differences circulate, the more affective value they may acquire while at the same time concealing how they were shaped by individual histories. I have suggested that aspects of individual histories that appear but are also concealed by the affective labour practices online are nonetheless important in trying to understand those practices online. Many of the narratives that I heard in the interviews were not made visible online. The tensions, contradictions, and wider dimensions that shaped the affective labour, and were likewise shaped by it, were hidden behind it. Similarly, the notion of lack that I outlined was both concealed and apparent through the labour practices on social media. 'I argue that affective structures mediate between the actual and the digital virtual' (Karatzogianni 2012, 245), as Karatzogianni puts it. While there is a relationship between the actual (we may also call it a realm beyond the digital sphere) and social media, such a relationship is partly obscured by the practices of affective labour that seek to bring such a relationship into focus. There are always elements that remain concealed, hidden, lacking, or glossed over.

Note

1 This project was carried out together with Diana Garrisi and funded by the University of Westminster Strategic Research Fund/The Quintin Hogg Trust. The particular interviews that form the basis of this chapter were conducted by me.

6 The Perverse Logic of Big Data

Introduction

This chapter shifts the book's focus from interview-based analyses to a more theoretical-exploratory discussion of big data and data mining processes by and through digital media today. In their overview of literature on big data, Ekbia et al. (2014) note that various discipline-specific definitions are floating around. Broadly speaking, the various perspectives on big data emphasise a process which has increased and accelerated in the past decades. Data volumes and how much data can be stored, for example, on a hard drive or online has dramatically increased in recent years. Similarly, the amount of data processed, for example, by Google on a daily basis (about 24 petabytes) is unprecedented to how much data was generated, say, 15 years ago. More and more data are being produced, stored, and used each day.

Some argue that the human mind is simply not equipped to work with such large amounts of data and that computers and computational processes are the answer as they can help humans make sense of data (boyd and Crawford 2012, 665). This has been widely discussed in media and communication studies and related disciplines with a focus on research methods that help researchers to work with large data sets (Rogers 2013). boyd and Crawford (2012) have put forward a useful definition of big data and I will be returning to some of the points they raise in it throughout this chapter. Big data rests on:

1   Technology: maximizing computation power and algorithmic accuracy to gather, analyze, link, and compare large data sets.
2   Analysis: drawing on large data sets to identify patterns in order to make economic, social, technical, and legal claims.
3   Mythology: the widespread belief that large data sets offer a higher form of intelligence and knowledge that can generate insights that were previously impossible, with the aura of truth, objectivity, and accuracy. boyd and Crawford 2012, 663

For this chapter, 'big data' can be defined as both a description of and the effort and mechanism itself through which to gather, extract, process, and analyse (digital) data or create such data in the first place through the conversion of other analogue data into the digital format. Those data are often made up of various smaller data and turned into large data sets. From the outset, big data is about 'high-volume, high-velocity and/or high-variety' (Gartner 2013, n. p.) data as information that is processed. Such processing is done, so it is often argued, by the actors engaged in it as well as by commentators, for 'enhanced insight and decision making' (ibid.). As has been pointed out, the purpose of big data is often commercial. Data sets are sold by companies to other companies or bodies who (think) they are useful to them. Data collection itself often takes place in order to know more about users through the process of collecting and analysing. This knowledge is generated through the use and analysis of user data (e.g., Facebook content and meta-data), and its ultimate aim is to persuade, guide, or manipulate users into (repeatedly) using a service or platform in a certain way. Needless to say, big data has various implications for users online; their data; and how users are constructed and constituted through them as data subjects and profiles by companies, governments, and others (Cheney-Lippold 2017).

While the processes of data mining may be automated, data mining is also at least partly conducted by individuals, who work for social media companies, for example. There is thus a subjective factor in how particular data are aggregated: 'making decisions about what attributes and variables will be counted, and which will be ignored. This process is inherently subjective' (boyd and Crawford 2012, 667). As noted, big data also marks an *automated* and code-based aggregating, sorting, extracting, and handling of user data. Such a combination has led to data discrimination as has been widely discussed, for instance when it comes to data sorting according to racialised algorithms (e.g., Sandvig et al. 2016; Cheney-Lippold 2017).

Big data does not only refer to the actual handling of existing data, but a turn towards *creating* data in the first place. For instance, attempts to capture user behaviour on social media and thereby turning it into data, or to track how many steps I walk through a wearable device and thereby turning my bodily movement into digital measures. Big data and its associated processes of data mining are thus attempts to turn *everything* into data, to datafy everything. Mayer-Schönberger and Cukier describe this as a process that aims 'to put it in a quantified format so that it can be tabulated and analysed' (2013, 78). Again, this has implications for how we think about subjectivity, how individuals experience an atmosphere of complete datafication, how they are changed by it and the wider social consequences of these changes that can be explored through psychoanalysis.

Data mining practices can be and are used by both corporations and individuals, and they make use of sophisticated, computational methods in order to produce the data (Kennedy, H. 2016, 32). Such tasks are, for example, performed by social media companies themselves, but data are also available from external companies that mine social media platforms in exchange for money. While such processes promise results that show objectively and rationally coded data that corresponds to real individuals, decisions, and content online, any form of data mining involves decisions made by algorithms and humans before the data have been created, repackaged, or visualised. 'Social media data, like other data, are not a window onto the world, but are shaped by decisions made about how to go about seeking and gathering those data' (Kennedy, H. 2016, 37). This not only has implications for how we see data mining but also for how questions of subjectivity inform or obfuscate (depending on the viewpoint) data mining. I return to this point in more detail later on. Data mining technologies already come with an inherent notion of who the human subject is or should be. Data 'need to be generated and, in order to be generated, they need to be *imagined*' (Kennedy, H. 2016, 50, my emphasis). Those acts of imagination simultaneously imagine a particular sense of subjectivity as well as particular relationalities which I am interested in exploring.

A number of scholars have criticised datafication processes because they amount to surveillance. The purpose of datafication on social media, for example, is primarily to be able to sell certain user data to enable targeted advertising (as discussed in Chapter 4). Data mining practices on social media are 'discriminatory by design' (Kennedy, H. 2016, 48, see also Barocas and Selbst (2014) and Gandy (2006)). Data mining involves the structuring of individual data profiles whereby they are classified according to criteria and often marked as more or less valuable (Golumbia 2009). The precise criteria according to which such data mining occurs are unknown to the general public and, in fact, carefully hidden by its creators and users (Gillespie 2014). Mark Andrejevic, Alison Hearn, and Helen Kennedy (2015) argue that this has led to a difficulty on the part of academic researchers to critically evaluate large data sets and the computational processes that produced them. Data mining processes are not only technical and complex, but often remain inaccessible. 'Most often, with so little insight available into their production, we are left only to theorize their effects' (Andrejevic et al. 2015, 380). I argue that we may still be able to theorise what happens more fundamentally during processes of data mining, even if we may lack the specific technical detail. More on this later. Following Andrejevic, Hearn, and Kennedy, I would like to draw on their call for an approach to data mining that specifically moves beyond the technical and includes questions of subjectivity, power, and autonomy, among others (ibid., 384).

This chapter begins with a discussion of the archive by offering a reading of Derrida's *Archive Fever* (1995) text in light of big data and contemporary data mining processes. I then go on to analyse how data can be used to be turned against the users they are supposed to mirror. Data mining processes are dis/individualising. They promise to provide a better experience of, for example, the Facebook newsfeed or Netflix by focussing on the individual user while at the same time merging their data with millions of others to make decisions that users cannot see or influence. I relate such phenomena to the psychoanalytic notion of perversion and argue that our relationship to services which mine our data resembles a perverse relationship in which we are loved/valued and abused at the same time.

While Nick Couldry and Alison Powell (2014) have called for a social analytics approach to big data which takes account of questions of agency, reflexivity, and the social embeddedness of big data, I propose a *psychosocial* analytics perspective in this chapter. This approach connects questions of the social implications of big data and its transindividual characteristics with questions of subjectivity by drawing on psychoanalysis and literature from media and communication studies. If we take Orit Halpern's argument about 'contemporary obsessions with storage, visualization, and interactivity in digital systems' (Halpern 2014, 17) as a starting point, we may ask what are its implications for a psychosocial analysis of big data?

Data Fever

As discussed in Chapter 1, Freud had a distinct interest in the relationship between the psyche and modes of storage and retrieval. His *Project* text (Freud 1981a) essentially postulated that the psyche worked like an information storage and processing system. Thirty years after the *Project*, he would return to these ideas in the *Mystic Writing Pad* essay (1981i) where he focussed on memory storage. These ideas have been taken up by Jacques Derrida in his work on the archive (1995). I feel that the archive is a useful metaphor for thinking about (big) data because of the permeability and osmosis between different subjects that contribute to an ever-expanding archive that the notion of the archive enables us to think about. Archives are never complete. Derrida (1995) wrote that the advances in technological inscription and recording systems, which have been epitomised by the ever-increasing and fine-tuned data mining practices across mediums, platforms, and objects today, mean that we record and archive in order to be able to forget. Recording makes the need to remember obsolete and fetishises that loss at the same time by placing an emphasis on the ability to retain everything (see also Lovink 2009). That 'mechanized loss' (Halpern 2014, 76) is rendered painless through the ability to immediately record our memories into digital form or to turn our creative outputs into digital memories.

However, what Halpern and Derrida seem to brush over here is that in many processes of archivisation, for example, in the creation and use of user data, there is a *double archivisation* in place. Taking the archive as a metaphor for digital processes around the production and distribution of information is not only about the externalisation of memory. To begin with, memories are not simply externalised in the production of data, but the very processes of creating data, for example, in the form of a Facebook post, involve unconscious, conscious, and affective forces within the subject that shape whatever they have posted or whichever image they have uploaded. While this may turn into a preserved digital memory that is to remain online, it is not simply something that is externalised unilaterally.

> Even in externalizing the archive, it is possible to trace the processes of internalization, and in the conscious and rational archival succession, there is a pervasive unconscious feature.
>
> (Ihanus 2007, 123)

Above all, it is psychoanalysis that should remind us that we never simply forget, that we cannot record to forget (as Derrida mistakenly argues) but that what we have forgotten may be repressed, negated, or simply not remembered, may nonetheless return to us. Not (only) in the form of a Facebook post that re-surfaces, but because the unconscious is dynamic and pushes towards consciousness. The data storage facilities of social networking sites are thus not mere extensions of memory, or external spaces for our psyches, but they are, as I have pointed to in the previous chapter, spaces that enable complex processes of psychic investment.

Derrida wrote eloquently that psychoanalysis is the paradigmatic discipline that can explore the archive, and processes around production, storage, preservation, and retrieval of information are important characteristics of the talking cure. For Freud, the psyche itself is a sort of archive which consists of different compartments or departments. The unconscious is a kind of infinite space which harbours repressed, negated, forgotten memories, affects, and fantasies. Yet the psyche, consciousness and the unconscious, is a spatial container which was mapped by Freud so that it comes to resemble an archive, as Derrida has noted. The free associative talking cure's goal, then, is to build an archive out of the psychic archive as it were to extract fragments, piece them together, and reconstruct or rebuild an archive together with the patient. Not only is this archive built by inviting free associative speech acts but also quite literally fixed discursively through written, anonymised case histories.

Data mining and psychoanalysis are both driven by a desire to know the other and to accumulate data. To some degree, the analyst and patient together extract data from the patient's (un)conscious life experiences and interpret them and use them in some way – with different goals of course. The analyst has a desire to know the patient in order to suggest potential solutions or ways of dealing with problems. Often, the patient would like to know more about the analyst's private life but this desire is prohibited for reasons of professional/ethical conduct. There are thus power relations involved and while there is a reciprocal relationship, it is not equal in terms of who knows what about whom. The same is true about the relationship between users and companies or agencies that mine their data for various purposes. Another characteristic shared between those two instances of data extraction is that they occur – albeit to varying degrees – automated. The purpose of free association is to enable a flow of utterances that bypass the conscious censorship and lay bare unconscious thoughts or ideas. This happens in a flowing, almost automatic manner. The same goes for data mining practices which are governed by algorithms and code that runs automatically beyond the users' knowledge and control. Code is hidden behind design interfaces that mask what is going on beneath the surface.

For Derrida, the archive implies a certain violence in its totalising quest for knowledge of the other. The archive comes into being through a form of surveillance (Derrida 1995, 12). Archives about certain individuals, historical periods, and themes are often constructed by others and not the ones who the archive is about. This is certainly applicable to data mining on social media and beyond. Derrida notes that the desire to archive and to create an archive is a defensive act against the death drive. In storing and maintaining data, the archive acts against the death drive. This desire is without end. The death drive continuously threatens the archive and ever more data needs to be accumulated to guard against destruction and loss. This desire to continuously add to the archive is the *archive fever*. We can see how this takes place on social media when users upload content and engage in communication with others. The reality principle is verified, and users feel connected to and recognised by others (Balick 2014). Audiences are of course not only creating one archive when they use Facebook or any other social networking platform, for example. They are creating numerous data across platforms, devices, and content. While the willingness of users to give and give off (Bunz and Meikle 2017) ever more data may be symptomatic of defences against loss and uncertainty by revealing, storing, and retaining information about ourselves, there is a further, deeper undercurrent beneath the surface: the algorithm. The algorithm and the more visible processes around it have become cathected objects that promise a sense of order, stability, and predictability to users. I will return to this later in more detail. First, I wish to look at the consequences of the vast amounts of user data creation.

There is a further dimension to the defensive creation of user data in order to guard against loss, which Halpern and Derrida do not take into account: *Something* happens with the archive. It is not just that data create or contribute to an archive but that these data are taken, extracted, repackaged, and used by social media companies, for example. The individual archive, and user subjectivity in that sense, is thus destroyed and merged with other data to be rendered meaningful and ultimately valuable to the platforms' economic desires. In the remaining parts of this chapter, I am more interested in the second step of what I have termed double archivisation: namely with the question of what happens to our archives as we have created them online. They are not preserved and guarded by us. Instead, they are kept, enlarged, reshuffled, appropriated, and used for other purposes.

> [W]e can think of the activated electronic record as pulsating from one form to another, between introflection and reflection, and between retroflection and projection. The record is created (cathected), deconstructed (decathected), and reconstructed (recathected) on the archival net.
>
> (Ihanus 2007, 124)

The archive that consists of an individual user's data on Facebook, for example, is thus always in flux. Open to modification by both the user and Facebook alike.

The archaeological metaphor of psychoanalysis which Freud evoked and which is similarly mobilised by Derrida may be highly pertinent to the movement of data and the excavation and reusage of various user data on the part of social media companies, data brokers, and various other actors. The desire to *unearth* and assemble as much data, from diverse localities, about us points to the exploitation of our psyches. The unconscious is commodified (Krüger and Johanssen 2014). In that sense, user data are a manifestation of unconscious traces that have come to bear upon our online interactions. Content created by users is not a mere externalisation of memory or a manifestation of consciousness. It is a complex depiction of psychic forces that have given rise to specific Facebook posts, for example. I have discussed this in more detail previously (Johanssen 2016a). It is an act of translation of memories into data. One cannot help but feel a certain inherent violence in the instrumental reason with which data are subjected to analytics and algorithmic processes.

Perversion

I would argue that something else is at stake in the processes of data mining: a perverse double bind that simultaneously treasures users and destroys their data/them, cherishes them as subjects, and abuses them as objects. Danielle Knafo and Rocco Lo Bosco (2017) have recently written about perversion as a psychosocial phenomenon in the contemporary age. As a clinical concept, perversion has been conceptualised by different psychoanalysts. Knafo and Lo Bosco name six characteristics that unite different psychoanalytic discussions of perversion. Perversion is universal; it functions across a spectrum of varying degrees; it may relate to trauma and loss which is disavowed and masked through perversion; it may feature sadomasochistic dynamics in relationships; it features experiences of excitement, mastery, and illusion; and it is expressed differently by men and women (Knafo and Lo Bosco 2017, 52–54).

While perversion is often linked to sexual deviance, sexual fetishes, and sexualities that go against norms and laws, object relations psychoanalysis in particular has stressed that perversion takes place in relationships. The perverse subject, or pervert, regards the other in a relationship as an object. They are treated with hatred, cruelty, and humiliation (Bach 1994; Stein 2005). A perverse relationship resembles one of recognition and care while those attributes are in reality betrayed. 'Perversion as a mode of relatedness points to relations of seduction, domination, psychic bribery and guileful uses of "innocence," all in the service of exploiting the other' (Stein 2005, 780–781). A perverse relationship constitutes the creation of a singular world that shuts out reality and external influences. New rules for and in the relationship are created. Perversion is thus always an attempt to ignore, subvert, or actively go against the law (Lacan 2002). The pervert's object – whether it be a real person or a physical object – is (ab)used and manipulated while at the same time being idealised and cherished (Khan 1979; Celenza 2014). Perversion is an act of mastery which denies human fragility, dependency on others, and ultimately death (McDougall 1972, 1995; Ogden 1996). A similar dynamic is at play in the relationship between many contemporary digital media and their users. Under the guise of communication and connection, Facebook lures its users into a relationship that is in reality based on exploitation. Users are addressed as unique individuals who are encouraged to express themselves online through the various functions of the platforms and yet they consent (whether to their knowledge or not) to being sold as data profiles to advertisers. This double mechanism with which Facebook, and other platforms, binds users has perverse tendencies. The psychoanalyst Masut Khan argued that the pervert's object resides in a space between her/him and the other, between fantasy and reality. Therefore, it can be 'invented, manipulated, used and abused, ravaged and discarded, cherished and idealized, symbiotically identified with and deanimated all at once' (Khan 1979, 26). This in-between space at the intersections of user and social media platform symbolises the rupture between a sense of who we are and who we are in the eyes of Google, Facebook, Twitter, and others. We are loved and instrumentally used at the same time. Theorising this relationship as one of perversion opens up a unique perspective through which to analyse it. It places an emphasis on the particular dynamics between users and platforms. I explore this more over the course of this chapter.

Inside Data Mining Processes

When it comes to some of the actual workings of data mining, Helen Kennedy has described social media data mining as follows:

> Calculations of each person's marketing value are produced, based on behavioural and other forms of data tracking, and each individual is categorised as target or waste.
>
> (Kennedy, H. 2016, 47)

Data mining often operates with a binary logic, target, or waste, 1 or 0. Users are automatically classified into categories which are often constructed based on market research metrics and economic characteristics, or in the case of government and security agencies based on security characteristics. John Cheney-Lippold has discussed this in his wide-ranging book *We are Data* (2017) and coined the term 'measurable type'. Based on the data we produce, any data and not just social media data, we are turned into measurable type, digital subjects. Barocas and Selbst write that data mining is discriminatory. 'The very point of data mining is to provide a *rational* basis upon which to distinguish between individuals' (2014, 6, my emphasis).

It is not only that our data are sold, they are also used to determine *who we are* for Google, Facebook, and Twitter. Based on our usage of their services, patterns are established that lead to the automatic creation of profiles of who we are in the eyes of those tech giants. Based on our browsing habits coupled with other data, Google, for example, assigns the person who is searching a gender and age range. This is algorithm-based and done automatically. The algorithm has been coded to distinguish between patterns of behaviour that are either female or male (Cheney-Lippold 2017, 60). Of course, there are many instances where this automated guesswork is incorrect. The algorithm may refine itself through 'semi-supervised learning' (ibid., 60) over time.

> Measurable types are most often subterranean, protected and unavailable for critique, all while we unconsciously sway to undulating identifications. Every time we surf the web, we are profiled with measurable types by marketing and analytic companies [...]. We are assigned identities when we purchase a product, walk down a street monitored by CCTV cameras, or bring our phones with us on vacation to Italy.
>
> (Cheney-Lippold 2017, 66)

This intense monitoring and datafication of subjectivities leads to a practice of being talked about, of subjects being coded 'as if' they are someone or fit to pre-defined categories rather than being directly addressed or talked about, Cheney-Lippold has argued. Additionally, our digital mirror images of our online selves are never fixed and always in flux, depending on if our behaviour online changes. This, at times, fundamental discrepancy and contradiction between who we think we are and who Facebook, Google, or security agencies think who we are introduces an 'alien' (ibid., 193) dimension into the contemporary moment of data-driven subjectivities. While the usage of our data and the creation of profiles by others may still be based on what information we have input, in that sense it may be better described by the Freudian notion of the uncanny than by that of an alien; this break and rupture between what we represent of ourselves online and how we are automatically turned into bits, patterns, and categories that are then thrown back at us and may even determine what we see on Facebook and Google, for example, is worthy of exploring some more. Those dynamics could be thought about in clinical terms, like personality disorder, schizophrenia, or psychosis. All denote, to different degrees, a breakdown of the subject's ability to understand who they are and what is real and what is not. While psychoanalysis may be credited with first arguing that subjectivity itself is dynamic, evolving, and unfixed, the kind of datafied subjectivities that are constituted because of our usage of social media and the Internet more generally display a far greater dynamic of liquidity than our own subjectivities beyond the digital realm. This perverse act of cherishing us and offering us connectivity, information, and communication, only to be then turned against us in the form of data mining and profiling, almost amounts to a neurotic projection on the part of someone else (data brokers, social media platforms) towards us. *This is how and who you are!*

This coded insistence on knowing us and therefore enabling us to see what we really want to see (e.g., on the Facebook newsfeed or on Google) comes close to the insistence of a psychotic or schizophrenic subject with whom it is impossible to talk about shared reality or if the things they see are not, in fact, fantasies. Smith (2018) has called such mechanisms the 'affective capacity to autonomously act on/against the data referent' (Smith 2018, 12). If Google thinks that I am female based on my search terms – how do I convince them otherwise? Once our data are turned back at us it they have the power to affect us in strong manners which are difficult to control and close to impossible to alter. There is thus a deep sense of alienation between users, their data, and how that data are turned into something unknowable and entirely new (Krüger and Johanssen 2014; Bucher 2016; Johanssen 2016a).

This sense of the unknown can be illuminated through psychoanalysis. How are our data mined? What happens to them? How are they used and for what purposes? Users know relatively little about such questions.

The Return of the Unknown: Data Talk Back

The following example can illustrate what I mean by the perverse relationship between users and contemporary digital media in more detail.

On 10 December 2017, the official Netflix US Twitter account posted the following tweet: 'To the 53 people who've watched A Christmas Prince every day for the past 18 days: Who hurt you?' (Netflix 2017, n. p.).

This statement is interesting on a number of levels. It is one rare example of companies revealing something about their data mining practices, if even in vague terms. It was not posted by an individual Twitter account or by a Netflix employee, for example, but was presented as a sort of disembodied voice that spoke for Netflix through its official account. It is even technically possible, if unlikely, that the tweet was composed by a bot. There is an uncanny quality about the tweet that is intensified when we look at its actual content. On a superficial level, the tweet reveals something that most Netflix users probably knew already. Netflix keeps track of user data, viewing figures, how often a particular user may view a film, and so on. However, this tweet was about a specific film, *The Christmas Prince*, a typical Christmas romcom produced for Netflix, and it provides statistics about selected viewership figures. It demonstrates that Netflix monitors individual profiles (and tracks their data as account IDs) and how often and on what days they watch content. From the tweet alone, it is unclear what specific data are captured and stored. On the official Netflix blog, some more information is given:

> Our system needs to know each member's entire viewing history for as long as they are subscribed. This data feeds the recommendation algorithms so that a member can find a title for whatever mood they're in. It also feeds the 'recent titles you've watched' row in the UI.
> (Netflix Tech Blog 2015, n. p.)

Searches, ratings, geolocation data, device information, time of the day and week a show is watched, and when a show is paused or aborted are also tracked. On its blog, Netflix reveals a tiny amount of what its algorithm is about (Finn 2017, 92). Viewers are likely aware of this, because the Netflix recommendation algorithm is a distinctive feature of the service. The tweet goes further than merely disclosing anonymised user data about a Netflix show. It *directly* addresses the group of people who are disclosed ('To the 53 people') and shames them with a short, added sentence which is meant to be tongue-in-cheek and funny: 'Who hurt you?' It is implied that this form of binge-watching is disproportionate and may be used by those viewers as a kind of working through of past relationships or broken hearts. This tweet is shaming and exposes viewers, who may recognise themselves in this description, for humour and attention purposes on Twitter.

Cheney-Lippold has argued that there is always an unquantifiable dimension added to the surveillance and data mining practices we are subjected to. This 'else' (2017, 24) may be felt or somewhat known by us, but we can never fully know what it is or who is watching us or doing what with our data at any given time. 'We can't really understand how we're talked about. We can't really experience, directly and knowingly what our algorithmic identities are. But they are there regardless, and their epistemic corruption alerts us to their presence' (ibid., 25). It is in such moments that we can experience them. The data talk back to us. This makes for an eerie and affective experience on the part of audiences. There is an affective quality to the data which are unknown and which seldom come to re-present itself to users. The *Christmas Prince* tweet is one example where they come back to haunt the users. Through the tweet, Netflix is presented as a powerful, all-knowing monolith, a kind of human-machine symbiosis, a humachine (Poster 2006, 34) which 'needs to know' its members 'entire viewing histories' in order for the algorithm to work properly. Minute data mining is presented here as a mandatory part of the service. These features are strongly worded and suggest a greedy, oral, accumulative machine that needs to be fed with and binge on ever more user data and shows in order to be satisfied. This is in line with the mystical quality attributed to the Netflix algorithm and the 36-page manual given to human taggers, who tag films and series based on complex schemata (Finn 2017, 93). While the question 'Who hurt you?' denotes a funny joke on the surface, it may speak to a desire common amongst many services and platforms which depend on data mining: Ideally, Netflix would indeed like to know who hurt the viewers of *The Christmas Prince* so that the algorithm can be fine-tuned and fed with more individual data about their desires, relationships, and heartaches.

> For the average Netflix subscriber, this also means we are no longer identified according to metrics we might choose ourselves (e.g., what we elect to share on a consumer survey) but according to a set of behavioral choices whose consequences are largely unknown. You might claim you love romantic comedies, but how much value does Netflix attribute to that statement if you watch The Matrix ten times in a summer? And how much value does Netflix ascribe to it if the new show Netflix needs to market is House of Cards? Who measures "happiness"? The same systems that quantify everything else.
> (Finn 2017, 109)

While such data may be collected, viewers did not expect to be confronted with them on social media. 'I don't need your judgment, Netflix!', one responds to the tweet. 'raise your hand if you've ever felt personally victimized by @netflix', another writes in the same thread. The tweet by Netflix is perhaps so powerful, because it works in an Althusserian manner by interpellating some specific viewers without distinctly addressing them as subjects. It is a message that clearly will find its addressee. The 53 viewers who watched the film every day for 18 days are able to recognise themselves from the tweet, and other Netflix viewers know that their viewing data are similarly collected. 'Hey, you there! We know what you have been watching'. I argue that there is a similar perverse dynamic to the social media – users dynamic discussed earlier laid bare in the Netflix tweet. Perhaps typical for Twitter, the majority of the responses added witty and funny comments that demonstrate a clear understanding of the Netflix tweet. For example,

USER A: Can you tell me who else has watched all 300 episodes of Greys [sic] Anatomy 5 times through? I'm looking for a husband.

USER B: I believe people need to relax. Have a sense of humor. They didn't put any names out there. @netflix, feel free to call me out if I watch a show too many times ... I may need it. haha! Carry on ...

USER C: netflix, how many hours have i watched the office in total?

(Netflix 2017, n. p.)

It may be that the majority of Netflix customers or Twitter users are not bothered by such a tweet. There are, however, some tweets which were more critical in nature:

USER D: This tweet raises a lot of important questions about Netflix policys [sic]. Who wrote this tweet? Can low level employees access private data? For whom is it possible to access data from specific users? What are the consequenses [sic] for employees misusing or accessing data they shouldn't?

USER E: cuz @netflix collects data on paying users; their official tweet demonstrates that they'll use that data to ridicule specific customers publicly; and that @netflix doesn't respect their larger customer base's concerns about other ways @netflix might misuse private data.

USER F: We all realize that folks at Netflix can access our viewing habits. Nothing is truly private on the internet. We get that this data is valuable and you're going to profit from it in lots of ways. I guess we held out this hope you won't publicly mock us. Our mistake.

USER G: Haven't seen this movie myself, but wtf Netflix? You do realize you have viewers who are autistic or who have OCD (or maybe

something else affecting them) that watch things repeatedly/compul-
sively. Way to shame, Netflix.
USER H: This is creepy as hell.

(Netflix 2017, n. p.)

These tweets demonstrate a sense of unease about Netflix's revelations.
Netflix has disclosed statistical information but the wider contexts sur-
rounding that information remained in the dark. Users expressed frus-
tration that they were being made fun of online. It is also unclear what
else Netflix might do with such data and how it may feed into the algorithm. Perhaps it might recommend similar romcoms; perhaps it might
also recommend self-help programmes or documentaries about dating,
therapy, or psychoanalysis? The interpretation by Netflix that those who
watched the film repeatedly were necessarily 'hurt' potentially results in
them being hurt by being shamed online. There is no option for them
to correct this judgment. Perhaps other motives played a role in the re-
peated viewing; perhaps the people were *happy* rather than hurt when
they streamed the film. Netflix has not responded to most of the thousands of comments to its tweet. One rare dialogue with a female user
looked as follows:

USER I: Why are you calling people out like that Netflix
NETFLIX: I just want to make sure you're okay
USER I: You're not my mom
NETFLIX: Ok sweetie

(Netflix 2017, n. p.)

Whoever composed those lines demonstrated a sexist and patronising
language. Netflix, or rather one employee, was worried about the users who watched *The Christmas Prince* and wanted to make sure they
are okay, or so it was said. This is akin to the pervert who has humili-
ated their partner publicly, only to then hug them and assure them they
wanted to make sure they were okay afterwards. Intrusion and humiliation are masked as care and love – or perhaps even meant/understood as
care and love. The difference between what the workers at Netflix and
how the users may think of such sentences is oblivious to the former. To
Netflix, composing such a Tweet is an act of care. To the rest of us, it
is an act of perverse care. There is a sense of affective disturbance here
that leaves audiences puzzled, hurt, and angry at how their data have
resurfaced and was used to speak back for cheap laughs on social media.
It also reinforces the experience for users of having little control over
what happens to their data. The tweets which reply to Netflix may thus
be seen as opportunities for discharging the affective unease that the users may have felt upon reading the tweet. The powerful dominance over

user data that can be transformed into any narrative of who users are that was articulated by Netflix may have resulted in a sense of affective unpleasure (Freud 1981e,f) for many users. The affective dimensions of powerlessness and that the users are somewhat complicit by using Netflix were discharged in the aforementioned tweets through criticising Netflix. The users dissociated themselves from Netflix and the affective feelings of not knowing, not fully understanding what happens to their data. As one user tweeted in reply to Netflix, 'I guess I don't like being reminded of how much data is out there about me'. The responses may thus only superficially have been about a critique of the shaming and mocking qualities of the tweet. They also articulate feelings of unease and perhaps even a diffuse sense of anxiety that are tied to the fact that users have, in this instance, suddenly been made aware of the fact that their user data are mined and can be used to make all sorts of interpretations based on their viewing habits. This may be something they rather not think about too much. The user tweets are an outlet for diffuse feelings of unease and of the unknown in relation to what happens to our data. Elsewhere, I have argued that there may be a 'kind of awareness' (Johanssen 2016a, 12) by users of the behind the scenes of digital media services, like Facebook and Netflix, but that this may be unconscious or denied by most users. It only re-emerges in instances where data are suddenly affecting us in a different manner. A type of affective knowledge has resurfaced and re-attached itself to the specific *idea* (in the Freudian sense, see Chapter 1) that Netflix tracks users' viewing habits. I further focus on this dichotomy between the subject who contributes their data to services and the subject who is in turn *created* by those services based on their data in the next section.

Dis/Individualising Users

Antoinette Rouvroy (2013) has argued that processes of data mining and algorithm-based profiling ignore the embodied subjectivity behind a user's data and instead construct a dichotomy between them and a statistical subject. For corporations and governments alike, 'the subjective singularities of individuals, their personal psychological motivations or intentions do not matter' (Rouvroy 2013, 157). Rouvroy is clearly writing from a Foucauldian standpoint here, but I would argue that such phenomena are both aimed at disindividualising and individualising at the same time. This is linked to the logic of perversion and how it articulates itself in relationalities. The perverse relationship is at once structured by dehumanisation and humanisation. Otto Kernberg (1995) has characterised perversion as a relationship consisting of complementary roles which manifest themselves in coercion which is masked as love over one subject by the other. The processes of data mining on social media are not only linked to commodification and the turning of user data into commodities; they are equally structured by feelings of care, love, community, and recognition on the part of social media companies. This relationship, which is structured along the axis of care/exploitation (Stein 2005), is created by social media through interface structures which interpellate and appeal to users' individual subjectivities. 'What is on your mind?', Facebook asks me. 'What is happening?', Twitter wishes to know. The more time we spend on those platforms and the more data we generate, the more are we rewarded through the inherent interface features of the platforms. At the end of 2017, Facebook sent me a celebratory message: 'Jacob, you've made 20 friends on Facebook this year! Thank you for making the world a bit closer. We think this is something to celebrate!'. A few months later, I received the following: 'Jacob, your friends have liked your posts 6,000 times! We're glad you're sharing your life with the people you care about on Facebook'. Another time, I was alerted to which friends had been responding the most to my shared content in a week. Such messages, distinctly aimed at myself as an *individual* subject who is in (data) relations with other users, denote a happy feeling of an affective community on the platform. They address me in positive ways and value my existence on Facebook. They do not say who else has been viewing part of my data and how much money Facebook has made from my data being sold for targeted advertising. In contrast to Rouvroy, I would argue that such messages are examples of the distinctly *individualising* features of Facebook that exist to enable communication on the platform and to express that users are valued as unique personalities. Personally, I cannot help but feel a sense of appreciation and acknowledgement by Facebook for using it. I felt like a truly social being who was popular and loved by others. A fundamental aspect of any human being's existence. The more you share, the more recognition is potentially awarded to you by social media platforms in the form of likes, shares, followers, and visibility. *The Globe and Mail* wrote in this context about Instagram, that it is

> common knowledge in the industry that Instagram exploits this craving by strategically withholding 'likes' from certain users. If the photo-sharing app decides you need to use the service more often, it'll show only a fraction of the likes you've received on a given post at first, hoping you'll be disappointed with your haul and check back again in a minute or two.
>
> (Andrew-Gee 2018, n. p.)

This withholding-reward dynamic is symptomatic of a perverse, sadomasochistic relationship where both partners complement each other in their (un)conscious desires for power and control, punishment, withdrawal, withholding, and reward.

Yet, at the same time, and I agree with Rouvroy here, such messages and features mask the dehumanisation that takes place once data are being mined. 'Perversion as a mode of relatedness points to relations of seduction, domination, psychic bribery and guileful uses of "innocence", all in the service of exploiting the other' (Stein 2005, 780–781). The sorting mechanisms that are at play in data mining processes, the differentiation between 'target or waste' (Kennedy, H. 2016, 47), the categorisation and valuation of users are deeply dehumanising practices. They are masked as innocence by social media companies and other services, and it is argued that they contribute to a better user experience, to more functionality, and so on.

Related to this is persuasive technology (Fogg 2003) which has become ever more important for social media platforms and other digital services of the contemporary. Such modes of operating and thinking about the relationship between technology and subjectivity are often behaviourist and simplistic. It is hoped that users can be *made* to do things through the design of software. Such modes of persuasion show themselves, for example, in Netflix's automated playing of the next episode after one has finished, or its automatic playing of a film after I have selected it long enough, but not confirmed the selection yet. Amazon tells me what other items were bought that are similar to mine in the hope that I may make an impulsive purchase of one or more of them. All those features exist in order to generate more data, more purchases, more time spent and, ultimately, more profit. A desire is implicit here that is aimed at the future. It is aimed at prolonging the psychic investment and positive cathexis users place in those services. They need to be hooked. In *Hooked: How to Build Habit-Forming Platforms*, the self-proclaimed 'behavioural designer' Nir Eyal (2014) puts it this way 'Habit-forming technologies leverage the user's past behavior to initiate an external trigger in the future' (Eyal 2014, 85). He proposes the 'hook model', which can be used, for example, when designing smartphone apps to get users hooked and returning to them: It consists of an internal or external trigger, an action, a variable reward, and an investment (2014, 10–11). Behaviour is triggered in the subject, for example, a push notification on my smartphone that I have a new Facebook friend request is followed by an action, logging onto Facebook; a reward for accepting the friend request, for example, Facebook congratulating me for it; and an investment, which means that I will return to Facebook in the future because potentially more friend requests, messages, and so on await. All of this is aimed at increasing my loyalty and maintaining my psychic investment in the platform. Those are inbuilt features that assume that all humans operate according to the same behaviourist principles. They are further examples of the negation of complexity and unconscious dynamics of human subjectivity on the part of the services, the individuals who have programmed them and the authors who write about them in popular books. But they are also aimed at controlling our behaviour through coded patterns that reward us like Pavlovian dogs. They assume that all subjects respond according to the same behaviourist logic. An individual sense of embodied subjectivity does not matter.

A further twist is added to this perhaps when we consider that media users themselves place a great amount of trust into the services that they use. We believe that targeted advertising, recommendation systems, or other automated mechanisms online enhance our lives – and perhaps to a degree they do. Through our actions we are complicit in the forms of dehumanisation we are subjected to.

> Dehumanization is no longer only what one human being does to another. Rather, it is what people do to themselves as mechanization and commodification move into them from the outside through the technical shaping of the social surround.
>
> (Knafo and Lo Bosco 2017, 23)

The fault thus does not only lie with the platforms in that sense. I cannot discuss this notion further here, but there is a user complicity at stake. Without the voluntary use of us, the platforms would not exist in the first place. In the next section, I wish to go beneath the surface of those practices of data mining in order to examine their underlying logic.

The Logic of the Algorithm

Time to step back a little at this point. Big data refers to much bigger developments that go beyond a focus on data mining and the like. It is part of, or perhaps symptomatic of, informational capitalism (Fuchs 2008) whereby information and information-based work has acquired a strong foothold within neo-liberal economies. I partly referred to this in Chapter 4.

A number of scholars, for instance Finn (2017) and Golumbia (2009), have argued that the underlying principle of not only technical but also cultural processes of any form today is *computation*. This applies to big data as it does to other phenomena. Computation not only acts as a referent to describe the functional processes of computing and technologies that make use of it but has also come to dominate sociocultural spheres as a kind of heuristic script. Above all, computation refers to rational calculation and *calculability* as a possibility. According to Golumbia, rational calculation 'might account for every part of the material world' today (Golumbia 2009, 1). Everything and everyone can be calculated and turned into complex equations. Computation becomes at once rhetoric and ideology as well as a *modus operandi* for social life. This is perhaps epitomised by the function of the algorithm. An algorithm can be crudely defined as a method for solving a problem (Finn 2017, 18).

According to Google, 'algorithms are the computer processes and formulas that take your questions and turn them into answers' (Google Canada n. d., n. p.). From a computer science perspective, algorithms are clearly defined guidelines to solve problems. Algorithms thus consist of steps and instructions that need to be executed to turn an input (by a user) into an output. One of Facebook's algorithms, for example, is responsible for selecting and curating my Newsfeed in order to show content based on profiles and pages that I have engaged with previously. The function of that algorithm is to provide orientation and manage/filter the amount of information that I see on the Newsfeed so that I am not overwhelmed by it. Algorithms are notoriously hidden, opaque, and complex. They 'remain outside our grasp, and they are designed to be' (Gillespie 2014, 192). They lie in the unconscious of many digital systems today. However, like any other computer-based process, they function according to a specific logic. It rests on the binary code that structures computational systems.

Rather than looking at the algorithm as a complex set of cultural-computational dimensions, I am interested in thinking about it psychosocially. Namely, to ask the question of how the social and the psyche are always already giving rise to, are within, as well as beyond the algorithm and algorithmic processes. What can a psychoanalytic-psychosocial perspective on algorithms and data mining offer?

Both Finn (2017) and Golumbia (2009) have linked the algorithm to the notion of instrumental reason (Horkheimer 1974). Algorithms, for example, in the form of recommender systems on Netflix or Amazon, friend suggestions on Facebook, automatic customer service emails from Amazon, suggest that those who have programmed them believe that they are capable of knowing better than humans and that they are capable of knowing better than us what we want. 'From the beginning, then, algorithms have encoded a particular kind of abstraction, the *abstraction of the desire for an answer*' (Finn 2017, 25, italics in original), as Finn notes. This desire for an answer is abstracted into calculability. Whatever the desire is, algorithms will have or can produce the answer. The object-cause of desire is identified by the algorithm and becomes the algorithm itself in our contemporary culture. As Finn notes, the underlying principles of computation are universal across its domain. With it comes a belief that 'algorithms embody and reproduce the mathematical substrate of reality in culturally readable ways' (ibid., 34). This instrumental reason makes algorithms so powerful. They articulate, similar to a kind of algorithmic superego, that they know what is best for us, and we believe them:

> There is a seductive quality to algorithmic models of digital culture even when they are only partially successful because they order the known universe. You listen to a streaming music station that *almost*

gets it right, telling yourself that these songs, not quite the right ones, are perfect for this moment because a magical algorithm se-lected them.

(Finn 2017, 50, italics in original)

The algorithm thus promises to know us better than we can ever hope to do. In so far as algorithms already make choices for us, or at least recom-mend particular things (e.g., shows on Netflix) for us, they have already dehumanised us because we cannot directly intervene or see how those choices have been made. Those mechanisms are conducted on a mass scale to, for example, all Netflix users, but they are always individual-ised and individualising at the same time because they target individual profiles. The promise of artificial intelligence only intensifies the poten-tial powers of algorithms.

There is something else present here: a pathological emphasis of ra-tionality. The logic of algorithms suggests that those who develop them have internalised a sense of subjectivity that is governed by rational-ity, or at least can be improved through rationality. This comes to be embodied in the algorithm. The relationality between data mining and algorithms is at once marked by a negation of unconscious and affec-tive processes of subjects as well as a desire to tap into the unconscious and to anticipate what users have repressed, negated, or would want in order to make choices on behalf of them. I will untangle this contra-dictory structure now. I have argued elsewhere (Johanssen 2013, 2014) that certain strands within posthumanism are effectively negating the unconscious and wish to do away with psychoanalysis. They advocate an instrumental sense of embodied subjectivity which can be altered and enhanced through technology, such as chip implants to 'rebalance' a brain suffering from depression, for example. This (allegedly) makes humans more durable, efficient, and productive. Bodies are enhanced through technology. A similar argument can be made with regard to the role of the algorithm, as well as artificial intelligence, today. There seems to be a general culture of rationalism which is about advocat-ing technology in order to enhance humanity. David Golumbia makes a provocative, and perhaps too generalising and pathologising, statement, which is nonetheless useful in this context:

The computer is, in some sense, sexually satisfying to the adolescent who already feels estranged from human social relations; the fact of its ultimately unsatisfactory nature powers the engineer's exaltation of the computer as the human itself: in a familiar psychoanalytic operation, the engineer introjects the inadequate hated/loved object, both blaming it for its failure and identifying with it in a profound way. Experiencing mastery over the computer, the individual also comes to see him/herself as a computer, in part so as to exercise computational mastery over others in the social world: 'you are all just machines anyway,' his/her unconscious says, 'why don't you all bend to my will?' The thought is accompanied with its opposite: 'I am a machine and can't provide what other humans want; my only recourse is to submit more and more to the abstract, absolute master I see elsewhere in the world.'

(Golumbia 2009, 187)

Be that as it may. The point is that algorithms and interfaces are constructed by humans, who themselves have internalised a particular philosophy of what it means to be a subject. This philosophy is characterised by rationalism, not by psychoanalysis. Algorithms embody a desire, as Finn has called it, for 'effective computability' (2017, 49) of humans and the way they express themselves online. Algorithms express a desire for universal knowledge, which is readily responded to by us because they promise to order the overload of information we are confronted with. I cannot possibly browse through all of Netflix's programmes, so the algorithm conveniently recommends some to me based on what I have previously watched. It promises to know more about myself than I can possibly know. How would I know that I may like those suggested programmes without knowing if their existence? The algorithm tells me so because it is a sophisticated technical mechanism that is always right, or so I might think to myself. Algorithms perfectly tap into the human desire for universal knowledge, both on the part of its producers and on the part of its users, Finn argues. However, an algorithm also expresses a dominance over its users. In the case of Netflix, for example, I am not able to refine the algorithm's parameters myself. It is the algorithm that, while being influenced by, also dominates over my subjectivity. Its implicit epistemology is that human decision-making can be optimised through influencing it through the algorithm. Such instrumentality effectively denies the complexity of psychoanalytic subjectivity and negates unconscious and affective processes that shape human decision-making. The oft-cited article by *Wired* editor Chris Anderson in which he proclaimed the end of theory is a case in point.

> Out with every theory of human behavior, from linguistics to sociology. Forget taxonomy, ontology, and psychology. Who knows why people do what they do? The point is they do it, and we can track and measure it with unprecedented fidelity. With enough data, the numbers speak for themselves.
>
> (Anderson 2008, n. p.)

This speaks to the dehumanising aspects of big data and algorithms which I have referred to earlier in the chapter. Not only does the algorithm remove part of my agency when I use Netflix or Facebook, for example, but it also amasses data about myself and relates it to millions of other users, ignoring the individual motives, goals, and desires *behind* that data. Rouvroy (2013) has called such phenomena, and how they are framed by companies, 'data behaviourism' that let the data speak for themselves. As I have discussed earlier, they amount to a schizophrenic division between 'data subject' and 'real subject'. Such narratives suggest a victory of reason over everything else that might intervene (emotion, affect, and irrationality).

In his book *Everybody Lies*, Seth Stephens-Davidowitz (2017), a former Google data scientist, has analysed Google search terms which are entered by millions. Following the big data logic, he argues that what people google can essentially reveal information about them which they would never share with anyone else:

> Some of this data will include information that would otherwise never be admitted to anybody. If we aggregate it all, keep it anonymous to make sure we never know about the fears, desires, and behaviors of any specific individuals, and add some data science, we start to get a new look at human beings—their behaviors, their desires, their natures.
>
> (Stephens-Davidowitz 2017, 19)

His book, intended for a mass audience, makes the argument that you can see patterns in Google searches tied to specific events, gender, or class categories. For example, he argues that Google searches for 'anxiety' and related keywords are more common in rural areas than in the city. The fundamental flaw of the argument here is of course that one cannot assume that Google searches really reflect reality or that they are necessarily representative of it. Leaving the simplicity of the argument aside, the book is interesting because it, like so many other popular books about big data, reveals the author's belief and desire to tap into domains of subjectivity that are not necessarily fully known by the subjects themselves, yet alone shared with anyone but the (assumed) anonymity of Google. Indeed, Stephens-Davidowitz goes as far as to say that 'Data science makes many parts of Freud falsifiable - it puts many of this famous theories to the test' (2017, 38). He claims that him analysing misspellings on search engines revealed that Freudian slips did not reveal unconscious, sexual desires because such typos were not more common than other, non-sexual ones. However, this claim blatantly ignores that the notion of the Freudian slip is primarily a verbal slip of the tongue, not a written one. In relation to this, Stephens-Davidowitz argues that big data, and the analysis of millions of search terms is one example, offers data that did not exist before the Internet. Big data is also 'honest' (ibid., 44) because it 'allows us to finally see what people really want and really do, not what they say they want and say they do' (ibid., 44). Third, because big data consists of multiple, refined data sets, data scientists and data owners (e.g., social media companies) are able to zoom in and compare very specific data sets. These claims are undoubtedly exaggerated. They reveal the hype with which big data is regarded by many commentators and corporations, but they also reveal another aspect: a belief that the data we share and leave behind online are mirrors of our true subjectivities and that in some instances they may even reveal things we or others do not yet know about ourselves (see Kennedy, H. 2016, 2 for a related example). Our true selves are thus in our data and not necessarily beyond them. This further dehumanises our online representations because an assumption is made that they are necessarily real and at times even more authentic than in the realm beyond the Internet. Such narratives are myths. They articulate a strong rationality that hinges on the computability of the human and their desires. Contexts and complexities are negated.

Datafying the Future

Such narratives also go beyond mere data mining but aim at predicting and anticipating what might follow from entering certain search terms on Google, or posting about certain things on social media. They go beyond creating data profiles in an afterward manner, following from and based on the data that have been mined, but are oriented towards the future. Related to this, the area of predictive analytics within informatics refers to computational models and code that are able to predict outcomes based on existing data. For example, Google data engineers (wrongly) argued that they would be able to predict flu epidemics by tracking emerging searches on flu symptoms (Butler 2013). This focus on the future adds another layer to my discussion of big data. Google's chairman Eric Schmidt told the *Wall Street Journal* in 2010 'I actually think most people don't want Google to answer their questions. They want Google to tell them what they should be doing next' (Schmidt 2010, n.p. cited in Finn 2017, 66). Such predictions are based on patterns across large data sets. They bring data mining to the next level in so far as it is no longer reactive and responds to data, but that it uses data to steer users into specific directions, for example. This is similar to the famous data analytics company Cambridge Analytica which played a part in Donald Trump's United States presidential election and the Brexit vote in the United Kingdom. It described its goal as 'To deliver Data-Driven Behavioral Change by understanding what motivates the individual and engaging with target audiences in ways that move them to action' (Cambridge Analytica n.d., n.p.).

CA Political will equip you with the data and insights necessary to drive your voters to the polls and win your campaign. We offer a proven combination of predictive analytics, behavioral sciences, and data-driven ad tech.

With up to 5,000 data points on over 230 million American voters, we build your custom target audience, then use this crucial information to engage, persuade, and motivate them to act.

(Cambridge Analytica n.d. n.p.)

A clear emphasis is placed on the future here. The future can be envisaged and in fact created by manipulating users thanks to data analytics. The mentioning of behaviourism, which is a simplistic and oppressive philosophy of the human mind, is rather telling in this context. It lays bare the kind of explicit understanding of subjectivity and agency that the employees of Cambridge Analytica have and according to which they act. This can be seen in relation to wider cultural narratives in the West fuelled by reality television and self-help literature which advocate that individuals look towards the future and ignore their past (Johanssen 2012, 2014).

Data mining is not just about capturing online output but about managing and influencing that output. This marks a state of dominance over users.

Alison Hearn (2017) has argued that mass datafication, targeting, and predictive analytics give rise to a, what she calls, 'speculative subject' (2017, 73). A subject, whose data are not only constantly anticipated and in flux but who becomes anticipatory and malleable herself: 'Anticipation, then, becomes a generalized affective condition that gives rise to modes of subjectivity' (2017, 73). The 'speculative self's value is predicated entirely on externally generated predictions about our future potential "optimization"' (2017, 74). Such narratives symbolise a subject whose self-expression online and in relation to digital devises, such as smartphones, has no future that she can fully control. To a large degree, how that future is going to look like is in the hands of automated data mining processes. This suggests that we have surrendered in our perverse relationships with those who own our data and that we have asked them to determine who and what we might become online. This leads to a state of a 'disavowal of the present in the interest of prediction' (Halpern 2014, 47).

Conclusion

This chapter presented a psychosocial approach to big data and data mining in order to explore those phenomena from a perspective that takes account of their social and individual dimensions. Through data mining social media companies believe that they are able to fully capture subjectivities and turn them into commodifiable data sets. In that sense, a subject is made to be mirrored in the various data sets they have created online and reassembled by social media companies, data brokers, and other stakeholders. This is done over and over on a large scale and gives rise to 'big data': large data sets that are made up of thousands of different data points. Individual, subjectively created data thus constitutes the elements of big data and is at the same disavowed through it being bundled together with vast amounts of other data such as meta-data or data that the subject may have left involuntarily. Social media are dependent on individuals who create and use data, but a real meaning and economic asset is only acquired through an accumulation into large data sets. Individual subjectivities and how they are expressed online thus become embraced and disavowed by social media companies at the same time. The subject is lured into producing ever more data and turned into a commodified entity that is surveilled and used. Subjects are thus affecting their data creation, voluntary and involuntary, and are likewise affected by data mining processes which often result in their data being merged with other data, sold and bought. Subjects have little knowledge and power over their data online, and once confronted with the knowledge that services such as Netflix have about them may respond with a sense of humour and understanding but also more affectively ambiguous states such as unease, anxiety, uncertainty, and unpleasure. Those latter states are felt bodily as a diffuse awareness and re-attach themselves to specific ideas, as in the case of the Netflix tweet about the *Christmas Prince*, for example. The level of complicity in the perverse relationship between users and data mining services may be more affectively felt than consciously known and reflected on.

Matthew Flisfeder, drawing on Lacan and Žižek, has argued that contemporary algorithmic media operate according to a logic of denying and withholding.

> But it is perhaps in this way that algorithmic logic is built, not upon giving us what we seem to desire, but by constantly *denying* us this. It has learned the practice of keeping us *dis*-satisfied, rather than satisfying our desire. That is to say, what if the algorithm learns, not to give us immediately the object of our desire – the thing we (think) we want – but instead prevents us from obtaining the object – keeps it constantly at a distance?
>
> (Flisfeder 2018, 473)

As I have argued in this chapter, I see contemporary algorithmic processes and how they articulate themselves in data mining as being about dynamics of withholding and rewarding. We are always provided with some satisfaction when using social media, for example; otherwise we would not be coming back. This presents the ideological lure facilitated by algorithms that we have ourselves invested positive psychic energy into. The relationship between us as subjects and the services and platforms which mine/use our data is complicated and symbiotic.

Metaphorically speaking, there is perhaps some resemblance of the mother-baby dyad of the skin ego (Anzieu 2016). We have become affectively embedded in a relationship which is structured by a degree of perversion. It is only in moments of glitches, ruptures, or the return of data, as I discussed by drawing on the Netflix tweet, that we are reminded of knowledge which had been present in us as affective states. Going back to the work of Didier Anzieu (2016), who I discussed in previous chapters, we can conceptualise the relation between users and social media such as Facebook as symbiotic and dependent, just like the skin ego. The skin ego of the Facebook – user dynamic as an interface is highly permeable and leaks and absorbs data from other services and third parties. This often happens unbeknownst to the users. The baby, being virtually and physically, contained in the skin ego envelope is a vulnerable being. She is dependent on the mother and other people for care, safety, and love. A sense of trust is felt and embodied between the two, rather than consciously known by the baby. While users have of course voluntarily agreed to their relationship with Facebook, Netflix, and other similar platforms, there is a sense of dependency and vulnerability for them. They know little about how and for what purposes their data are used. The sense of vulnerability is to a degree managed/contained by algorithmic platforms through offering interfaces that are easy, useful, and rewarding to users, while a different logic operates beneath the surface. There is thus a kind of affective imbalance between how the users perceive the relation to Facebook and how Facebook perceives its relation to users. While users are, so it appears, contained by Facebook in so far as they are given a platform that they can use, where rules are laid down and enforced (Balick 2014; Johanssen 2018), beneath the surface, this containment is broken and users are denied mastery over their data and their destiny. Users are subjected to Eros, a life-affirming drive, and to the death drive at the same time by Facebook, Netflix, and others through enabling communication and sociality as well as destruction and reshaping of their online subjectivities through data mining. Their data are situated in a strange borderline, netherworld where they have agency over them and are simultaneously denied it. Writing about a borderline patient, whose body 'has no owner' (Anzieu 2016, 231), Anzieu notes how the body floats between themselves and others, being abused and appropriated by others:

> The patient is nothing but a body of need, and that need is abused. The result: the body functions in a way that they cannot appropriate as theirs: as a possible object of knowledge or intense pleasure; the distinction between what is mine and what comes from others has not been acquired; there is nothing but a lament, not even accusations levelled at a cause, culprit or persecutor.
>
> (Anzieu 2016, 232)

There is some analogy to the status of users who are subject to data mining here. Users are essentially vulnerable because they have little control over what happens to their data. They cannot fully appropriate their data but instead it belongs to them and Facebook in a strange borderline space where they are valued and devalued at once. Hearn's (2017) notion of the anticipating self is helpful in this context because it suggests a state of subjectivity that is marked by an affective sense of uncertainty, unease, and unpleasure with regard to the control one has over their data online and how that data might be used in the future. The fact that we, as anticipating selves, see ourselves confronted with machinic processes structured by algorithms may further complicate a sense of agency on our parts. In *Archive Fever*, Jacques Derrida asks the question,

> Is the psychic apparatus *better represented* or is it *affected differently* by all the technical mechanisms for archivization and for reproduction, for prostheses of so-called live memory, for simulacrums of living things which already are, and will increasingly be, more refined, complicated, powerful than the 'mystic pad' (microcomputing, electronization, computerization, etc.)?
>
> (Derrida 1995, 16, italics in original)

Have technology and digital media in particular helped us to store and retrieve our memories and thoughts? Or, have our subjectivities been so fundamentally altered by digital media that they have radically changed?

If so much of the content we produce online and of other data that are gathered along the way can be used in ways we may anticipate but do not know about, subjectivities in relation to the digital, then, are characterised by a sense of paranoia and uncertainty. More transparency of how data are used could potentially ease such affective impressions. I return to the notion of the anticipating self in the book's Conclusion.

Conclusion

This book's aim has been to show how media audience research in particular and digital media research more generally can benefit from psychoanalysis in terms of theoretical and methodological input.

I have shown that a psychosocial approach to digital media audiences enables complex and ambivalent analyses to emerge. Rather than resorting to the rationalistic and dualistic (passive vs. active) ideas of the media user that are still often present in media research, I have offered a theorisation of the media user in different contexts that is marked by many complex layers. Psychoanalysis is here understood as a mode of attention (Highmore 2007) that consists of specific epistemological and methodological angles. Jo Whitehouse-Hart (2014b) makes an important point when she argues that mainstream media studies which often focus 'on "pleasures", "uses" and "needs" must also acknowledge that the meaning of such terms is not transparent and that they mask complex emotional and affective processes' (ibid, 131). The terms 'watching', 'using', 'needs', and 'choices' have been used endlessly within media studies, mostly referring to rational or cognitive dimensions that lack complexity. Media use in general is more than just 'watching', 'viewing', 'doing', 'participating', 'using', 'communicating', 'affording', 'interacting'. All these labels denote something on the surface that has far deeper implications and dimensions. They are important but can be rendered more complex. As a paradigm, psychoanalysis can add new perspectives to media and communication studies which open up perspectives beyond the rational.

Chapters 2 and 3 featured discussions of *Embarrassing Bodies* viewers. Many of my interviewees said that *Embarrassing Bodies* was one of their favourite programmes, and I would suggest that there is a special connection that binds them to it. This connection is an indirect one that binds them to experiences related to their bodies that are invested with meaning in the viewing process, particularly through scenes with the doctors that offer explanations for any kind of medical condition. Furthermore, this connection complicates notions of media choice or how and why people select and choose to engage with particular media texts. It is the process of choosing and watching a programme that is overall characterised as an embodied-affective as well as cognitive-agentic one that enriches media studies audience research. The agency of the viewer and the choice to consume certain programmes are not simply of a cognitive nature that is structured by willpower, rationality, and clear thinking. The body as a whole – and this includes rationality but also exceeds it – has made a choice as it were. This kind of embodied viewing that I have suggested in this book goes beyond a Cartesian dualism that is implicit in many theoretical models or empirical works (that stress entertainment or voyeurism). It is not the mind that has decided to watch something so that the body may follow and be informed, aroused, shocked, pleased, or in any other way stimulated by it, but instead it is the body as a whole with its affective forces as well as its ability for reflexive judgment that is situated in front of the television screen. This body-in-tension was, I argue, also present in the narratives of the viewers. At times, they spoke very clearly about their viewing experiences and at times they were looking for words or lost for words when they described their affective responses. Furthermore, I looked at the interviewees' social media use in Chapter 3. Rather than regarding the interviewees' passiveness and silence in relation to the show on Twitter as conscious forms of disengagement or resistance, I argued that unconscious and affective inhibitions may have played a role in shaping their social media use.

Chapter 4 set up the case study in Chapter 5. Drawing on the digital labour paradigm as well as Hardt and Negri's use of affective labour, I argued that a closer engagement with the notion of affective labour on social media can add a level of complexity to those terms. I presented and analysed interview data from a research project with social media users with facial disfigurements. Similar to my study on *Embarrassing Bodies* audiences, I drew on the free associative interview method (Hollway and Jefferson 2012) that also paid attention to the interviewees' biographies. I was able to show how affective labour is a form of embodied use of social media that reflects the individuals' embodied subjectivities and also is about maintaining particular affective atmospheres on Twitter, Facebook, YouTube, or Instagram. I developed Freud's affect model so as to steer it slightly away from the sole focus on discharge. I supplemented my use of it with Lacan's notion of lack and Green's 'negative hallucination' to show how the particular interview narratives point to a type of digital labour which is about coming to terms with the self in relation to (real and imagined) others as well as wider aspects around agency.

Chapter 6 was more explorative than the other chapters and did not discuss interview data. It dealt with the term 'big data' and processes of data mining on social media and also Netflix. I paid particular attention to the role of the algorithm in such processes and examined its underlying logic through the prisms of dis/individualisation and perversion. Audiences today are, similar to a perverse relationship, cherished and valued while at the same time being reconstructed and turned into data which they have no control over. Given the revelations about Cambridge Analytica and Facebook's role in the UK EU referendum as well as the Trump campaign in 2016, such theoretical discussions are of even stronger relevance. I would like to use this concluding chapter to further think about the psychoanalytic notion of affect that I have put forward in this book in relation to digital media. I am also teasing out some common themes from the various chapters that speak to the book as a whole.

Further Thoughts on Affect and Digital Media

In drawing on Freud and Anzieu, I suggested in Chapter 1 that the very ability to relate to moving images is born in the relationality and affective communication between baby and mother/father/others (Cartwright 2008; Kavka 2009). Cartwright and Kavka only mention this idea *in passim* and I will further explore it here. It is of significance for media studies in so far as it can shed light on the fascination with and saturation of audio-visual based media texts and mediums in the world. Furthermore, it introduces a biographical dimension to media consumption. I will return to Freud's scene of the hungry baby from the *Project* that I discussed in Chapter 1. A baby is hungry and cries as a result in order to discharge the (unpleasurable) affective experience of being hungry. The discharge is only completed when the mother (or another caregiver) responds and offers her breast or the bottle. For Freud, this sequence of discharge is the first form of communication between the baby and an other. It is deeply relational because it is not only about the baby's crying but equally connected to the way that the m/other responds. It is thus the different segments and sequences of the whole scene that characterise the affective communication of m/other and baby. The baby's crying is of a bodily affective nature and that experience is stored in the baby's memory in the form of memory traces. Specifically it is stored as *moving images*.

The scene that Freud depicted is of significance on a number of levels. It describes one of the first experiences of affect for the subject and designates affect as the earliest form of social communication. It may be that one is so taken by subsequent affective experiences in response to media content because they unconsciously resonate with our earliest form of communication.

For Freud, there is a link in this case between (any) subsequent affective experience of being hungry and the baby's history. How the mother responded to the baby's cries and fed the baby is of significance. The scene acts as a kind of blueprint in shaping (but not determining) the baby and others' relationships, communications, and affective responses. In describing the scene, Freud thus made a link between affect, relationality, and a subject's biography. Affective responses that do not seem to have an origin or explanation that can be pinpointed or known (as many interviewees discussed) may thus be aroused because of (unconscious) memory traces that relate to past affective experiences. The scene is of further significance for media research because, as Freud said, the baby's memory traces consist of moving images (i.e., filmic sequences). Cartwright (2008) and Kavka (2009) argue that it is this earliest scene of communication that lays the basis for a subject's ability and ways to be affected by technologically produced, moving images. Communication *per se* is thus initially defined through affect and a kind of '*Ur- Erlebnis*', a primary experience that is stored in the form of moving images as mnemic traces. The subject's first experience with 'media content' is thus of her own making in terms of remembering and storing a scene like a film sequence.

Furthermore, in returning to the scene, I have conceptually explored the primary moment of relationality between mother and baby in order to discuss the relationality between viewer and *Embarrassing Bodies* that makes any viewing experience come into being. It is only because of the viewer – *Embarrassing Bodies* relationship that the viewer may be affected (in any sense) by the programme. Freud's work on affect, in particular the *Project*, helps us to think about the complex entanglements of affect, relationality, biography, and the process of watching and engaging with *Embarrassing Bodies*. What is additionally important is Freud's conceptualisation of affect as process. In his description of the scene in the *Project*, he highlighted its sequential and process-like nature, particularly with regard to affect. An affective experience is a process that consists of different stages and is itself embedded in wider psychic and social processes. An affective experience occurs in a certain time and space that the subject is situated in. This processual character of affect is, I argue, a key aspect of Freud's thinking that can be applied to analyses of television viewing and other forms of media use. Television viewing itself is a process that lasts for a certain amount of time (e.g., for the duration of an episode of *Embarrassing Bodies*). In turn, this process is partially characterised by the process of affect as well as other sequences. I will return to the notion of the viewing process and how it may relate to affect, the skin ego, and the more conscious elements (entertainment, voyeurism, education, comparison of bodies) throughout this chapter. But how is an affective experience felt? As discussed, there is space for more phenomenological modes of affective communication to be explored via Anzieu, particularly in the light of some of the interviewees' narratives about the programme. This process can be further underscored by drawing on the sensual, affective, virtual-material, embodied relationality of the baby in the skin envelope. Before returning to Anzieu, I will briefly dwell on Freud's affect theory in relation to media a little more.

The *Erlebnis* of Affect

A connection between a subject's psyche and technological media had already been emphasised by Freud himself in other writings besides the *Project* (1981g). He wrote of the psyche bearing similarities to the mystic writing pad that is essentially a medium (see Chapter 1). This relationship between the psyche and technology has been explored by a number of scholars (Derrida 1978, 1995; Hansen 2000, 2006; Elsaesser 2009; Halpern 2014). It is the work of Anzieu – and of Freud – that opens up space for conceptualising embodied modes of watching television and using the Internet that are not always of a rational nature and as I have argued in the previous chapters cannot always be fully captured by language when being asked about them in interviews.

As Hansen has remarked, 'An actual worldly machine capable of modeling [sic] the process of psychic production, the writing pad furnishes a metaphor not just for the [...] functioning of the mind but for the ontogenesis of the psyche itself' (Hansen 2000, 144). For Freud, then, the psyche is distinctly technological and technology likewise has a psychological quality as he illustrated with the example of the writing pad (Freud 1981g). This relates to my discussion of the scene from the *Project*; Freud already conceived of the psyche as a medium that is capable of storing and 'replaying' film-like sequences. If we hold on to this claim, what follows is that 'technology cannot simply be opposed to psyche' (ibid). Instead, Hansen maintains that media technology is 'an essential part of the very *movement that generates* psychic life' (ibid, my italics). The terms 'movement' and 'generates' point to, I argue, an essential – if not *the* essential – *modus operandi* of psychic life: affect. In Chapter 1, I defined the Freudian notion of affect by drawing on André Green as 'a movement awaiting a form' (Green 1999, 265). Affect designates a movement of the body in response. In our contemporary age of media saturation, not only is affect distinctly technological and machinic in its sequential, circuit-like ontology, but media in particular, reality/makeover television, social media, and many other forms, are distinctly affect triggering. *Embarrassing Bodies* embodies in its scripted sequences moments that produce affect in the viewer and allow for discharge. The use of social media similarly allows for moments of affectivity to occur, as I discussed.

For example, we see affectivity in the extreme close-ups of body parts during surgery sequences of *Embarrassing Bodies* and also those that show the patient after the successful treatment. The rawness and affective authenticity are pushed to a new level through those scenes. Affective experiences do occur suddenly in the viewing process but it is their *patterned* form of (re-)occurrence that resembles a machinic mechanism of the psyche. Interviewees told me that they would record the show and watch it every week. This repetition that is initiated through the conscious act of recording the show, as well repetitive affective experiences, puts the affect centre stage. It has no apparent relation to an ideational referent, as I discussed. Week by week, affects are 'lived out' (Green 1999, 280) and discharged in front of the television screen. For Freud, affect may be understood here as 'essentially a residue, aroused by repetition, a kind of memory of some experience [...], and it only indirectly refers to, or relies upon, external or fresh impressions' (Stein 1999, 131). This indirect relation could, I suggest, also be found in the data. It was a relation that was not spoken of by the interviewees as such but could be found as separate narratives in most interviews. It is thus not only the content *of Embarrassing Bodies* that results in affective experiences but the relation and intertwinement of content and viewers' life histories. *Embarrassing Bodies*' ability to generate psychic life can be found in its movements that are affect triggering. It can also be found in other characteristics that the interviewees spoke of that point to containment and compassion. These moments designate a heightened, excessive production of viewing experiences. It is the makeover genre that is marked by a particular type of *excess* that has the ability to affect the viewer bodily, or, as Jagodzinski puts it,

> The release of bodily fluids, a sure sign that the body is under stress, approaches a threshold experience, an *Erlebnis*, where the dividing line between sublimity and trauma can easily slip into an excess, an overload, like a drug overdose. What was once experienced as an ecstatic bodily state becomes a "bad trip".
>
> (Jagodzinski 2004, 55)

This quotation points to the generative power of media in their ways of affecting us and to generate, what Hansen calls, 'psychic life'. Jagodzinski's vivid description of the process-like and sequential nature of media reception mirrors some of the interviewee's narratives about their viewing experiences that I have quoted in the previous chapter. It is the shift in the viewer from an ecstatic to a different, visceral viewing experience that is marked by affect. These reactions take place as a result of the matrix of self-other. For Jagodzinski, this is the psychic impact that many different media have on us, be it watching a romantic comedy like *The Christmas Prince* on Netflix, attending a rock concert, reading horror fiction, using Twitter to raise awareness of facial disfigurement, or watching *Embarrassing Bodies*. As he writes, 'It is through their very *exaggeration*, in their excess, that such transference of emotionality succeeds. We want to see and hear something "larger than life" to make its impact *felt* on us' (ibid, 58, italics in the original).

I have illustrated moments that point to this 'larger than life' threshold experience, which Jagodzinski describes in Chapters 2 and 3. I would claim that his description is a little too vivid and poetic but he nonetheless has a point. The interviewees did feel – and this includes myself – an *Erlebnis* at times. This *Erlebnis* (which roughly translates as 'a lived experience' or 'a heightened form of experience') precisely lets them slip into a sort of excessive state (without necessarily releasing bodily fluids) that is characterised by an affective response. There are moments in their consumption of *Embarrassing Bodies* that result in a 'bad trip' experience for the interviewees in, for example, their being shocked, turning away, or being excited, or by something indicated as 'eurgh' in a deferred way during the interview. These moments of *something* 'being too much' are discharged by these responses and fade away and the viewing process returns to a more rational viewing mode again. The same goes for some of the experiences in using social media of the interviewees from Chapter 5. They spoke of unpleasurable experiences when affected by other users online but also narrated pleasurable experiences that come with their affective labour on social media.

Hansen (2000) defines the term *Erlebnis* in relation to contemporary media technology – by drawing on Walter Benjamin (1968) and Freud's *Project* text (1981a) – as a process that 'absorbs infelicitous or alien stimuli that can only be integrated into experience as something lived through rather than reflected on' (Hansen 2000, 237) in the first instance. In supplementing the Freudian model of affect with Jagodzinski's and Hansen's writings on the *Erlebnis* of media use, I am able to further set up a counter-argument against an implicit 'cognitive monopoly' (ibid, 238) which is often present in media studies. The term *Erlebnis* 'marks the irreducibility of life to language, of experience to meaning' (ibid, 239). Similar to Freud's affect model, *Erlebnis* 'is made to designate what is most fleeting and transitory – those shocks that impact us immediately and corporeally' (ibid, 239) and are not buffered or blocked by the protective shield and the skin envelope.

Waiting for Something to Happen

The other major theme in the data of the *Embarrassing Bodies* project was that of containment and I supplemented it with the theoretical notion of the skin ego. Jan Jagodzinski (2004, 2005) has developed a psychoanalytic approach to media that is mainly based on Jacques Lacan's work. In *Youth Fantasies* (2004), he also draws on Didier Anzieu's *Skin Ego* (2016). He reads Anzieu with Lacan when he writes that the

> skin-ego acts as both a protection as well as an organ of rupture that exposes the body to the affects of the Real — such as anxiety, fear, hysterical laughter, and so on, as moments when the body is out of control.
>
> (2004, 54)

As previously discussed, the skin ego is 'the membrane that complexly mediates the body's inside and its outside as an enfolded space of exchange' (ibid, 54). Just like the skin, the eyes and ears (and other bodily orifices) that are of course partly covered by skin mediate between the inner and outer world. To reiterate, Anzieu characterises the skin ego as follows:

> I can now give a precise account of my conception of the Skin Ego. The maternal environment [*entourage maternant*] is so called because it surrounds [*entoure*] the baby with an external envelope made up of messages. This adjusts itself with a certain flexibility - and leaving some free space between - to the inner envelope, the surface of the baby's body, which is the site and instrument of the transmission of messages: to be an Ego is to feel one has the capacity to send out signals that are received by others.
>
> (Anzieu 1989, 62, translations in the original)

The similarity, or rather analogy, of the skin as a technological medium that receives, stores, and responds to messages is striking here and presents a further development of Freud's notion of the bodily ego (see Chapter 1). Anzieu makes explicit the fruitfulness of drawing on psychoanalysis when thinking about current media technologies in relation to a subject's history.

In *Music in Youth Culture* (2005), Jagodzinski gives a further, more detailed summary of the skin ego. He writes that the formation of an ego in the subject 'always takes place in the past tense' (ibid, 19) – just like the sensemaking of an affective experience takes place after its occurrence (Green 1999; Stein 1999). The skin ego is affected by experiences that have been felt. It is always in tension with drives, the orifices of the body and pores of skin that feel *something*. It is affected and responds, as felt by the baby. The skin ego exists as an 'invisible image' (ibid, 19) that is not recognised by the baby as her own but as being shared with mother. As was discussed, for the baby it acts as a mental image. The relationship between the interior and exterior of the body is mediated by 'a virtual body' (2005, 39). 'The skin-ego presents the space-time of an excluded middle between the body's inside and outside', writes Jagodzinski, 'a vacuum zone as a field of forces that is filled with potential for exchange. *This is the enfolded space-time of fantasy*' (ibid, 39, italics in the original). To repeat, it is through sensations on the skin, the skin being affected, that the baby has the illusion of sharing a skin envelope with mother. This materialist-sensory but at the same time 'virtual envelope' (ibid, 39) makes possible an ego and the very formation of fantasy and ultimately, as mentioned in Chapter 1, thinking.

It is the idea of the skin envelope that makes it a fruitful concept for thinking about media and audiences because of its emphasis on the virtual and material qualities of the medium of the skin. It protects against outer stimuli and at the same time against inner, unconscious feelings, affects, memories, or thoughts that cannot pass through the skin layer to the outside. I have argued in the previous chapters that the viewing experience of *Embarrassing Bodies* – which was so strongly structured by feelings and desires for containment as well as seeing suffering bodies for purposes of comparison on part of many of the interviewees – can be metaphorically regarded as an enfolded skin that enwraps the viewers with their television sets (or tablet or smartphone screens) in a cocoon-like envelope. It is primarily the doctors who make the viewers feel held and contained in the skin envelope. This idea allows for affective responses (that may invade the skin and pass through it) *as well as* the desire for containment to exist simultaneously in the same concept. I would argue that in the affective 'bad trip' moments described earlier, something happens that makes the ego, precisely the protective shield, *crack*, and subjects are confronted with (unconscious and mostly unpleasurable) aspects of their subjectivities that they did not reckon with in that moment:

> A film [or a television series], by catching us unawares, by taking us by surprise can, I would argue, effectively break through defences and take the viewer to an experiential place that they may not have consciously chosen.
>
> (Diamond 2013b, 79)

It is in the affective 'bad trip' moments that the permeable skin (envelope) receives a *crack* and something emerges that interviewees mostly associated with unpleasure. This similarly occurred for the interviewees who spoke about their use of social media (Chapter 5) and for the Netflix viewers, who responded to the tweet about *The Christmas Prince* (Chapter 6). These associations are then responded to through affective discharge. The 'affect breaks the screen of consciousness' (Green 1999, 212) in such moments. We can picture this vividly; in a moment when we cover our eyes when confronted with a sudden scene of *Embarrassing Bodies*, the skin that rests on the eyelid folds over an orifice that has allowed for something to pass through. The crack is closed by covering or averting the gaze. In the case of the user replies to the Netflix tweet, the affect is discharged by drawing a discursive boundary between the users and Netflix. One can underscore this idea further with Anzieu and the complexity of the skin ego that has at once a material as well as virtual ontology. This goes back to Freud and his idea of the skin as a projection of a surface. As Diamond writes,

> The skin as a surface always relates to other surfaces from sensory mirroring surfaces derived from others, to social surfaces such as

media surface projections, billboard advertising surfaces; from glossy magazine surfaces to screen surfaces, the skin surface is never fully owned. This is one way of understanding and developing Freud's reference to the skin ego as not only based in being a surface entity but in fact existing as a surface projection.

(Diamond 2013a, 123)

The television screen is also a surface and it is the screen and the content showing that metaphorically acts as the skin that enwraps viewers with *Embarrassing Bodies*. This desire to be contained and held in the skin envelope is particularly heightened in the reality genre. Misha Kavka (2009) defined reality television as 'an interface' (ibid, 29) that connects viewers with the subjects on screen. In that sense, it is the television screen as 'affective glue' (ibid, 37) that is capable of triggering affective responses as well as generating the desire and feeling of being enwrapped – both mentally and physically. In the same way the skin between mother and baby is capable of holding, containing, generating, and discharging affect and ways of communicating, feeling, sensing, and so on.

On the other hand, the skin envelope is capable of holding and containing the baby. The feeling and desire of being contained on the part of the viewers may be imagined to take place through the doctors' speech acts when they diagnose a patient's problem and tell him/her about the plan of action as well as through the successful medical procedures (such as operations) and the 'after' shots that follow the treatment that are shown. This kind of containment – that always remains incomplete because it does not occur off the television screen – is momentarily felt on the body and the skin, for example, after a patient has been healed or his condition has improved. It is also registered mentally (virtually) as the viewers' reflect on and make sense of what they have seen.

Watching and interacting with *Embarrassing Bodies*, then, can partly be seen as a regressive move to piece the torn and lost skin envelope back together, to reunite in the skin ego.[1] It is the idea of containment (as discussed previously) that may illustrate the skin ego's ability of patching up broken or uncertain parts of the ego and the body as a whole. The relationality of media and viewer resembles the relationality between mother and baby. It is precisely the media's potential to excite and frustrate, to attract and repel, to shock and embrace us on a conscious, sensory and unconscious level that resembles the skin ego's mother-baby dyad. It is also the rhythms of watching that stabilise an uncertain viewing experience. As I have mentioned, most interviewees watched *Embarrassing Bodies* whenever it was on. They also recorded it. The show was watched by them every week. It is always on (during its period of running) while offering new and unknown cases. There is a continuity of sameness (every week the same doctors in the same studio, etc.) and uncertainty and curiosity (what cases will be on the show?) that also contributes to the entertaining aspect of the show for audiences. As one interviewee said in this context, 'it just takes my mind off things and it is just reliable, you kinda know what you're getting with it, even when you don't know what you're getting with it, kind of, you know' (I10, 173–175). 'I'm always excited to watch it, cos' I wanna see what's on next! [laughs]. Erm, I just find it really interesting' (I3, 222–223). A third interviewee expressed one of their thoughts upon seeing the programme for the first time: 'one of my first thoughts was: "When is this next programme on, when is this programme on next?"' (I4, 98–99). All quotes speak of a continuity and sameness while at the same time leaving space for something as yet unknown to happen. One interviewee was 'always' excited and the other found the show to be 'reliable' and he knew what he was getting with it. At the same time, all three seemed to want to see what is on 'next' and did not know what they were getting with the programme. It is this attachment to the show – and we could argue to television series in general – that holds and contains the viewers to some degree. Such containment is particularly amplified through the format characteristics of *Embarrassing Bodies* that always remain the same. The programme was a structure in the interviewees' lives that may have acted in a containing manner and responded to the interviewees expectations by being there, by being on television at the same time every week over the course of a season while at the same time leaving space for uncertainty and agency in terms of the interviewees making sense of whatever they will see each week.

Yet the containment is never fully completed, and this may also be one of the reasons why the viewers in the sample tune in again every week. The notion of an enwrapping skin envelope may figure as the other side of a particular, dialectical moment in the viewing process that is also characterised by affective discharge. Both occur in a repetitive, patterned manner in the same process of viewing the programme. The skin may hold, yet it is always already broken and fragile. Every new episode, a possibility of mastery and a final containment presents itself. There seems to be an underlying notion of *waiting* in the viewing process: for another affective experience, for a new patient, for another successful operation, for a new episode, and so on. Just like the skin ego designates a phase that is characterised by the growing baby who – we could say – unconsciously and consciously awaits the ego and a degree of separation from the mother to gain more independence (Anzieu 2016), the watching of *Embarrassing Bodies* is on one level characterised by a waiting for a final containment. It is the skin ego's status of the *not yet*, of the potential to develop an ego, of 'virtual potentiality' (Jagodzinski 2004, 19), that not only make it subject to culture (and the super ego) as the ego develops but it is mirrored in the media viewing process. As McCarthy has emphasised, media are fundamentally structured by waiting:

How much is the experience of waiting built into the format of TV programming and images in general – waiting for an upcoming program, a better music video, the resumption of a narrative interrupted by commercials? In other words, is waiting a 'deep structure' of television spectatorship regardless of where we watch TV?

(McCarthy 2001, 218–219)

This waiting for mastery, waiting for containment, waiting for a healthy and functioning body, a different life even, may continue as long as *Embarrassing Bodies* is broadcast. It is beyond speculation whether the interviewees ever felt really contained over the course of a season. This idea of waiting is of significance to the format of the television series in general and of the reality and makeover genres in particular because it is amplified by the structural characteristics of television (a programme that can be recorded is scheduled to run on a certain day every week over a set period of time).

States of Anticipation

I touched on a similar notion of waiting and anticipating in Chapters 5 and 6. Some of the narratives about the affective labour on social media were narratives of affective anticipation of specific scenes, discourses, and ways of being affected online that the interviewees were trying to encourage as well as pre-empt or prevent. They attempted to do so through the creation of an atmosphere of ease, satisfaction, and well-being. Such moments are less characterised by affective discharge but more by a lingering nature of affect, which I discussed in Chapter 5. Those forms of labour revolved around a lack and often a reference point for speaking about their self-representation online was for interviewees who or what they were not and wanted to become. There was nonetheless a sense of empowerment for interviewees and their ability of contesting and subverting body images on social media. Communication on social media is perhaps so attractive and pleasurable because it reinforces a sense of our own existence and being in the world, as Aaron Balick (2014) has argued at length. The interfaces of social media platforms enable such modes of communication. Didier Anzieu has put it beautifully when he wrote that 'to be an Ego is to feel one has the capacity to send out signals that are received by others' (Anzieu 1989, 62). This capacity is without a doubt enabled and amplified by social media and other services that make use of personalised data. However, users never know *how* their signals (content) are received and responded to by others. This applies both to other users and to data brokers. Hearn's (2017) notion of the anticipating self is a good description of the state of subjectivity which is cultivated through the ownership and interface structures at the heart of social media and other platforms today. Users unconsciously wait for the next recommended friend, the next targeted advertisement, the next suggested episode on Netflix, the next affectively charged exchange on Twitter, and so on. All of this happens while data are being collected in the background and while the very experience of using those services is shaped by algorithms.

There is thus some common ground between the *Embarrassing Bodies* viewers and the social media users I spoke to. They are all in a state of anticipation and of being anticipated as audiences/users at the same time. All types of media use discussed in this book constitute efforts to achieve a sense of mastery over subjects either by the mastery of media users over their (un)conscious fears and fantasies in relation to their bodies, or their use of social media and affective engagement with other users, and algorithmic processes by data mining platforms (Facebook, Netflix, Twitter, etc.) that aim to influence user behaviour. The skin ego relationship between users and the services and platforms they use is symbiotic yet highly osmotic and fragile. It is partly constituted by an affective sense of anticipation on the part of users of what happens to their data, and on the part of data mining platforms of how a sense of mastery over users can be obtained so that they can be persuaded to click on targeted advertisements, or follow the algorithm's recommendations.

The digital subject, then, constructs and reconstructs herself and is constructed and reconstructed by others whereby past, present, and future elements are merged into a dynamic, floating subjectivity. The states of anticipation we find ourselves in when using contemporary digital media point to a sense of expressed and experienced subjectivity that is always open and in flux (Turkle 1985). This may sound positive on the surface, but it also points to more damaging elements which threaten a sense of who we are in relation to digital technologies. We, as media users, as well as social media companies and other digital media services, never really know who we are. The lack, which I have discussed in Chapter 5, is a fundamental characteristic of the human condition which applies to all subjects according to Lacan. It is this lack which is exploited when we are told that contemporary media will enable us to know ourselves better and in fact will be able to know us better than we could ever know ourselves. This results in a state of affective fragility we find ourselves in. Always subject to modification based on our own doings as well as that of others. It points to forms of media use which have fundamentally shifted our ways of cathecting media and media texts. Whereas I discussed the kind of media engagement of the *Embarrassing Bodies* viewers as inward directed and inhibited, a state which perhaps points to forms of 'old' mass media use more generally, other forms of media use in the networked age are much more outward directed and self-invasive. This applies to the kind of affective-digital labour I discussed in Chapter 5 and how we are (ab) used through data mining processes (Chapter 6). The book's chapters thus detail a shift from the internal and inhibited media use towards the external and a drive for externalisation. From a psychoanalytic perspective, such a transformation from inward to outward, from internal to external may not be as clear cut as I have described it here. The two are more messily interlinked. Where there is inward-directedness, there is also outward-directedness and vice versa. The skin ego like symbiosis of the contemporary subject and digital media, however fragile and affectively mobile it may be, will surely remain and even increase. Subjects will be in close proximity to the media services and technologies they use. A welcome impetus for the field of psychoanalytic media studies and its future.

Note

1 This notion of television viewing as a regressive experience has been differently theorised by Silverstone (1994) in relation to the transitional object. As I have made clear, *Embarrassing Bodies* and television *per se* may not always fulfil the function of a transitional object, particularly in terms of the affective experiences of the viewers.

Bibliography

Abidin, C. (2014). 'Privacy for Profit: Commodifying Privacy in Lifestyle Blogging. Paper Presented at Internet Research 15: The 15th Annual Meeting of the Association of Internet Researchers. Daegu, Korea: Aoir'. *Aoir Selected Papers of Internet Research*, 4. https://spir.aoir.org/index.php/spir/article/view/918 (13 December 2017).

Abidin, C. (2015). 'Communicative Intimacies: Influencers and Perceived Interconnectedness'. *Ada: A Journal of Gender, New Media, and Technology*, 8. http://adanewmedia.org/2015/11/crystalabidin/2912/ (13 December 2017).

Abidin, C. (2016). 'Visibility Labour: Engaging with Influencers' Fashion Brands and #OOTD Advertorial Campaigns on Instagram'. *Media International Australia*, 161, 1, pp. 86–100.

Ahmed, S. (2004). 'Affective Economies'. *Social Text*, 22, 2, pp. 117–139.

Ahmed, S. (2014). *The Cultural Politics of Emotion*. Second Edition. Edinburgh: Edinburgh University Press.

Anderson, B. (1983). *Imagined Communities*. London: Verso.

Anderson, B. (2009). 'Affective Atmospheres'. *Emotion, Space and Society*, 2, 2, pp. 77–81.

Anderson, C. (2008). *The End of Theory: The Data Deluge Makes the Scientific Method Obsolete*. www.wired.com/2008/06/pb-theory/ (05 March 2018).

Andrejevic, M. (2011). 'The Work That Affective Economics Does'. *Cultural Studies*, 25, 4–5, pp. 604–620.

Andrejevic, M., Hearn, A. and Kennedy, H. (2015). 'Cultural Studies of Data Mining: Introduction'. *European Journal of Cultural Studies*, 18, 5, pp. 379–394.

Andrew-Gee, E. (2018). *Your Smartphone Is Making You Stupid, Antisocial, and Unhealthy. So Why Can't You Put It Down?* www.theglobeandmail.com/technology/your-smartphone-is-making-you-stupid/article37511900/ (04 January 2018).

Ang, I. (1985). *Watching Dallas: Soap Opera and the Melodramatic Imagination*. London: Routledge.

Angerer, M. (2015). *Desire After Affect*. London: Rowman & Littlefield International.

Anzieu, D. (1984). *The Group and the Unconscious*. London: Routledge and Kegan Paul.

Anzieu, D. (1989). *The Skin Ego*. New Haven, CT: Yale University Press.

Anzieu, D. (2016). *The Skin-Ego. A New Translation by Naomi Segal*. London: Karnac Books.

Arvidsson, A. (2005). 'Brands. A Critical Perspective'. *Journal of Consumer Culture*, 5, 2, pp. 235–258.

Bach, S. (1994). *The Language of Perversion and the Language of Love*. Northvale, NJ: Aronson.

Bagdasarov, Z., Greene, K., Banerjee, S., Krcmar, M., Yanovitzky, I. and Ruginyte, D. (2010). 'I Am What I Watch. Voyeurism, Sensation Seeking, and Television Viewing Patterns'. *Journal of Broadcasting & Electronic Media*, 54, 2, pp. 299–315.

Bainbridge, C. (2012). 'Psychotherapy on the Couch. Exploring the Fantasies of In Treatment'. *Psychoanalysis, Culture & Society*, 17, 2, pp. 153–168.

Bainbridge, C. and Yates, C. (2010). 'On Not Being a Fan: Masculine Identity, DVD Culture and the Accidental Collector'. *Wide Screen Journal*, 2, 3, pp. 1–22.

Balick, A. (2014). *The Psychodynamics of Social Networking: Connected-Up Instantaneous Culture and the Self*. London: Karnac Books.

Ball, K. (Ed.) (2007). *Traumatizing Theory: The Cultural Politics of Affect in and Beyond Psychoanalysis*. New York: Other Press.

Ball, K. (2015). 'LOSING STEAM AFTER MARX AND FREUD: On Entropy as the Horizon of the Community To Come'. *Angelaki*, 20, 3, pp. 55–78.

Banet-Weiser, S. (2012). *AuthenticTM: The Politics of Ambivalence in a Brand Culture*. New York: NYU Press.

Barker, M. (2005). 'The *Lord of the Rings* and "Identification": A Critical Encounter'. *European Journal of Communication*, 20, 3, pp. 353–378.

Barocas, S. and Selbst, A. (2014). 'Big Data's Disparate Impact'. *Social Science Research Network*. http://papers.ssrn.com/sol3/papers.cfm?abstract_id=2477899 (05 May 2017).

Baruh, L. (2009). 'Publicized Intimacies on Reality Television. An Analysis of Voyeuristic Content and Its Contribution to the Appeal of Reality Programming'. *Journal of Broadcasting & Electronic Media*, 53, 2, pp. 190–210.

Baruh, L. (2010). 'Mediated Voyeurism and the Guilty Pleasure of Consuming Reality Television'. *Media Psychology*, 13, 3, pp. 201–221.

Basch, M. F. (1976). 'The Concept of Affect: A Re-Examination'. *Journal of the American Psychoanalytic Association*, 24, 4, pp. 759–777.

Baym, N. (2002). 'Interpersonal Life Online'. In: Lievrouw, L. A. and Livingstone S. (Eds.) *The Handbook of New Media*. London: Sage, pp. 35–54.

Baym, N. K. (2015). *Personal Connections in the Digital Age*. London: John Wiley & Sons.

Belk, R. (2009). 'Sharing'. *Journal of Consumer Research*, 36, 5, pp. 715–734.

Benjamin, W. (1968). *Illuminations*. New York: Schocken Books.

Berardi, F. (2009). *The Soul at Work: From Alienation to Autonomy*. New York: Semiotext(e).

Bereswill, M., Morgenroth, C. and Redman, P. (2010). 'Alfred Lorenzer and the Depth Hermeneutic Method'. *Psychoanalysis, Culture & Society*, 15, 3, pp. 221–250.

Billig, M. (1999). *Freudian Repression: Conversation Creating the Unconscious*. Cambridge: Cambridge University Press.

Bion, W. (1963). *Elements of Psycho-Analysis*. London: Heinemann.

Blackman, L. and Cromby, J. (2007). 'Editorial. Affect and Feeling'. *International Journal of Critical Psychology*, 21, pp. 5–22.

Boellstorff, T. (2008). *Coming of Age in Second Life: An Anthropologist Explores the Virtually Human*. Princeton: Princeton University Press.

Bolton, S. C. (2009). 'The Lady Vanishes: Women's Work and Affective Labour'. *International Journal of Work Organisation and Emotion*, 3, 1, pp. 72–80.

Bonner, F. (2005). 'Looking inside. Showing Medical Operations on Ordinary Television'. In: King, G. (Ed.) *The Spectacle of the Real. From Hollywood to Reality TV and Beyond*. Bristol: Intellect, pp. 105–116.

Borch-Jacobsen, M. (1993). *The Emotional Tie Psychoanalysis, Mimesis, and Affect*. Palo Alto, CA: Stanford University Press.

Bordwell, D. (1996). 'Contemporary Film Studies and the Vicissitudes of Grand theory'. In Carroll, N. and Bordwell, D. (Eds.) *Post-theory: Reconstructing Film Studies*. Madison: University of Wisconsin Press, pp. 3–36.

Bore, I. L. K., Graefer, A. and Kilby, A. (2018). 'This Pussy Grabs Back: Humour, Digital Affects and Women's Protest'. *Open Cultural Studies*, 1, 1, pp. 529–540.

boyd, D. (2007). *Why Youth Heart Social Networking Sites: The Role of Networked Publics in Teenage Social Life*. http://research.fit.edu/sealevel-riselibrary/documents/doc_mgr/1006/Boyd._2008_Why_Teens_Love_Social_Media.pdf (15 May 2016).

boyd, D. and Crawford, K. (2012). 'Critical Questions for Big Data: Provocations for A Cultural, Technological, and Scholarly Phenomenon'. *Information, Communication & Society*, 15, 5, 662–679.

Bratich, J. (2007). 'Programming Reality. Control Societies, New Subjects and the Powers of Transformation'. In: Heller, D. (Ed.) *Makeover Television. Realities Remodelled*. London: I.B. Tauris, pp. 6–22.

Bratich, J. (2011). 'Affective Convergence in Reality Television. A Case Study in Divergence Culture'. In: Kackman, M., Binfield, M., Payne, M. T., Perlman A. and Sebok, B. (Eds.) *Flow TV. Television in the Age of Media Convergence*. London: Routledge, pp. 55–74.

Breu, C. (2014). *Insistence of the Material: Literature in the Age of Biopolitics*. Minneapolis: University of Minnesota Press.

Breuer, J. and S. Freud. (2001). *On the Psychical Mechanism of Hysterical Phenomena: Preliminary Communication. Complete Psychological Works of Sigmund Freud. Volume II. Studies on Hysteria. By Josef Breuer and Sigmund Freud*. London: Penguin Books.

Brierley, M. (1937). 'Affects in Theory and Practice'. *The International Journal of Psychoanalysis*, 18, pp. 256–268.

Brinkema, E. (2014). *The Forms of the Affects*. Durham: Duke University Press.

Brody, S. (1980). 'Transitional Objects: Idealization of a Phenomenon'. *Psychoanalytic Quarterly*, 49, pp. 561–605.

Bucher, T. (2016). 'The Algorithmic Imaginary: Exploring the Ordinary Affects of Facebook Algorithms'. *Information, Communication & Society*, 20, 1, pp. 30–44.

Bunz, M. and Meikle, G. (2017). *The Internet of Things*. Cambridge: Polity.

Burgess, J. and Green, J. (2009). *YouTube*. Cambridge: Polity.

Butler, D. (2013). 'When Google Got Flu Wrong'. *Nature*, 494, pp. 155–156.

Butler, J. (1990). *Gender Trouble and the Subversion of Identity*. London: Routledge.

Calvert, C. (2004). *Voyeur Nation. Media, Privacy and Peering in Modern Culture*. Oxford: Westview Press.

Cambridge Analytica. (No Date). *Mission Statement*. https://ca-political.com/missionstatement (13.03.2018).

Cambridge Analytica. (No Date). *The CA Advantage*. https://ca-political.com/ca-advantage (13.03.2018).

Cammaerts, B. (2011). 'Disruptive Sharing in a Digital Age: Rejecting Neoliberalism?' *Continuum*, 25, 1, pp. 47–62.

Campbell, F. (2009). *Contours of Ableism: The Production of Disability and Abledness*. Basingstoke: Palgrave Macmillan.

Caraway, B. (2011). 'Audience Labor in the New Media Environment: A Marxian Revisiting of the Audience Commodity'. *Media, Culture & Society*, 33, 5, pp. 693–708.

Carpentier, N. (2014a). 'Participation as a Fantasy: A Psychoanalytical Approach To Power-Sharing Fantasies'. In: Kramp, L., Carpentier, N., Tomanić Trivundža, I., Nieminen, H., Kunelius, R., Olsson, T., Sundin, E. and Kilborn, R. (Eds.) *Media Practice and Everyday Agency in Europe*. Bremen: Edition Lumière, pp. 319–330.

Carpentier, N. (2014b). '"Fuck the Clowns From Grease!!": Fantasies of Participation and Agency in the YouTube Comments on a Cypriot Problem Documentary'. *Information, Communication & Society*, 17, 8, pp. 1001–1016.

Carpentier, N. and Trioen, M. (2010). 'The Particularity of Objectivity: A Poststructuralist and Psychoanalytical Reading of the Gap Between Objectivity-As A-Value and Objectivity-As-A-Practice in the 2003 Iraqi War Coverage'. *Journalism*, 11, 3, pp. 311–328.

Cartwright, L. (2008). *Moral Spectatorship. Technologies of Voice and Affect in Postwar Representations of the Child*. Durham: Duke University Press.

Cavanagh, S., Failler, A. and Hurst, R. (Eds.) (2013). *Skin, Culture and Psychoanalysis*. Basingstoke: Palgrave Macmillan.

Celenza, A. (2014). *Erotic Revelations: Clinical Applications and Perverse Scenarios*. London: Routledge.

Centonze, D., Siracusano, A., Calabresi, P. and Bernardi, G. (2004). 'The Project for a Scientific Psychology (1895). A Freudian Anticipation of LTP-Memory Connection Theory'. *Brain Research Review*, 46, pp. 310–314.

Chalaby, J. K. (2015). *The Format Age. Television's Entertainment Revolution*. London: Wiley.

Cheney-Lippold, J. (2017). *We Are Data: Algorithms and the Making of Our Digital Selves*. New York: NYU Press.

Cho, A. (2015). 'Queer Reverb: Tumblr, Affect, Time'. In: Hillis K., Paasonen S. and Petit M. (Eds.) *Networked Affect*. Cambridge, MA: MIT Press, pp. 43–58.

Chun, W. H. K. (2011). *Programmed Visions: Software and Memory*. Cambridge, MA: MIT Press.

Clarke, S. (2002). 'Learning From Experience. Psycho-Social Research Methods in the Social Sciences'. *Qualitative Research*, 2, 2, pp. 173–194.

Clarke, S. and Hoggett, P. (2009). *Researching Beneath the Surface. Psycho Social Research Methods in Practice*. London: Karnac Books.

Clough, P. (2007). 'Introduction'. In: Clough, P. and Halley, J. (Eds.) *The Affective Turn. Theorizing the Social*. Durham: Duke University Press, pp. 1–33.

Clough, P. T. (2000a). *Autoaffection. Unconscious Thought in the Age of Tele-technology*. Minneapolis: University of Minnesota Press.

Clough, P. T. (2000b). 'The Technical Substrates of Unconscious Memory: Re-reading Derrida's Freud in the Age of Teletechnology'. *Sociological Theory*, 18, 3, pp. 383–398.

Clough, P. T. (2008). '(De) Coding the Subject-in-Affect'. *Subjectivity*, 23, 1, pp. 140–155.

Clough, P. T. (2009). 'Reflections on Sessions Early in an Analysis: Trauma, Affect and "Enactive Witnessing"'. *Women & Performance: A Journal of Feminist Theory*, 19, 2, pp. 149–159.

Clough, P. T. (2013). 'The Digital, Labor, and Measure Beyond Biopolitics'. In: Trebor, S. (Ed.) *Digital Labor: The Internet as Playground and Factory*. London: Routledge, pp. 112–126.

Clough, P. T., Goldberg, G., Schiff, R., Weeks, A. and Willse, C. (2007). 'Notes Towards a Theory of Affect-Itself'. *Ephemera: Theory and Politics in Organization*, 7, 1, pp. 60–77.

Cohen, R. (2013). 'Investments in Cinematic Constructions of the Female Serial Killer. Re-Conceptualising Spectatorial "Identification"'. *Free Associations*, 64, pp. 37–63. http://freeassociations.org.uk/FA_New/OJS/index.php/fa/article/view/80 (04.08.2014).

Comor, E. (2010). 'Digital Prosumption and Alienation'. *Ephemera: Theory & Politics in Organization*, 10, 3, pp. 439–454.

Connor, S. (2009). *The Book of Skin*. London: Reaktion Books.

Copjec, J. (1989). 'The Orthopsychic Subject: Film Theory and the Reception of Lacan'. *October* 49, pp. 53–72.

Coté, M. and Pybus, J. (2011). 'Learning To Immaterial Labour 2.0: Facebook and Social Networks'. In: Peters, Michael A. and Bulut E. (Eds.) *Cognitive Capitalism, Education and Digital Labor*. New York: Peter Lang, pp. 169–194.

Couldry, N. (2000). *Inside Culture: Re-Imagining the Method of Cultural Studies*. London: Sage.

Couldry, N. (2012). *Media. Society. World*. Cambridge: Polity.

Couldry, N. and Powell, A. (2014). 'Big Data from the Bottom Up'. *Big Data & Society*, 1, 2, pp. 1–5.

Cowie, E. (1990). 'Fantasia'. In: Adams, P. and Cowie, E. (Eds.) *The Woman in Question: m/f*. London: Verso, pp. 149–196.

Cramer, F. and Fuller, M. (2008). 'Interface'. In: Fuller, M. (Ed.) *Software Studies: A Lexicon*. Cambridge, MA: MIT Press, pp. 168–173.

Cronan, T. (2013). *Against Affective Formalism. Matisse, Bergson, Modernism*. Minneapolis: University of Minnesota Press.

Dahlgren, P. (2013). 'Tracking the Civic Subject in the Media Landscape. Versions of the Democratic Ideal'. *Television & New Media*, 14, 1, pp. 71–88.

Day Sclater, S., Jones, D. W., Price, H. and Yates, C. (Eds.) (2009). *Emotion. New Psychosocial Perspectives*. Basingstoke: Palgrave Macmillan.

De Lauretis, T. (1984). *Alice Doesn't: Feminism, Semiotics, Cinema*. Bloomington: Indiana University Press.

Dean, J. (2009). *Democracy and Other Neoliberal Fantasies: Communicative Capitalism and Left Politics*. Durham: Duke University Press.

Dean, J. (2010). *Blog Theory: Feedback and Capture in the Circuits of Drive*. Cambridge: Polity.

Dean, J. (2016). *Crowds and Party*. London: Verso.

Deery, J. (2004). 'Reality TV as Advertainment'. *Popular Communication*, 2, 1, pp. 1–20.

Deleuze, G. and Guattari, F. (1983). *Anti-Oedipus: Capitalism and Schizophrenia*. Minneapolis: University of Minnesota Press.

Deleuze, G. and Guattari, F. (1987). *A Thousand Plateaus: Capitalism and Schizophrenia*. Minneapolis: University of Minnesota Press.

Derrida, J. (1978). *Writing and Difference*. Chicago: University of Chicago Press.

Derrida, J. (1995). 'Archive Fever: A Freudian Impression'. *Diacritics*, 25, 2, pp. 9–63.

Devereux, G. (1967). *From Anxiety to Method in the Behavioral Sciences*. The Hague: Mouton & Co.

Di Mattia, J. (2007). 'The Gentle Art of Manscaping. Lessons in Heteromasculinity from the Queer Eye Guys'. In: Heller, D. (Ed.) *Makeover Television. Realities Remodelled*. London: I.B. Tauris, pp. 133–149.

Diamond, N. (2013a). *Between Skins. The Body in Psychoanalysis. Contemporary Developments*. London: Wiley.

Diamond, N. (2013b). 'The Body and Film. Estranged Body States. A Case of Das Unheimlich'. *Journal of Psycho-Social Studies*, 7, 1, pp. 78–97. www. psychosocial-studies-association.org/wp-content/uploads/2017/01/UN-HEIMLICH.pdf (15 November 2013).

Doane, M. A. (1987). *The Desire to Desire: The Woman's Film of the 1940s*. Bloomington: Indiana University Press.

Dowling, E. (2007). 'Producing the Dining Experience: Measure, Subjectivity and the Affective Worker'. *Ephemera: Theory and Politics in Organization*, 7, 1, pp. 117–132.

Dyer-Witheford, N. (2001). 'Empire, Immaterial Labor, the New Combinations, and the Global Worker'. *Rethinking Marxism*, 13, 3–4, pp. 70–80.

Bleuler, E. (1952). *Dementia Praecox or the Group of Schizophrenias*. New York: International Universities Press.

Ekbia, H., Mattioli, M., Kouper, I., Arave, G., Ghazinejad, A., Bowman, T. and Sugimoto, C. R. (2014). 'Big Data, Bigger Dilemmas: A Critical Review'. *Journal of the Association for Information Science and Technology*, 66, 8, pp. 1523–1545.

Elerding, C. and Risam, R. (2018). 'Introduction: A Gathering of Feminist Perspectives on Digital Labor'. *First Monday*, 23, 3. www.firstmonday.dk/ojs/index.php/fm/article/view/8278 (04 April 2018).

Elliott, A. and Urry, J. (2010). *Mobile Lives*. London: Routledge.

Ellis, J. (2000). *Seeing Things: Television in the Age of Uncertainty*. London: I.B. Tauris.

Ellis, D., Tucker, I. and Harper, D. (2013). 'The Affective Atmospheres of Surveillance'. *Theory & Psychology*, 23, 6, pp. 716–731.

Elsaesser, T. (2009). 'Freud as Media Theorist. Mystic Writing-Pads and the Matter of Memory'. *Screen*, 50, 1, pp. 100–113.

Eyal, N. (2014). *Hooked: How to Build Habit-Forming Platforms*. New York: Penguin.

Facebook. Our Mission. https://newsroom.fb.com/company-info/ (14 August 2017).

Farman, J. (2011). *Mobile Interface Theory: Embodied Space and Locative Media.* London: Routledge.

Federici, S. (2004). *Caliban and the Witch. Women, the Body and Primitive Accumulation.* New York: Autonomedia.

Fenichel, O. (1995). *The Psychoanalytic Theory of Neurosis.* London: Routledge.

Finn, E. (2017). *What Algorithms Want: Imagination in the Age of Computing.* Cambridge, MA: MIT Press.

Flisfeder, M. & Willis, L. (Eds.) (2014). Žižek and Media Studies: A Reader. Basingstoke: Palgrave Macmillan.

Flisfeder, M. (2015). 'The Entrepreneurial Subject and the Objectivization of the Self in Social Media' *South Atlantic Quarterly,* 114, 3, pp. 553–570.

Flisfeder, M. (2018). 'The Ideological Algorithmic Apparatus: Subjection before Enslavement'. Theory & Event, Forthcoming.

Fogg, B. J. (2003). *Persuasive Technology. Using Computers to Change What We Think and Do.* London: Morgan Kaufmann Publishers.

Fortunati, L. (1995). *The Arcane of Reproduction: Housework, Prostitution, Labor and Capital.* New York: Autonomedia.

Fortunati, L. (2007). 'Immaterial Labor and Its Machinization'. *Ephemera: Theory and Politics in Organization,* 7, 1, pp. 139–157.

Freud, S. (1949). *Inhibitions, Symptoms and Anxiety.* London: The Hogarth Press and the Institute of Psycho-Analysis.

Freud, S. (1978). *Five Lectures on Psycho-Analysis. The Standard Edition of the Complete Psychological Works of Sigmund Freud. Volume XI. Five Lectures on Psycho-Analysis, Leonardo Da Vinci and Other Works.* London: The Hogarth Press and the Institute of Psycho-Analysis.

Freud, S. (1981a). *Project for a Scientific Psychology. The Standard Edition of the Complete Psychological Works of Sigmund Freud. Volume I. Pre-Psycho Analytic Publications and Unpublished Drafts.* London: The Hogarth Press and the institute of Psycho-Analysis, pp. 283–346.

Freud, S. (1981b). *Sketches for the 'Preliminary Communication' of 1893. The Standard Edition of the Complete Psychological Works of Sigmund Freud. Volume I. Pre-Psycho-Analytic Publications and Unpublished Drafts.* London: The Hogarth Press and the Institute of Psycho-Analysis, pp. 147–156.

Freud, S. (1981c). *The Neuro-Psychoses of Defence. The Standard Edition of the Complete Psychological Works of Sigmund Freud. Volume III. Early Psycho-Analytic Publications.* London: The Hogarth Press and the Institute of Psycho-Analysis.

Freud, S. (1981d). *The Interpretation of Dreams. The Standard Edition of the Complete Psychological Works of Sigmund Freud. Volume V. The interpretations of Dreams (Second Part) and On Dreams.* London: The Hogarth Press and the Institute of Psycho-Analysis.

Freud, S. (1981e). *Recommendations to Physicians Practicing Psycho Analysis. The Standard Edition of the Complete Psychological Works of Sigmund Freud. Volume XII. The Case of Schreber, Papers on Technique and Other Works.* London: The Hogarth Press and the Institute of Psycho-Analysis.

Freud, S. (1981f). *Remembering, Repeating and Working-Through. Further Recommendations on the Technique of Psycho-Analysis II. The Standard Edition of the Complete Psychological Works of Sigmund Freud. Volume*

XII. The Case of Schreber, Papers on Technique and Other Works. London: The Hogarth Press and the Institute of Psycho-Analysis.

Freud, S. (1981g). *Repression. The Standard Edition of the Complete Psychological Works of Sigmund Freud. Volume XIV. On the History of the Psycho-Analytic Movement, Papers on Metapsychology and Other Works*. London: The Hogarth Press and the Institute of Psycho-Analysis.

Freud, S. (1981h). *Anxiety. The Standard Edition of the Complete Psychological Works of Sigmund Freud. Volume XVI. Introductory Lectures on Psycho-Analysis (Part III)*. London: The Hogarth Press and the Institute of Psycho-Analysis.

Freud, S. (1981i). *A Note Upon the 'Mystic Writing Pad'. The Standard Edition of the Complete Psychological Works of Sigmund Freud. Volume XIX. The Ego and the Id and Other Works*. London: The Hogarth Press and the Institute of Psycho-Analysis.

Freud, S. (1981j). *Civilization and its Discontents. The Standard Edition of the Complete Psychological Works of Sigmund Freud. Volume XXI. The Future of an Illusion, Civilization and Its Discontents and Other Works*. London: The Hogarth Press and the Institute of Psycho-Analysis.

Freud, S. (1981k). *Fetishism. The Standard Edition of the Complete Psychological Works of Sigmund Freud. Volume XXI. The Future of an Illusion, Civilization and Its Discontents and Other Works*. London: The Hogarth Press and the Institute of Psycho-Analysis.

Freud, S. (1981l). *The Future of an Illusion. The Standard Edition of the Complete Psychological Works of Sigmund Freud. Volume XXI. The Future of an Illusion, Civilization and Its Discontents and Other Works*. London: The Hogarth Press and the Institute of Psycho-Analysis.

Freud, S. (1981m). *Negation. The Standard Edition of the Complete Psychological Works of Sigmund Freud. Volume XIX. The Ego and the Id and Other Works*. London: The Hogarth Press and the Institute of Psycho-Analysis.

Freud, S. (1991a). 'Beyond the Pleasure Principle'. In: Freud, S. (Ed.) *On Metapsychology*. London: Penguin, pp. 269–337.

Freud, S. (1991b). 'The Ego and the Id'. In Freud, S. (Ed.) *The Essentials of Psycho-Analysis*. London: Penguin, pp. 439–483.

Frosh, S. (2010). *Psychoanalysis Outside the Clinic. Interventions in Psychosocial Studies*. Basingstoke: Palgrave Macmillan.

Frosh, S. and Baraitser, L. (2008). 'Psychoanalysis and Psychosocial Studies'. *Psychoanalysis, Culture & Society*, 13, 4, pp. 346–365.

Frosh, S. and Young, L. S. (2008). 'Psychoanalytic Approaches to Qualitative Psychology'. In Willig, C. (Ed.) *The Sage Handbook of Qualitative Research in Psychology*. London: Sage, pp 109–126.

Fuchs, C. (2008). *Internet and Society: Social Theory in the Information Age*. New York: Routledge.

Fuchs, C. (2010). 'Labor in Informational Capitalism and on the Internet'. *The Information Society*, 26, 3, pp. 179–196.

Fuchs, C. (2012). 'Dallas Smythe Today—the Audience Commodity, the Digital Labour Debate, Marxist Political Economy and Critical theory. Prolegomena to a Digital Labour theory of Value'. *Triple C—Journal for a Global Sustainable Information Society*, 10, 2, pp. 692–740.

Fuchs, C. (2014). *Digital Labour and Karl Marx*. London: Routledge.

Fuchs, C. and Sevignani, S. (2013). 'What Is Digital Labour? What Is Digital Work? What's their Difference? And Why Do these Questions Matter for Understanding Social Media?' *Triple C—Journal for a Global Sustainable Information Society* 11, 2, pp. 237–293.

Galloway, A. R. (2012). *The Interface Effect*. Cambridge: Polity.

Gandy Jr, O. (2006). 'Data Mining, Surveillance, and Discrimination in the Post-9/11 Environment'. In: Haggerty, D. K. and Ericson, R. V. (Eds.) *The New Politics of Surveillance and Visibility*. Toronto: University of Toronto Press, pp. 363–384.

Garde-Hansen, J. and Gorton, K. (2013). *Emotion Online: Theorizing Affect on the Internet*. Basingstoke: Palgrave Macmillan.

Garrisi. D. and Johanssen, J. (Eds.) (forthcoming). *Disability, Media, and Representations: Other Bodies*. London: Routledge.

Gartner (2013). *What Is Big Data?* www.gartner.com/it-hlossary/big-data (12 February 2018).

Georgis, D. (2013). *The Better Story: Queer Affects from the Middle East*. New York: Suny Press.

Ghai, A. (2006). *(Dis)Embodied Form: Issues of Disabled Women*. Delhi: Shakti Books.

Gibbs, A. (2011). 'Affect Theory and Audience'. In: Nightingale, V. (Ed.) *The Handbook of Media Audiences*. Oxford: Blackwell, pp. 251–266.

Gillespie, T. (2014). 'The Relevance of Algorithms'. In: Gillespie, T., Boczkowski, P. and Foot K. (Eds.) *Media Technologies. Essays on Communication, Materiality, and Society*. Cambridge, MA: MIT Press, pp. 167–194.

Goffman, E. (1959). *The Presentation of Self in Everyday Life*. Harmondsworth: Penguin Books.

Golumbia, D. (2009). *The Cultural Logic of Computation*. Cambridge, MA: Harvard University Press.

Goodley, D. (2011). *Disability Studies: An Interdisciplinary Approach*. London: Sage.

Google Canada. (No Date). *Algorithms*. www.google.ca/insidesearch/how-searchworks/algorithms.html (12 February 2018).

Graefer, A. (2016). 'The Work of Humour in Affective Capitalism: A Case Study of Celebrity Gossip Blogs'. *Ephemera: Theory and Politics in Organization*, 16, 4, pp. 143–162. www.ephemerajournal.org/contribution/work-humour-affective-capitalism-case-study-celebrity-gossip-blogs (12 April 2017).

Green, A. (1999). *The Fabric of Affect in the Psychoanalytic Discourse*. London: Routledge.

Grossberg, L. (1987). 'The in-Difference of Television'. *Screen*, 28, 2, pp. 28–46.

Guattari, F. (1990). 'Ritornellos and Existential Affects'. *Discourse*, 12, 2, pp. 66–81.

Guattari, F. (2005). *The Three Ecologies*. New York: Bloomsbury Publishing.

Gutierrez, C. (2016). 'The Other Self in Free Fall: Anxiety and Automated Tracking Applications'. *CM: Communication and Media*, 11, 38, pp. 111–134. www.fpn.bg.ac.rs/wp-content/uploads/2017/03/CM38-Ceo.pdf#page=111 (05 May 2016).

Gutwill, S. and Hollander, N. C. (2002). 'Zero Tolerance or Media Literacy: A Critical Psychoanalytic Perspective on Combating Violence among Children'. *JPCS: Journal for the Psychoanalysis of Culture & Society*, 7, 2, pp. 263–273.

Hagman, G. (2002). 'The Sense of Beauty'. *The International Journal of Psychoanalysis*, 83, 3, pp. 661–674.

Hall, A. (2006). 'Viewers' Perceptions of Reality Programs'. *Communication Quarterly*, 54, 2, pp. 191–211.

Hall, S. (1980). 'Encoding/Decoding'. In: Hall, S., Hobson, D., Lowe, A. and Willis, P. (Eds.) *Culture, Media, Language: Working Papers in Cultural Studies, 1972–79*. London: Hyman, pp. 117–127.

Halpern, O. (2014). *Beautiful Data: A History of Vision and Reason Since 1945*. Durham: Duke University Press.

Handyside, S. and Ringrose, J. (2017). 'Snapchat Memory and Youth Digital Sexual Cultures: Mediated Temporality, Duration and Affect'. *Journal of Gender Studies*, 26, 3, pp. 347–360.

Hansen, M. B. N. (2000). *Embodying Technesis. Technology Beyond Writing*. Ann Arbor: University of Michigan Press.

Hansen, M. B. N. (2006). *Bodies in Code. Interfaces With Digital Media*. London: Routledge.

Hardt, M. (1999). 'Affective Labor'. *Boundary 2*, 26, 2, pp. 89–100.

Hardt, M. (2007). 'Foreword: What Affects Are Good For'. In: Clough, P. and Halley, J. (Eds.) *The Affective Turn. Theorizing the Social*. Durham: Duke University Press, pp. IX–XIII.

Hardt, M. and Negri, A. (2000). *Empire*. Cambridge, MA: Harvard University Press.

Hardt, M. and Negri, A. (2004). *Multitude*. New York: Penguin.

Hardt, M. and Negri, A. (2009). *Commonwealth*. Cambridge, MA: Harvard University Press.

Harrington, C. L. and Bielby, D. D. (2013). 'Pleasure and Adult Development: Extending Winnicott into Late(r) Life'. In: Kuhn, A. (Ed.) *Little Madnesses: Winnicott, Transitional Phenomena and Cultural Experience*. London: I.B. Tauris, pp. 87–102.

Harrington, C. L. and Bielby, D. (1995). *Soap Fans: Pursuing Pleasure and Making Meaning in Everyday Life*. Philadelphia, PA: Temple University Press.

Hearn, A. (2010). 'Reality Television, the Hills and the Limits of the Immaterial Labour Thesis'. *Triple C: Communication, Capitalism & Critique. Open Access Journal for a Global Sustainable Information Society*, 8, 1, pp. 60–76.

Hearn, A. (2017). 'Verified: Self-Presentation, Identity Management, and Selfhood in the Age of Big Data'. *Popular Communication*, 15, 2, pp. 62–77.

Hemmings, C. (2005). 'Invoking Affect: Cultural theory and the Ontological Turn'. *Cultural Studies*, 19, 5, pp. 548–567.

Hesmondhalgh, D. and Baker, S. (2008). 'Creative Work and Emotional Labour in the Television Industry'. *Theory, Culture & Society*, 25, 7–8, pp. 97–118.

Highfield, T., Harrington, S. and Bruns, A. (2013). 'Twitter as a Technology for Audiencing and Fandom: The #Eurovision Phenomenon'. *Information, Communication & Society*, 16, 3, pp. 315–339.

Highmore, B. (2007). 'Michel De Certeau and the Possibilities of Psychoanalytic Cultural Studies'. In: Bainbridge, C., Radstone, S., Rustin, M., Yates, C. (Eds.) *Culture and the Unconscious*. Basingstoke: Palgrave Macmillan, pp. 88–101.

Hill, A. (2005). *Reality TV. Audiences and Popular Television*. London: Routledge.

Hill, A. (2007). *Restyling Factual TV. Audiences and News, Documentary, and Reality Genres*. London: Routledge.

Hills, M. (2002). *Fan Cultures*. London: Routledge.

Hills, M. (2005). Patterns of Surprise. 'The "Aleatory Object" in Psychoanalytic Ethnography and Cyclical Fandom'. *American Behavioral Scientist*, 48, 7, pp. 801–821.

Hills, M. (2014). 'Playing and Pathology: Considering Social Media as "Secondary Transitional Objects"'. In: Bainbridge, C. and Yates, C. (Eds.) *Media and the Inner World: Psycho-Cultural Approaches to Emotion, Media and Popular Culture*. Basingstoke: Palgrave Macmillan, pp. 185–200.

Hills, M. (2017). 'Always-On Fandom, Waiting and Bingeing. Psychoanalysis as an Engagement with Fans' "infra-Ordinary" Experiences'. In: Click, M. A. and Scott, S. (Eds.) *The Routledge Companion to Media Fandom*. London: Routledge, pp. 18–26.

Hochschild, A. R. (1983). *The Managed Heart: Commercialization of Human Feeling*. California: University of California Press.

Hoggett, P. (2008). 'What's in a Hyphen? Reconstructing Psychosocial Studies'. *Psychoanalysis, Culture and Society*, 13, 4, pp. 379–384.

Hollway, W. (2006). 'Paradox in the Pursuit of a Critical theorization of the Development of Self in Family Relationships'. *Theory and Psychology*, 16, pp. 465–482.

Hollway, W. (2008) 'Doing Intellectual Disagreement Differently?' *Psychoanalysis, Culture and Society*, 13, 4, pp. 385–396.

Hollway, W. and Jefferson, T. (2000). *Doing Qualitative Research Differently. Free Association, Narrative and the Interview Method*. First Edition. London: Sage.

Hollway, W. and Jefferson, T. (2005). 'Panic and Perjury. A Psychosocial Exploration of Agency'. *British Journal of Social Psychology*, 44, pp. 146–167.

Hollway, W. and Jefferson, T. (2008). 'The Free Association Narrative Interview Method'. In: Given, L. M. (Ed.) *The Sage Encyclopedia of Qualitative Research Methods*. London: Sage, pp. 296–315.

Hollway, W. and Jefferson, T. (2012). *Doing Qualitative Research Differently. Free Association, Narrative and the Interview Method*. Second Edition. London: Sage.

Holman, W. J. (2010). *Google and the Search for the Future. Interview with Eric Schmidt*. www.wsj.com/articles/SB1000142405274870490110457542329 4099527212 (22 May 2017).

Hookway, B. (2014). *Interface*. Cambridge, MA: MIT Press.

Horbury, A. (2016). 'Digital Feminisms and the Split Subject: Short-Circuits Through Lacan's Four Discourses'. *CM: Communication and Media*, 11, 38, pp. 135–166. www.fpn.bg.ac.rs/wp-content/uploads/2017/03/CM38-Ceo.pdf#Page=135 (05 May 2017).

Horkheimer, M. (1974). *Eclipse of Reason*. London: Continuum.

Houzel, D. (1990). 'The Concept of the Psychic Envelope'. In: Anzieu, D., Houzel, D., Missenard, A., Enriquez, M., Anzieu, A., Guillaumin, J., Doron, J., Lecourt, E. and Nathan, T. (Eds.) *Psychic Envelopes*. London: Karnac Books, pp. 27–58.

Ihanus, J. (2007). 'The Archive and Psychoanalysis: Memories and Histories Toward Futures'. *International Forum of Psychoanalysis*, 16, 2, pp. 119–131.

Jackson, K. (2007). 'Editing as Plastic Surgery. The Swan and the Violence of Image-Creation'. *Configurations*, 15, 1, pp. 55–76.

Jagodzinski, J. (2004). *Youth Fantasies. The Perverse Landscape of the Media.* Basingstoke: Palgrave Macmillan.

Jagodzinski, J. (2005). *Music in Youth Culture. A Lacanian Approach.* Basingstoke: Palgrave Macmillan.

Jarrett, K. (2015). *Feminism, Labour and Digital Media: The Digital Housewife.* New York: Routledge.

Jarrett, K. (2018). 'Laundering Women's History: A Feminist Critique of the Social Factory'. *First Monday*, 23, 3. http://journals.uic.edu/ojs/index.php/fm/article/view/8280 (04 April 2018).

Jenkins, H. (2006). *Convergence Culture: Where Old and New Media Collide.* New York: New York University Press.

Jhally, S. and Livant, B. (1986). 'Watching as Working. The Valorization of Audience Consciousness'. In: Jhally, S. (Ed.) *The Spectacle of Accumulation. Essays in Culture, Media, and Politics.* New York: Peter Lang, pp. 24–43.

Johanssen, J. (2012). 'Subjects in Labour. A New Self in "My Strange Addiction"'. In: Henderson, D. (Ed.) *Psychoanalysis, Culture and Society.* Newcastle: Cambridge Scholars Publishing, pp. 144–162.

Johanssen, J. (2013). 'We Shall Overcome. The Posthuman Discourse as a Symptom of Today's Negation of the Unconscious'. In: Rambatan. B. and Johanssen, J. (Eds.) *Cyborg Subjects: Discourses On Digital Culture.* Seattle, WA: Createspace Publishing, pp. 42–52.

Johanssen, J. (2014). 'Posthumanists on the Couch'. In: Tamboukou, M. (Ed.) *Crossing Conceptual Boundaries VI.* London: University of East London, pp. 31–40. www.uel.ac.uk/wwwmedia/crossing-conceptual-boundaries-VI.pdf (03 October 2016).

Johanssen, J. (2016a). 'Not Belonging to One's Self: Affect on Facebook's Site Governance Page'. *International Journal of Cultural Studies*, 21, 2, pp. 207–222. http://journals.sagepub.com/doi/full/10.1177/1367877916666116 (01 February 2017).

Johanssen, J. (2016b). 'The Subject in the Crowd: A Critical Discussion of Jodi Dean's "Crowds and Party"'. *Triplec: Communication, Capitalism & Critique. Open Access Journal for a Global Sustainable Information Society*, 14, 2, pp. 428–437. www.triple-c.at/index.php/tripleC/article/view/759 (03 February 2017).

Johanssen, J. (2017). 'Immaterial Labour and Reality TV: The Affective Surplus of Excess'. In: Briziarelli, M. and Armano, E. (Eds.) *The Spectacle of 'Free' Labor: Reading Debord in the Context of Digital Capitalism.* London: University of Westminster Press, pp. 197–208.

Johanssen, J. (2018). 'Gaming–Playing on Social Media: Using the Psychoanalytic Concept of "Playing" to Theorize User Labour on Facebook'. *Information, Communication & Society.* https://doi.org/10.1080/1369118X.2018.1450433 (20 April 2018).

Johanssen, J. and Krüger, S. (Eds.) (2016). 'Digital Media, Psychoanalysis and the Subject'. *Special Issue of CM: Communication and Media*, 38, 11. *http://aseestant.ceon.rs/index.php/comman/issue/view/467/showtoc (03 January 2017).*

John, N. A. (2013). 'The Social Logics of Sharing'. *The Communication Review*, 16, 3, pp. 113–131.

John, N. A. (2014). 'File Sharing and the History of Computing: Or, Why File Sharing Is Called "File Sharing"'. *Critical Studies in Media Communication*, 31, 3, pp. 198–211.

Johnson, C. (2007). 'Tele-Branding in TVIII: The Network as Brand and the Programme as Brand'. *New Review of Film and Television Studies*, 5, 1, pp. 5–24.

Johnson, C. (2012). *Branding Television*. London: Routledge.

Johnston, A. and Malabou, C. (2013). *Self and Emotional Life: Philosophy, Psychoanalysis, and Neuroscience*. New York: Columbia University Press.

Jones, D. W. (2008). *Understanding Criminal Behaviour. Psychosocial Approaches to Criminality*. Uffculme: Willan Publishing.

Jones, M. (2017). 'Expressive Surfaces: The Case of the Designer Vagina'. *Theory, Culture & Society*, 34, 7–8, pp. 29–50.

Karatzogianni, A. (2012). 'Epilogue: The Politics of the Affective Digital'. In: Karatzogianni, A. and Kuntsman, A. (Eds.) *Digital Cultures and the Politics of Emotion*. Basingstoke: Palgrave Macmillan, pp. 245–249.

Karatzogianni, A. and Kuntsman, A. (Eds.) (2012). *Digital Cultures and the Politics of Emotion*. Basingstoke: Palgrave Macmillan.

Kavka, M. (2009). *Reality Television, Affect and Intimacy. Reality Matters*. Basingstoke: Palgrave Macmillan.

Kennedy, H. (2016). *Post, Mine, Repeat: Social Media Data Mining Becomes Ordinary*. Basingstoke: Palgrave Macmillan.

Kennedy, J. (2013). 'Rhetorics of Sharing: Data, Imagination and Desire'. In: Lovink, G. and Resch, M. (Eds.) *Unlike Us Reader. Social Media Monopolie and their Alternatives*. Amsterdam: Institute of Network Cultures, pp. 127–136.

Kennedy, J. (2016). 'Conceptual Boundaries of Sharing'. *Information, Communication & Society*, 19, 4, pp. 461–474.

Kernberg, O. (1995). *Love Relations: Normality and Pathology*. New Haven, CT: Yale University Press.

Khan, M. (1979). *Alienation in Perversions*. New York: International Universities Press.

Khanna, R. (2012). 'Touching, Unbelonging, and the Absence of Affect'. *Feminist Theory*, 13, 2, pp. 213–232.

Klein, M. (1988a). *Love, Guilt and Reparation and Other Works. 1921–1945*. London: Virago.

Klein, M. (1988b). *Envy and Gratitude and Other Works. 1946–1963*. London: Virago.

Knafo, D. and Lo Bosco, R. (2017). *The Age of Perversion: Desire and Technology in Psychoanalysis and Culture*. London: Routledge.

Kristeva, J. (1982). *Powers of Horror. An Essay on Abjection*. New York: Columbia University Press.

Krüger, S. (2013). 'How Far Can I Make My Fingers Stretch? – A Response to Vivian Sobchack'. *Free Associations* 64, pp. 104–131. http://freeassociations.org.uk/FA_New/OJS/index.php/fa/article/view/73/103 (02 March 2013).

Krüger, S. (2016). 'Understanding Affective Labor Online: A Depth Hermeneutic Reading of the My 22nd of July Webpage'. *Ephemera: Theory and*

Politics in Organization, 16, 4, pp. 185–208. http://ephemerajournal.org/contribution/understanding-affective-labor-online-depth-hermeneutic-reading-my-22nd-july-webpage (05 July 2017).

Krüger, S. (2017). 'Dropping Depth Hermeneutics into Psychosocial Studies – A Lorenzerian Perspective'. *The Journal of Psycho-Social Studies*, 10, 1, pp. 47–66. www.psychosocial-studies-association.org/wp-content/uploads/2017/05/Steffen-Krueger-Dropping-Depth-Hermeneutics-into-Psychosocial-Studies-A-Lorenzerian-Perspective.Pdf (05 July 2017).

Krüger, S. and Johanssen, J. (2014). 'Alienation and Digital Labour—A Depth Hermeneutic Inquiry into Online Commodification and the Unconscious'. *Triple C: Communication, Capitalism & Critique. Open Access Journal for a Global Sustainable Information Society*, 12, 2, pp. 632–647. (04 July 2016).

Krüger, S. and Johanssen, J. (2016). 'Thinking (with) the Unconscious in Media and Communication Studies: Introduction to the Special Issue'. *CM: Communication and Media*, 38, 11, pp. 5–40. http://aseestant.ceon.rs/index.php/comman/article/view/13131 (03 January 2017).

Krüger, S. and Rustad, G. C. (2017). 'Coping with Shame in a Media-Saturated Society: Norwegian Web-Series *Skam* as Transitional Object'. *Television & New Media*, Online First, pp. 1–24. http://journals.sagepub.com/doi/pdf/10.1177/1527476417741379 (12 April 2018).

Krzych, S. (2010). 'Phatic Touch, or the Instance of the Gadget in the Unconscious'. *Paragraph*, 33, 3, pp. 376–391.

Kücklich, J. (2005). 'Precarious Playbour: Modders and the Digital Games Industry'. *Fibreculture Journal* 5. http://five.fibreculturejournal.org/fcj-025-precarious-playbourmodders-and-the-digital-games-industry/ (20 April 17).

Kuhn, A. (Ed.) (2013). *Little Madnesses: Winnicott, Transitional Phenomena and Cultural Experience*. London: I.B. Tauris.

Lacan, J. (2002). *Écrits*, New York: Norton.

Lacan, J. (2014). *Anxiety: The Seminar of Jacques Lacan. Book X*. Cambridge: Polity Press.

Lanoix, M. (2013). 'Labor as Embodied Practice: The Lessons of Care Work'. *Hypatia*, 28, 1, pp. 85–100.

Laplanche, J. (1999). *Essays on Otherness*. London: Routledge.

Laplanche, J. and Pontalis, J.-B. (1973). *The Language of Psycho-Analysis*. New York: Norton.

Lazzarato, M. (1996). 'Immaterial Labor'. In: Virno, P. and Negri, A. (Eds.) *Radical Thought in Italy: A Potential Politics*. Minneapolis: University of Minnesota Press, pp. 133–147.

Lee, M. (2014). 'A Feminist Political Economic Critique of Women and Investment in the Popular Media'. *Feminist Media Studies*, 14, 2, 270–285.

Lemma, A. (2017). *The Digital Age on the Couch. Psychoanalytic Practice and New Media*. London: Routledge.

Löchel, E. (2006). 'Versuch Über Das Lesen Und Schreiben. Zur Psychodynamik Alter Und Neuer Medien'. *Psychosozial* 29, 104, pp. 113–124.

Lorenzer, A. (1986). *Kultur Analysen: Psychoanalytische Studien Zur Kultur*. Frankfurt/M.: Fischer.

Lovink, G. (2009). 'Society of the Query. The Googlization of our Lives'. In: Becker, F. and Stalder, F. (Eds.) *Deep Search: The Politics of Search Engines Beyond Google*. Innsbruck: Studienverlag, pp. 45–53.

Lundy, L. K., Ruth, A. M. and Park, T. D. (2008). 'Simply Irresistible. Reality TV Consumption Patterns'. *Communication Quarterly*, 56, 2, pp. 208–225.

Lury, C. (2004). *Brands: the Logos of the Global Economy*. London: Routledge.

Malinowska, A. and Miller, T. (Eds.) (2017). 'Media and Emotions'. *Open Cultural Studies*, 1, 1. www.degruyter.com/view/j/culture.2017.1.issue-1/issue-files/culture.2017.1.issue-1.xml (03 March 2018).

Marwick, A. E. (2013). *Status Update: Celebrity, Publicity, and Branding in the Social Media Age*. New Haven, CT: Yale University Press.

Marwick, A. E. and boyd, D. (2011). 'I Tweet Honestly, I Tweet Passionately: Twitter Users, Context Collapse, and the Imagined Audience'. *New Media & Society*, 13, 1, pp. 114–133.

Marx, K. (1973). *Economic and Philosophical Manuscripts*. London: Lawrence and Wishart.

Marx, K. (1976). *Capital: A Critique of Political Economy. Volume 1*. Harmondsworth: Penguin Books.

Massumi, B. (2002). *Parables for the Virtual: Movement, Affect, Sensation*. Duhram: Duke University Press.

Matviyenko, S. (2015). 'FCJ-184 Interpassive User: Complicity and the Returns of Cybernetics'. *The Fibreculture Journal*, 25, 2015 http://twentyfive.fibreculturejournal.org/fcj-184-interpassive-user-complicity-and-the-returns-of-cybernetics/ (12 April 2017).

Mayer-Schönberger, V. and Cukier, K. (2013). *Big Data: A Revolution that Will Transform How We Live, Work, and Think*. New York: Houghton Mifflin Harcourt.

Mccarthy, A. (2001). *Ambient Television. Visual Culture and Public Space*. Durham: Duke University Press.

Mccarthy, A. (2007). 'Reality Television: A Neoliberal Theater of Suffering'. *Social Text*, 25, 493, pp. 17–42.

McDougall, J. (1972). 'Primal Scene and Sexual Perversion'. *International Journal of Psychoanalysis*, 53, pp. 371–384.

McDougall, J. (1995). *The Many Faces of Eros*. New York: Norton.

McLaughlan, R. (2015). 'The Trauma of Form: Death Drive as Affect in À La Recherche Du Temps Perdu'. In: Taylor, J. (Ed.) *Modernism and Affect*. Edinburgh: Edinburgh University Press, pp. 39–55.

McRobbie, A. (2004). 'Notes On: "What Not To Wear" and Post-Feminist Symbolic Violence'. In: Adkins, L. and Skeggs, B. (Eds.) *Feminism After Bourdieu*. London: Wiley, pp. 99–109.

McRobbie, A. (2009). *The Aftermath of Feminism. Gender, Culture and Social Change*. London: Sage.

McRobbie, A. (2011). 'Reflections on Feminism, Immaterial Labour and the Post-Fordist Regime'. *New Formations*, 70, pp. 60–76.

Meikle, G. (2016). '*Social Media: Communication, Sharing and Visibility*'. London: Routledge.

Metzl, J. (2004). 'From Scopophilia to Survivor. A Brief History of Voyeurism'. *Textual Practice*, 18, 3, pp. 415–434.

Mies, M., Bennholdt-Thomsen, V. and Von Werlhof, C. (1988). *Women: The Last Colony*. London: Zed Books.

Minsky, R. (2013). *Psychoanalysis and Culture: Contemporary States of Mind*. London: Wiley.

Modleski, T. (1990). 'Hitchcock, Feminism, and the Patriarchal Unconscious'. In: Erens, P. (Ed.) *Issues in Feminist Film Criticism*. Indianapolis: Indiana University Press, pp. 58–74.

Moran, A. (Ed.) (2009). *TV Formats Worldwide. Localizing Global Programs*. Bristol: Intellect.

Morley, D. (1986). *Family Television: Cultural Power and Domestic Leisure*. London: Routledge.

Morley, D. (1992). *Television, Audiences and Cultural Studies*. London: Routledge.

Moseley, R. (2000). 'Makeover Takeover on British Television'. *Screen*, 41, 3, 299–314.

Mulvey, L. (1975). 'Visual Pleasure and Narrative Cinema'. *Screen*, 16, 3, pp. 6–18.

Muñoz, J. E. (2009). 'From Surface to Depth, Between Psychoanalysis and Affect'. *Women & Performance: A Journal of Feminist Theory*, 19, 2, pp. 123 129. www.tandfonline.com/doi/abs/10.1080/07407700903064854 (12 September 2017).

Murthy, D. (2013). *Twitter*. London: Wiley.

Nabi, R., Biely, E. N., Morgan, S. J. and Stitt, C. R. (2003) 'Reality-Based Television Programming and the Psychology of Its Appeal.' Media Psychology, 5, pp. 303–330.

Nabi, R. (2009). 'Cosmetic Surgery Makeover Programs and intentions to Undergo Cosmetic Enhancements. A Consideration of Three Models of Media Effects'. *Human Communication Research*, 35, 1, pp. 1–27.

Nakamura, L. (2015). 'The Unwanted Labour of Social Media: Women of Colour Call Out Culture as Venture Community Management'. *New Formations*, 86, 86, pp. 106–112.

Negri, A. (1999). 'Value and Affect'. *Boundary* 2, 26, 2, pp. 77–88.

Netflix. (2017). *A Christmas Prince Tweet*. https://twitter.com/netflix/status/940051734650503168 (03 January 2018).

Netflix Tech Blog. (2015). *Netflix's Viewing Data. How We Know Where You Are in House of Cards*. https://medium.com/netflix-techblog/netflixs-viewing-data-how-we-know-where-you-are-in-house-of-cards-608dd61077da (03 January 2018).

Ngai, S. (2005). *Ugly Feelings*. Cambridge, MA: Harvard University Press.

Nunn, H. and Biressi, A. (2005). *Reality TV. Realism and Revelation*. London: Wallflower Press.

Ogden, T. (1996). 'The Perverse Subject of Analysis'. *Journal of the American Psychoanalytic Association*, 44, 4, pp. 1121–1146.

Ogden, T. (2004). 'On Holding and Containing, Being and Dreaming'. *International Journal of Psychoanalysis*, 85, 6, pp. 1349–1364.

Ouellette, L. (2004). '"Take Responsibility for Yourself". Judge Judy and the Neoliberal Citizen'. In: Murray, S. and Ouellette, L. (Eds.) *Reality TV. Remaking Television Culture*. New York: New York University Press, pp. 243–259.

Ouellette, L. (2014). 'Introduction'. In: Ouellette, L. (Ed.) *A Companion to Reality TV*. London: Wiley, pp. 1–8.

Ouellette, L. and Hay, J. (2008a). *Better Living through Reality TV. Television and Post-Welfare Citizenship*. Oxford: Blackwell.

Ouellette, L. and Hay, J. (2008b). 'Makeover Television, Governmentality and the Good Citizen'. *Continuum. Journal of Media and Cultural Studies*, 22, 4, pp. 471–484.

Paasonen, S., Hillis, K. and Petit, M. (2015). 'Introduction: Networks of Transmission: Intensity, Sensation, Value'. In: Hillis, K., Paasonen, S. and Petit, M. (Eds.) *Networked Affect*. Cambridge, MA: MIT Press, pp. 1–24.

Pahl, R. (2005). 'Are All Communities in the Mind?' *Sociological Review*, 53, pp. 621–40.

Papacharissi, Z. (2015). *Affective Publics: Sentiment, Technology, and Politics*. New York: Oxford University Press.

Papacharissi, Z. and Mendelson, A. (2007). 'An Exploratory Study of Reality Appeal. Uses and Gratifications of Reality TV Shows'. *Journal of Broadcasting*, 51, 2, pp. 355–370.

Papacharissi, Z. and de Fatima Oliveira, M. (2012). 'Affective News and Networked Publics: The Rhythms of News Storytelling on #Egypt' Journal of Communication, 62, 2, pp. 266–282.

Parker, I. (2015). *Critical Discursive Psychology*. Second Edition. Basingstoke: Palgrave Macmillan.

Pile, S. (2009). 'Topographies of the Body-and-Mind. Skin Ego, Body Ego, and the Film "Memento"'. *Subjectivity*, 27, pp. 134–154.

Pile, S. (2011). 'Spatialities of Skin. The Chafing of Skin, Ego and Second Skins in T. E. Lawrence's Seven Pillars of Wisdom'. *Body & Society*, 17, 4, pp. 57–81.

Portwood-Stacer, L. (2013). 'Media Refusal and Conspicuous Non-Consumption: The Performative and Political Dimensions of Facebook Abstention'. *New Media & Society*, 15, 7, pp. 1041–1057.

Poster, M. (2006). *Information Please: Culture and Politics in the Age of Digital Machines*. Durham: Duke University Press.

Prokop, U. (2006). 'Spiel-Strategien in Der Zweiten Staffel Der Sendung "Big Brother"'. In: Prokop, U. and Jansen, M. (Eds.) *Doku-Soap, Reality-TV, Affekt Talkshow, Fantasy-Rollenspiele. Neue Sozialisationsagenturen Im Jugendalter*. Marburg: Tectum, pp. 243–274.

Pybus, J. (2013). 'Social Networks and Cultural Workers: Towards an Archive for the Prosumer'. *Journal of Cultural Economy*, 6, 2, pp. 137–152.

Pybus, J. (2015). 'Accumulating Affect: Social Networks and their Archives of Feelings'. In: Hillis, K., Paasonen, S. and Petit, M. (Eds.) *Networked Affect*. Cambridge, MA: MIT Press, pp. 235–250.

Qiu, J. L., Gregg, M. and Crawford, K. (2014). 'Circuits of Labour: A Labour theory of the Iphone Era'. *Triple C: Communication, Capitalism & Critique. Open Access Journal for a Global Sustainable Information Society*, 12, 2, 564–581.

Radway, J. A. (1984). *Reading the Romance: Women, Patriarchy, and Popular Literature*. Chapel Hill: University of North Carolina Press.

Rapaport, D. (1953). 'On the Psychoanalytic Theory of Affects'. *International Journal of Psychoanalysis*, 34, pp. 177–98.

Ribak, R. (2009). 'Remote Control, Umbilical Cord and Beyond: The Mobile Phone as a Transitional Object'. *British Journal of Developmental Psychology*, 27, 1, pp. 183–196.

Ribak, R. and Rosenthal, M. (2015). 'Smartphone Resistance as Media Ambivalence'. *First Monday*, 20, 11. www.firstmonday.dk/ojs/index.php/fm/article/view/6307 (05 April 2016).

Richard, F. (2005). 'Mnemic Trace / Memory Trace'. In: Mijolla, A. (Ed.) *International Dictionary of Psychoanalysis*. Detroit, MI: Thomson Gale, pp. 1062–1065.

Richards, B. (2007). *Emotional Governance. Politics, Media and Terror.* Basingstoke: Palgrave Macmillan.

Rogers, R. (2013). *Digital Methods.* Cambridge, MA: MIT Press.

Rouvroy, A. (2013). 'The End(s) of Critique: Data-Behaviourism Vs. Due Process'. In: Hildebrandt, M. and De Vries, K. (Eds.) *Privacy, Due Process and the Computational Turn: The Philosophy of Law Meets the Philosophy of Technology.* London: Routledge, pp. 143–168.

Ruckenstein, M. (2014). 'Visualized and Interacted Life: Personal Analytics and Engagements with Data Doubles'. *Societies*, 4, 1, pp. 68–84.

Sandvig, C., Hamilton, K., Karahalios, K. and Langbort, C. (2016). 'When the Algorithm itself is a Racist: Diagnosing Ethical Harm in the Basic Components of Software.' *International Journal of Communication*, 10, p. 4972–4990.

Sampson, T. (2012). *Virality: Contagion Theory in the Age of Networks.* Minneapolis: University of Minnesota Press.

Sampson, T., Maddison, S. and Ellis, D. (Eds.) (2018). *Affect and Social Media: Emotion, Mediation, Anxiety, and Contagion.* London: Rowman & Littlefield International.

Sandvoss, C. (2005). *Fans: The Mirror of Consumption.* Cambridge: Polity Press.

Schore, A. N. (1997). 'A Century after Freud's Project. Is a Rapprochement Between Psychoanalysis and Neurobiology At Hand?'. *Journal of the American Psychoanalytic Association*, 45, 3, pp. 807–840.

Sedgwick, E. K. (2003). *Touching Feeling: Affect, Pedagogy, Performativity.* Durham: Duke University Press.

Segal, N. (2009). *Consensuality. Didier Anzieu, Gender and the Sense of Touch.* Amsterdam: Rodolphi.

Seigworth, G. (2003). 'Fashioning a Stave, Or, Singing Life'. In: Daryl Slack, J. (Ed.) *Animations of Deleuze and Guattari.* Oxford: Peter Lang, pp. 75–105.

Seigworth, G. J. and Gregg, M. (2010). 'An Inventory of Shimmers'. In: Gregg, M. and Seigworth, G. J. (Eds.) *The Affect theory Reader.* Durham: Duke University Press, pp. 1–25.

Sender, K. (2012). *The Makeover. Reality Television and Reflexive Audiences.* New York: New York University Press.

Sherman, Y. D. (2008). 'Fashioning Femininity. Clothing the Body and the Self in What Not To Wear'. In: Palmer, G. (Ed.) *Exposing Lifestyle Television. The Big Reveal.* Aldershot: Ashgate, pp. 49–64.

Shields, R. (2006). 'Virtualities'. *Theory, Culture & Society*, 23, 2–3, pp. 284–286.

Silverman, K. (1992). *Male Subjectivity at the Margins*. London: Routledge.

Silverstone, R. (1994). *Television and Everyday Life*. London: Routledge.

Singh, G. (2016). 'Youtubers, Online Selves and the Performance Principle: Notes from a Post-Jungian Perspective'. *CM: Communication and Media*, 11, 38, 167–194. www.fpn.bg.ac.rs/wp-content/uploads/2017/03/CM38-ceo. pdf#page=167 (05 May 2016).

Skeggs, B. and Wood, H. (2012). *Reacting to Reality Television. Performance, Audience and Value*. London: Routledge.

Smith, G. J. (2018). 'Data Doxa: The Affective Consequences of Data Practices'. *Big Data & Society*, 5, 1, pp. 1–15.

Smythe, D. W. (1981). *Dependency Road*. Norwood, NJ: Ablex.

Soler, C. (2016). *Lacanian Affects: The Function of Affect in Lacan's Work*. London: Routledge.

Solove, D. J. (2007). 'I've Got Nothing to Hide and Other Misunderstandings of Privacy'. *San Diego Law Review*, 44, pp. 745–772.

Spezzano, C. (2013). *Affect in Psychoanalysis: A Clinical Synthesis*. London: Routledge.

Stacey, J. (1994). *Star Gazing: Hollywood Cinema and Female Spectatorship*. London: Routledge.

Stein, R. (1999). *Psychoanalytic Theories of Affect*. London: Karnac Books.

Stein, R. (2005). 'Why Perversion? "False Love" and the Perverse Pact'. *International Journal of Psychoanalysis*, 86, 3, pp. 775–799.

Stephens-Davidowitz, S. (2017). *Everybody Lies. Big Data, New Data and What the Internet can Tell Us About Who We Really Are*. New York: Bloomsbury Publishing.

Stern, D. (1998). *The Interpersonal World of the Infant. A View from Psychoanalysis and Developmental Psychology*. London: Karnac.

Studdert, D. (2006). *Conceptualising Community: Beyond the State and the Individual*. Basingstoke: Palgrave Macmillan.

Stutzman, F., Gross, R. and Acquisti, A. (2012). 'Silent Listeners: The Evolution of Privacy and Disclosure on Facebook'. *Journal of Privacy and Confidentiality*, 4, 2, pp. 7–41.

Suler, J. (2004). 'The Online Disinhibition Effect'. *Cyberpsychology & Behavior*, 7, 3, pp. 321–326.

Terranova, T. (2000). 'Free Labor: Producing Culture for the Digital Economy'. *Social Text*, 18, 2, pp. 33–58.

Tiidenberg, K. and Gómez Cruz, E. (2015). 'Selfies, Image and the Re-Making of the Body'. *Body & Society*, 21, 4, pp. 77–102.

Timpanaro, S. (2010). *Freudian Slip: Psychoanalysis and Textual Criticism*. London: Verso.

Tomkins, S. (1962). *Affect, Imagery, Consciousness: Vol. 1. The Positive Affects*. New York: Springer.

Turkle, S. (1984). *The Second Self: Computers and the Human Spirit*. Cambridge, MA: MIT Press.

Turkle, S. (1985). *Life on the Screen*. New York: Simon & Schuster.

Turkle, S. (2009). *Simulation and Its Discontents*. Cambridge, MA: MIT Press.

Turkle, S. (2011). *Alone Together: Why We Expect more from Technology and Less from each other*. New York: Basic Books.

Turkle, S., Essig, T. and Russell, G. I. (2017). 'Afterword: Reclaiming Psychoanalysis. Sherry Turkle in Conversation with the Editors'. *Psychoanalytic Perspectives*, 14, 2, pp. 237–248.

Tzankova, V. (2015). 'Affective Politics or Political Affection: Online Sexuality in Turkey'. In: Hillis, K., Paasonen, S. and Petit, M. (Eds.) *Networked Affect*. Cambridge, MA: MIT Press, pp. 59–74.

Van Dijck, J. (2013). *The Culture of Connectivity: A Critical History of Social Media*. Oxford: Oxford University Press.

Vanheule, S. (2001). Inhibition: 'I Am Because I Don't Act'. *The Letter*, 23, pp. 109–126.

Virno, P. (1996). 'The Ambivalence of Disenchantment'. In: Virno, P. and Negri, A. (Eds.) *Radical Thought in Italy: A Potential Politics*. Minneapolis: University of Minnesota Press, pp. 12–33.

Virno, P. (2004). *A Grammar of the Multitude: For an Analysis of Contemporary Forms of Life*. New York: Semiotext(e).

Walkerdine, V. (1986). 'Video Replay'. In: Burgin, V., Donald, J. and Kaplan, C. (Eds.) *Formations of Fantasy*. London: Verso, pp. 167–199.

Walkerdine, V. (2010). 'Communal Beingness and Affect: An Exploration of Trauma in an Ex-industrial Community'. *Body & Society*, 16, 1, pp. 91–116.

Weber, B. R. (2009). *Makeover TV. Selfhood, Citizenship, and Celebrity*. Durham: Duke University Press.

Wegenstein, B. and Ruck, N. (2011). 'Physiognomy, Reality Television and the Cosmetic Gaze'. *Body and Society*, 17, 4, pp. 27–54.

Wetherell, M. (2012). *Affect and Emotion: A New Social Science Understanding*. London: Sage.

Whitehouse-Hart, J. (2014a). *Psychosocial Explorations of Film and Television Viewing. Ordinary Audience*. Basingstoke: Palgrave Macmillan.

Whitehouse-Hart, J. (2014b). '"Programmes for People who are Paranoid About the Way they Look". Thoughts on Paranoia, Recognition, Mirrors and Makeover Television'. In: Bainbridge, C. and Yates, C. (Eds.) *Media and the Inner World. Psycho-Cultural Approaches to Emotion, Media and Popular Culture*. Basingstoke: Palgrave Macmillan, pp. 135–153.

Wilson, E. A. (2004). *Psychosomatic: Feminism and the Neurological Body*. Durham: Duke University Press.

Wilson, E. A. (2010). *Affect and Artificial Intelligence*. Seattle, WA: University of Washington Press.

Wilson, N. (2005). 'Excessive Performances of the Same. Beauty as the Beast of Reality TV'. *Women & Performance. A Journal of Feminist theory*, 15, 2, pp. 207–229.

Winnicott, D. W. (2002). *Playing and Reality*. London: Routledge.

Wittel, A. (2004). 'Culture, Labour and Subjectivity: For a Political Economy From Below'. *Capital & Class*, 28, 3, pp. 11–30.

Wittel, A. (2011). 'Qualities of Sharing and their Transformations in the Digital Age'. *International Review of Information Ethics*, 15, 9, pp. 3–8.

Wood, H. and Skeggs, B. (2004). 'Notes on Ethical Scenarios of Self on British "Reality" TV'. *Feminist Media Studies*, 4, 2, pp. 205–208.

Woodstock, L. (2014). 'Media Resistance: Opportunities for Practice theory and New Media Research'. *International Journal of Communication*, 8, 19, pp. 1983–2001.

Woodward, K. (2015). *Introduction to Psychosocial Studies*. London: Routledge.

Yates, C. (2007). *Masculine Jealousy and Contemporary Cinema*. Basingstoke: Palgrave Macmillan.

Zajc, M. (2015). 'Social Media, Prosumption, and Dispositives: New Mechanisms of the Construction of Subjectivity'. *Journal of Consumer Culture*, 15, 1, pp. 28–47.

Žižek, S. (2007). *Enjoy Your Symptom! Jacques Lacan in Hollywood and Out*. London: Routledge.

Index

Printed in the United States
by Baker & Taylor Publisher Services